'A very important and timely book that contribute
and public debates about the wider purpose of vol
Written by and for both academics and practition
and highly readable collection that provides valu
ethical dimensions of voluntary action. It makes a unique contribution to
the existing voluntary sector literature by embracing a broader focus on
the potential for, and obstacles to, civil society in re-kindling critical voices
and creating democratic spaces for collective action. This book will be of
interest to a wide audience including academics, students, practitioners,
and policymakers.'

**Dr Armine Ishkanian, Department of Social Policy, London School of
Economics**

'This book is a hugely important, critical reflection on the challenges
facing civil society organizations in neo-liberal times. Its contributors raise
fundamental questions about autonomy, resilience and resistance, and
demand the imagination to face them.'

**Jon Burnett, Researcher and Assistant Editor, IRR News,
Institute of Race Relations**

'This book is required reading for those seriously interested in thinking
about the future of civil society in the UK in a post-Brexit, post-Trump
world. It makes the case for our need to find spaces for resistance, and
poses a stark question: is civil society a consensual glue, or a place for
dissenting voices? The contributors to this edited volume draw in their
experiences of the voices of those they work with. It is rooted in critical
practice but while located in the UK it is not solely of the UK. It invites an
international perspective and is all the more thought provoking for that.
Do read it!'

**Professor John Diamond, Director of the Institute for Public Policy and
Professional Practice, Edge Hill University UK**

Civil Society Organizations in Turbulent Times

Civil Society Organizations in Turbulent Times

A gilded web?

Edited by Linda Milbourne and Ursula Murray

 is an imprint of

First published in 2017 by the UCL Institute of Education Press, 20 Bedford Way, London WC1H 0AL

www.ucl-ioe-press.com

©2017 Linda Milbourne and Ursula Murray

British Library Cataloguing in Publication Data:
A catalogue record for this publication is available from the British Library

ISBNs
978-1-85856-815-7 (paperback)
978-1-85856-816-4 (PDF eBook)
978-1-85856-817-1 (ePub eBook)
978-1-85856-818-8 (Kindle eBook)

Every effort has been made to trace copyright holders and to obtain their permission for the use of copyright material. The publisher apologizes for any errors or omissions and would be grateful if notified of any corrections that should be incorporated in future reprints or editions of this book.

The opinions expressed in this publication are those of the author and do not necessarily reflect the views of the UCL Institute of Education.

Typeset by Quadrant Infotech (India) Pvt Ltd
Printed by CPI Group (UK) Ltd, Croydon, CR0 4YY
Cover image ©Freiheit/Alamy Stock Photo

Contents

Acknowledgements

This book owes much to the efforts and encouragement of others. As editors we are indebted to our contributors, without whose knowledge of diverse welfare fields this book would have been considerably poorer. As the notes on the authors attest, each adds a wealth of background experience. The chapters have emerged from research exploring everyday working lives and understandings in larger and smaller civil society organizations and have often been written despite exacting work demands and time pressures as well as difficult personal circumstances. Our thanks also go to colleagues, especially members of the Voluntary and Community Studies Masters team, including Jan Etienne, who supported several of these contributors during their studies and encouraged us to realize this project. We are also grateful to our families and friends, who have willingly discussed ideas and offered intellectual advice during the course of the book's development.

About the authors

Cate Evans has worked in the social housing sector for over ten years, in both housing associations and local authorities. Currently she works for a local authority housing department exploring ways to improve services for residents. Cate's first degree was a BSc in Economic History; in 2011 she graduated from Birkbeck, University of London, with an MSc in Voluntary and Community Sector Studies.

Truly Johnston has been working in the voluntary sector for over ten years. She has taught ESOL (English for Speakers of Other Languages), managed volunteers, and been a development officer at a Council for Voluntary Services (CVS). She is currently the Director of Social Action at Community Southwark, where she manages the social action and volunteering services, helping people to get involved in their local community. Truly studied English Literature at Cambridge University and completed an MSc in Voluntary and Community Sector Studies at Birkbeck, University of London, in 2013.

Linda Milbourne has worked as an academic in higher education since 1998, at King's College and Birkbeck, University of London, and is also an associate of the Third Sector Research Centre, Birmingham. At Birkbeck, she headed a Social Policy and Education department and led postgraduate programmes in voluntary, community, and youth studies, also teaching public sector management courses. As a critical researcher she has focused on social policy, civil society organizations, changing welfare relationships, and the suppression of alternatives. Her recent publications include: *Voluntary Sector in Transition: Hard Times or New Opportunities?* (2013, Policy Press); articles for *Journal of Social Policy* and *Voluntas* on austerity, Big Society, and policy resistance; co-authored work with Ursula Murray and Mike Cushman; and book chapters for the OU, Presses Sorbonne Nouvelle, and Sage. She has some 30 years' experience of public and voluntary organizations, including as a manager, teacher, trustee, and active campaigner.

Alexandra Molano-Avilan has worked in various settings including NGOs, community resilience, youth participation, and mental health for ten years. Alexandra's first degree was a BSc in International Relations; in 2014, she graduated from Birkbeck, University of London, with an MSc in Voluntary and Community Sector Studies.

Antony Moore qualified as a social worker in 1993 and worked within local authority children's services as a social worker and senior practitioner until 1998. He has additional experience of working within social care in both the private and third sectors and is currently employed in a specialist service with a national children's charity working with young people who engage in harmful sexual behaviours and their families. Antony graduated with an MSc in Voluntary and Community Sector Studies from Birkbeck, University of London, in 2014. He also has a Diploma in Social Work, a Certificate in Life Coaching, and the CCETSW (Central Council for Education and Training in Social Work) Accredited Social Work Practice Teacher qualifications.

Ursula Murray taught on public sector management, gender studies, and lifelong learning courses, as well as the MSc in Voluntary and Community Sector Studies, at Birkbeck, University of London. She previously undertook action-research around local economic change and women's employment. Following a decade in senior management in local government, she studied for an MSc in Group Relations, Organizations and Society (2000), and her subsequent doctorate explored the meaning of the public sector, using narrative, complexity, and psycho-social methodologies (2005). As an activist academic, she has published papers on reasserting a relational model of teaching and learning (2011) and on the loss of 'publicness' in *Public Service on the Brink* (2012). The National Coalition for Independent Action (NCIA) published 'Has the voluntary sector been colonised by neo-liberal thinking?' (2013). This was followed by joint working papers with Linda Milbourne for the NCIA Inquiry into the Future of Voluntary Services (2015).

Wale Olulana has worked in various settings including the private business sector and voluntary community services for about 30 years.

Currently he works for Harmony Christian Ministries, a Christian organization, on their voluntary services and joint public venture initiatives both in the UK and West African countries. Wale's first degree was a BSc in Geography in 1985. He graduated from Obafemi Awolowo University (formerly University of Ife, Ile Ife, Nigeria) and subsequently gained an MSc in Voluntary and Community Sector Studies from Birkbeck, University of London, in 2015.

Rachel Potts has worked in the public and voluntary sectors for 30 years in various settings, including mental health, domestic violence, and specialist housing provision. Currently she works for a local authority. In 2014 she graduated from Birkbeck, University of London, with an MSc in Voluntary and Community Sector Studies.

Dawn Thorpe has worked in the field of learning disabilities in various settings including hospitals, residential units, supported living, and advocacy for 25 years. Currently she works for Brighton and Hove Speak Out, an advocacy organization, on their Learning Disabilities Voices network. Dawn's first degree was a BSc in Anthropology (1998); in 2011 she graduated from Birkbeck, University of London, with an MSc in Voluntary and Community Sector Studies.

Palmela Witter has 20 years' experience in schools and youth services as a manager. More recently, she has worked on promoting community development, networking, and collaboration between public and third sector partners across a London local authority to source external and entrepreneurial funding for project management and organizational development and to support effective tendering and commissioning. She is also a voluntary organization chair and trustee in her local community. Her research interests are around young people, mental health, and the survival of African Caribbean voluntary and community organizations. In 2014, she graduated with an MSc in Voluntary and Community Sector Studies from Birkbeck, University of London, and in 2015 the annual UK Voluntary Sector and Volunteering Research Conference awarded her the first prize for the best new researcher's paper on black mental health organizations' potential to survive mainstreaming.

Preface

'All that glitters is not gold.' Familiar allegories or fairy tales encourage us to adopt ethical behaviours. Yet current society promotes the idea that we should chase all that promises gold. These allegorical stories invariably illustrate that entrapment, whether in a web of deceit, an impenetrable forest, or a prison with no doors, follows this pursuit of mythical gold, which also turns out to be worthless. In the stories, escape from the impenetrable forest or an elaborately woven spider's web is sometimes achieved via a magic wand. However, this book is not a fairy tale. It is about real society and people and, specifically, the civil society role of voluntary organizations finding ways back to ethical paths in turbulent times.

Like many books, we have had to complete it while the world is changing rapidly. The EU referendum of June 2016 was followed by a new Conservative government in the UK and in November, by the US presidential elections. A still-dominant neo-liberal paradigm, seemingly uncaring governments and elites, and a rise in populist and anti-establishment movements provide a turbulent backcloth for the themes in this book, underlining the challenges and acute dilemmas now facing voluntary organizations.

Chapter 1

Civil society organizations in turbulent times: Contested terrain

Linda Milbourne and Ursula Murray

This is a challenging time to write about voluntary organizations, charities, and wider civil society. All have experienced a series of far-reaching changes both in the UK and internationally. Since the 2010 Coalition and subsequent Conservative governments came to power in the UK, cultures and arrangements surrounding welfare provision and previously independent civil society activities have been in flux, following the combined effects of austerity measures and shifts in the balance of relationships between the state, market interests, and civil society. The recasting of these relationships has ensued over three decades, with the increasing dominance of neo-liberal political ideology gradually drawing voluntary service organizations into its gilded web. When the recent Conservative administration took up power in 2015, however, changes in the socio-economic and political landscape accelerated, and for-profit organizations were increasingly privileged in public service contracts, while local governments and voluntary organizations experienced rapidly declining funds and status.

In parallel with the privatization of public services, restrictions on key aspects of civil society activity are growing. Independent non-profit organizations seeking to provide flexible, locally based welfare activities are experiencing increasing regulation, while constraints on organizing independently and voicing dissent have multiplied. Some of these changes have been enshrined in law, others promoted through ideology deprecating the local state and allied civil society organizations while extolling the virtues of market economics and large corporations.

This picture is exacerbated by an increasingly austere economic environment impacting most on the poorest in society (Hills *et al.*, 2015; JRF, 2016) as financial cuts to public services deepen. Fields of service, including housing, health, social care, and criminal justice, discussed in later chapters, are all experiencing major policy upheavals, leading to impoverished services for the most vulnerable and a transfer of the burden of addressing growing gaps in welfare services to unpaid volunteers. In a modern, ostensibly democratic society with a long tradition of public welfare, how have our social support systems broken down to the extent that volunteer food banks should become normalized rather than for emergency use only (Perry *et al.*, 2014)?

The consequences of international conflict are also evident within UK and European politics and policy, with a new wave of far-right political parties challenging any social democratic consensus (Marquand, 2015) and exhibiting intolerance towards refugees and economic migrants. Since the EU referendum, such intolerance has become more overt in the UK. Globally, civil society movements play a crucial role in challenging attacks on democracy and human rights, which is reflected currently in the UK as the government seeks to withdraw from the European Human Rights Act. Fraught political debate and a conflict of ideas have clearly re-entered UK politics, not least because of the erosion of social and welfare systems, increased impoverishment and growing suppression of outlets for criticism.

These multiple changes affect civil society organizations and wider movements in different ways, but whatever their roles, it has become a critical time for civil society groups to reassess their goals and directions. This book mainly explores the parts of civil society involved in providing service activities, and the fates of organizations discussed in later chapters are closely bound with the state of social welfare overall. Thus the book offers insights into ways that complex changes are affecting the well-being of services in different fields and for different groups in society more widely.

Throughout the book we refer to 'voluntary organizations' and 'charities' as the most frequently used terms in the UK[1], whereas the terms 'non-profit organization' (NPO) (North America, Australia), 'third sector', and 'non-government organization' (NGO) have wider international currency. Wider civil society encompasses everything and everyone beyond the business and public sectors, and comprises diverse sub-groups including registered charities, voluntary service organizations, micro-community groups, membership associations, mutual aid groups, co-operatives, trade unions, and multiple campaign organizations and social movements. Of the nearly 1 million civil society groups in the UK, fewer than a fifth are registered charities, ranging from very large organizations including international NGOs to small local support and campaign groups. Many

---

1   Terminology commonly used in the UK, including 'voluntary', 'community', and 'third sector', has been influenced by policy terms at different times, whereas 'charity', though used widely, defines a small fraction of organizations registered with the Charity Commission.

trust funds, research think tanks, universities, school academies, and faith-based organizations are also registered charities, benefiting from favourable tax exemptions in exchange for regulation by the Charity Commission or other bodies.

Our focus

The snapshot above of rapidly changing political and policy climates provides the context for a book concerned with critical reflection on voluntary organizations in turbulent times. Actors within such organizations are not, of course, innocent bystanders – those who are simply 'done to'. They may be compliant or resistant, intentionally or unintentionally; and the strategies adopted when facing change, together with the everyday dilemmas, challenges, and tensions faced in cross-sector and intra-organizational contexts are integral to examples explored in the book.

While subsequent chapters offer insights into distinct examples of pressures on everyday frontline activities in voluntary service organizations, the book overall aims to locate these in the bigger socio-economic picture and to extend conceptual thinking into how and why arrangements have developed as they have, and how they could be different. We argue that conventional theory on the rationale for voluntary organizations within British welfare, which we discuss briefly in chapter 2, no longer appears adequate for the present turbulent times. Similarly, normative concepts widely applied to civil society serve the dominant ideology but negate more oppositional models. The chapters speak to our overarching arguments about the entrapment of many voluntary services and the turbulence now surrounding contemporary civil society organizations in the UK. However, our reading of recent studies from other parts of the world, including Australia, New Zealand, the USA, Canada, and some other parts of Europe, indicates a resonance among civil society experiences elsewhere.

Defining limits for a book is challenging, and naming our focus treads contested ground, since language and labels and their related meanings invariably reflect cultural, political, and policy legacies. We have chosen to emphasize civil society and not simply the commonly used UK terms: 'voluntary sector', 'third sector', or 'charity', to acknowledge the diversity of organizations involved in terms of both size and purpose, and to signify our broader concerns beyond the often limited focus in UK voluntary sector research. This emphasis also recognizes the advocacy and campaign roles that voluntary organizations have undertaken alongside service activities, and refocuses thinking on rekindling alliances across different civil society activities and groups. In this sense, our book deviates from much UK research around voluntary organizations, which has been reluctant to express political criticism. It explores issues of societal concern, be they welfare, austerity, democratic participation, political ideology, or social justice, analysing contemporary examples of voluntary services through a critical lens.

Historical signs of a chill wind?

By defining the book's focus within a wider civil society perspective, we are conscious of sharply opposed views on the role that civil society should play: put simply, the contradiction between acting as consensual glue to avoid civil disorder and acting independently to promote critical or dissenting voices. Voluntary action is increasingly called upon to tackle problems and unmet needs in social welfare, becoming a form of community-based first aid, but the climate for expressing criticism and dissent around such needs has chilled, with policy changes constraining both service activities and campaign groups. Civil society promises a space in which citizens can organize freely, with their priorities, objectives, and ways of working arising from negotiated beliefs and aspirations and from shared ethical and moral values (NCIA, 2015). However, spaces to organize and speak freely have been significantly curtailed. Historically, close relationships between civil society and the state over services invariably entailed conditionality, but the recent levels of regulation and legal restraint on diverse civil society activities are of a different order and, as they become more restrictive, may provoke increased dissent.

Earlier shifts in the socio-political landscape affected relationships between voluntary organizations and the state, some more than others. The advent of the post-war welfare state in 1946 was one such conjuncture, and the more recent shifts to outsourcing public services since the 1990s represents another (Prochaska, 2014). Since this period, welfare provision has increasingly depended on a mixed economy and plurality of forms (Baines *et al.*, 2011), characterized by three broad features. The first is an ideological commitment to the superiority of the market, rationalized as a means to improve efficiency and effectiveness in public services. The second is the establishment of new public management cultures (Clarke and Newman, 1997), involving increasingly centralized policy objectives and associated accountability systems. The third involves governance models based on networks and localism (Barnes and Prior, 2009): planning, managing, and delivering services through local and regional co-ordinating bodies, ostensibly collaborative, devolved forms of working. The latter imply consensual forms of governance and management, but like the managerial command and control mechanisms associated with new public management and contractualism (Brown and Calnan, 2010), they are underpinned by powerful technocratic arrangements and hierarchies, which suppress dissent and displace creativity and trust relationships.

When the New Labour government came to power in 1997, it promised significant changes, while effectively consolidating the neo-liberal turn to market economics, with a social democratic ideological veneer, via the Third Way agenda. This applauded third sector or voluntary organizations as locally trusted and responsive service providers, according them a higher profile in government policy and service delivery than they had experienced since the 1940s. Close links between third sector leaders and senior politicians encouraged a form of sofa politics around a small web of contacts (Murray, 2013), marginalizing dissenting voices and enabling a significant reorientation of third sector ethos. This followed an era when neo-liberal corporations had come to dominate the way organizational arrangements were understood, reshaping thinking about management, which over time exerted multiple pressures on voluntary organizations to professionalize and adopt business models of operation, displacing previous relational approaches. Entrapment for voluntary service organizations had begun.

Renewed voluntary sector importance brought costs as well as benefits, raising questions around compromised independence and mission drift (Cairns, 2009). Overall income grew, but small local organizations were also drawn into delivering diverse government-led initiatives, especially those intended to tackle social exclusion, neighbourhood regeneration, and community engagement. In effect, New Labour had instituted the third sector as governable terrain (Carmel and Harlock, 2008), not only through involving them in growing procurement and performance management regimes, but also through drawing them into numerous projects and collaborative bodies, in which powerful agencies defined the rules of play (Clegg, 1989). Rapid growth in income and service provision during the 13 years of New Labour effectively induced resource dependency (Pfeffer and Salancik, 2003) and ensured the entrapment of many voluntary organizations in a complex web involving an increasingly competitive contract culture. Figures illustrating growth patterns from central and local government funding from 2004–5 to 2013–14 (Keen, 2015; NCVO, 2016) demonstrate the rapid rise in income up to 2010, followed by a subsequent decline. They underline the extent to which voluntary organizations had become embedded in remodelling and modernizing public services.

Gilded web or cold climate?

Recession following the economic crisis of 2008 saw public services budgets decline in real terms year on year, with funding to local governments falling by £800 million over five years up to 2013–14, compared to only a £1 billion reduction to central government budgets overall. The Coalition government in 2010 initially welcomed voluntary organizations, but its references swiftly changed to the 'private and voluntary sector' as apparently interchangeable service providers, and it became clear that voluntary organizations had lost any preferred status as alternatives to public sector providers (Milbourne, 2013). The ideological territory had shifted significantly towards privatization, marketization, and financialization of the public realm, cemented in the Open Public Services White Paper (Cabinet Office, 2011), an unambiguous statement of the government's intentions to outsource public services to corporate providers. Voluntary organizations were significantly disadvantaged by the scale and financial criteria built into new contracts, and few could compete as primary contractors. Instead, many adopted new roles, as sub-contractors to corporate contractors. Despite criticisms of being used as a Trojan horse (Murray, 2012), voluntary organizations were now firmly ensconced in a contractual culture aimed at dismantling the public sector and ultimately the foundations of the welfare state.

The nearly 163,000 voluntary organizations registered as charities in 2013–14 had accrued a total income of some £44 billion, of which £15 billion came from the state, largely for service contracts (NCVO, 2016). Roughly half of this was for central government-funded programmes, such as welfare to work and transforming rehabilitation, and the rest for local government-commissioned services. Less than a fifth of this income reaches medium and smaller organizations, with most going to 3 per cent of the largest charities, which, in contrast to declining trends in public funding to other voluntary organizations, received increased funding from central government during 2013–14 (NCVO, 2016). While large charities continued to grow, smaller, locally based organizations suffered disproportionately from the overall reduction in resources available, with reports nationally of one in five small service providers at risk of closure (CSJ, 2013) and many more closing since (Civil Exchange, 2016).

The policy focus for small voluntary groups transferred to the much trumpeted Big Society agenda, but closures far outstripped the minimal funding granted to encourage self-organized community groups and volunteers to plug the service gaps emerging from local state withdrawals. Localism similarly promised much; however, as Padley (2013) argues, it located responsibility but little power and no new resources locally, while retaining controls centrally. Thus, local voluntary organizations dependent on progressively reduced local government funding have found themselves as much a target of funding cuts. As Walker (2015) concludes, 'the love affair with the voluntary sector that Cameron announced back in 2007 is well and truly over'. However, their entrapment in this service culture had induced dependency.

If these transitions were not sufficiently damaging, restrictions on key aspects of civil society activity have ensued, curtailing voluntary organizations' local flexibility and responsiveness in welfare activities, in organizing independently, and in voicing dissent. In service provision, contracts and sub-contracts including gagging clauses have ensured that underfunding, service failures, and poor practices are concealed from public knowledge (Milbourne and Cushman, 2015). Scaled-up, homogenized contracts and highly specified targets and outcomes have eroded flexibility and distanced commissioners and contractors from knowledge about localized needs (Rees *et al.*, 2013). Despite notable exceptions, these strictures have been compounded by widespread self-censorship and silence jeopardizing independent voices and activities (Baring Foundation, 2015), and by an absence of interventions from influential large charities or infrastructure bodies challenging the overall policy directions.

Turbulent times

The cold climate for voluntary organizations has intensified since 2014, with right-wing think tank and political attacks on lobbying and the Civil Society Minister stating that voluntary organizations should 'stick to knitting and stay out of politics' (Mason, 2015). Recent criticisms of charity 'fat cat' salaries, aggressive fund-raising, and politicized interventions have followed. Much of this censure has been disseminated ideologically, promoting restrictive behaviours and arrangements. Yet since 2014, a series of legal reforms have compounded restrictions on freedoms to protest, speak out, and lobby, exacerbating regulation of charities and trade unions, including the loosely termed 'TU and Lobby Act' (Cabinet Office, 2014a) and the Charities Act (UK Parliament, 2016).

Worse still was the imposition of an anti-lobbying clause, with far-reaching consequences on silencing government-opposed views, potentially muzzling the research findings of multiple independent bodies and university departments (McKie, 2016). While campaigns highlighting serious contradictions in the clause have effectively led to its withdrawal, the jury is still out on the level of monitoring required. The chilling effects of various recent measures extend well beyond voluntary service organizations, and it is important to recognize the wider public interest in not suppressing well-researched information and in ensuring a voice for diverse social groups. Voluntary service providers, for example, have a long history of campaigning and advocacy work on behalf of disparate and often marginal groups in society, but many have now withdrawn from overt advocacy due to fear of losing funding. Together with other constraints and legislation, such as new contracts for junior NHS doctors, changes to electoral registration, and funding rules for opposition parties, there is disturbing evidence of a government seeking to prevent organized opposition and dissent.

Several factors underlie the intense chill for voluntary organizations. The 2015 Conservative government appears wholly focused on achieving a smaller state sector, a low welfare state, to be reduced to 36 per cent of GDP by 2020 (HM Treasury, 2015), which is justified by the myth that lower spending produces better services. With corporate contractors now involved in a growing number of services and such achievements now applauded in a progress report on the Open Public Services legislation (Cabinet Office, 2014b), voluntary organizations are no longer useful as a rhetorical cover for dismantling the public sector. Future involvement in services will mean them shedding dependency on public funding and increasing private and social investments, such as social impact bonds, which were recently signalled in policy as a key means to financing future social services (Keen, 2015). However, chasing money comes at a high price, which risks losing public trust and active membership. For some major charities, dependency on corporate funds is already becoming an indispensable habit, which, like dependency on public service contracts, may rebound in damaging ways (LeBaron and Dauvergne, 2014), as charitable activities morph into corporate behaviours in financial investment, marketing, and branding. These trends not only restrict activities and silence opinions, but they also empower big business models and undermine alternatives, ironically reinforcing the social and economic systems that many charities were established to reform.

Political ideology: Co-opted or resisting?

Research in British social welfare policy has often focused predominantly on statutory services (Jones *et al.*, 1983). Yet voluntary organizations have a long history of providing humanitarian social welfare and have played an important role in social action and change, not only in developing British welfare provision, but also in mutual aid, in campaigning and advocacy, and in influencing values and policies. Underlining the conflicting roles of different civil society organizations identified earlier, they have also been characterized as reactive do-gooders, perpetuating existing patterns of privilege (Brenton, 1985) and a useful means of exerting social control over potentially disruptive groups in society (Taylor and Kendall, 1996).

The renewal of international movements campaigning on poverty and injustice saw the upsurge of a new strand of politically motivated voluntary organizations and community development workers in the UK during the 1970s and 1980s, with organizations such as the Child Poverty Action Group and Shelter established. It was a time during which diverse social movements flourished, producing a potent voice for social justice and change and the development of alternative service models, involving both state and voluntary sector practitioners in challenging existing approaches (Challis *et al.*, 1988). Underlying practical alternatives was also a desire to reclaim 'the ethical vision' (Hoggett, 2000: 198) of the post-war welfare state from increasingly bureaucratized, professionalized, and perfunctory public services, often experienced as inaccessible by those that most needed them.

The increased emphasis on redressing social inequities encouraged a proliferation in new voluntary groups through the 1980s. A vibrant sub-sector emerged combining services and campaigning, securing funding for innovative projects largely from Labour local authorities and metropolitan councils, including the Greater London Council (GLC). A more overtly political focus on welfare rights; initiatives ranging from gender, race, sexuality, disability and class to free schools; non-hierarchical organizational forms; and growing criticisms of the social controls associated with public services permeated both theoretical and practical debates. The extent of the cultural shift of these new voluntary organizations away from the voluntary sector's earlier philanthropic roots (Kendall and Knapp, 1996) was significant. However, a decade later, as many local councils, the GLC, and other metropolitan authorities were rate-capped or broken up by the Conservative government, innovative funding streams were lost and related political alliances disintegrated, leaving projects to sink or swim unaided, as later chapters illustrate.

Kendall (2010) highlights the 1990s as starting an 'erosion of political innocence' among voluntary organizations, eager to expand or mainstream by engaging in outsourced public service contracts, often in the initial belief that they would provide better services than those delivered previously. However, many had failed to grasp the extent of the political changes among local government agencies and their effects on service arrangements in a burgeoning quasi-market. This was not the only avenue open to voluntary organizations, and Kendall also highlights two other roles that voluntary organizations assumed: renewal of civil order and revival of democratic life.

The latter received less attention in policy ideology and had less prominence in research.

Many voluntary organizations engaged in government projects concerned with social inclusion, neighbourhood regeneration, and community participation were drawn into socially valuable government agendas, effectively renewing civil order. However, this largely harnessed them in a consensual civil society role and deterred critical models. Revival of democratic life was undoubtedly the poor relation in terms of public visibility, although many pre-existing grassroots groups continued to organize at community levels. In some neighbourhoods, wider participation in local policy forums took place, but these were often criticized for being consultative exercises that failed to generate practical changes (Barnes *et al.*, 2010). This revival strand was effectively Labour's precursor to the later Big Society initiative, which, however, both the Coalition and Conservative governments have subsumed within a civil order agenda, now integral to shoring up welfare but masked as worthy voluntary action.

It is often assumed that voluntary organizations are driven by social values and philanthropic motives, but as organizations relate more closely with other sectors, they demonstrate isomorphic tendencies (Powell and Di Maggio, 1991), adopting dominant cultures and practices that gradually displace and undermine earlier approaches (Buckingham, 2011). Amid the recent trends described above, assumptions about the values and features of voluntary organizations must then come under question. Emulating features more characteristic of the state or private sectors raises questions about whether an organization really belongs to civil society or, indeed, whether pursuing growth, competing aggressively for contracts, undermining small local providers, and becoming delivery agents for corporate contractors are activities compatible with charitable purposes.

For many years, voluntary organizations were able to act both within and against the state (Holloway, 2005): a critical voice, highlighting deficiencies in welfare, while also delivering services on behalf of the state and adding value through supplementary provision; and over time many gained seats at the policy table. Discussions above, however, make clear that the climate has changed irreversibly, and this dual role has become severely compromised. Many voluntary organizations have become resource and status dependent on service contracts, trapped but complicit in current welfare changes and in relinquishing their voice and independence. Nevertheless, some voluntary organizations are opting out of the contracts race, and a critical debate on the jeopardy of recent changes is surfacing (NCIA, 2015).

Research approach

As the discussions above illustrate, our concern is with the political and policy environment surrounding voluntary organizations and the dilemmas that they face in rapidly changing and more punitive welfare settings. Our research purposely assumes a social responsibility for revealing aspects of apparent injustice, reflecting on how these might be addressed differently. Research also carries an important role of exploring beneath the surface (Cooper and Lousada, 2005) of macro-policies and organizational trends to shed light on the lived experiences of change in practical settings. The empirical material gathered in the book draws on a series of small-scale studies, using mainly qualitative methods, including case studies, interviews, and observations, framed within critical and interdisciplinary lenses.

There is still insufficient contemporary work that considers in-depth research situated in small community organizations or specific localities, and insights from this kind of detailed focus often remain hidden. In parallel, larger social forces also influence the actors involved in these settings, and subsequent chapters locate the research subjects within wider social contexts and meanings, so as not to lose 'the bigger picture' (Maguire and Ball, 1994: 8). In this sense, our research is committed to uncovering patterns of local events and linking them with broader patterns of social change, recognizing the interwoven nature of governmental strategies, structures, and agencies in accounting for local experiences and outcomes. Through this analysis, we can start to identify how some seemingly inevitable patterns could be contested or resisted and to imagine alternative ways forward.

The frontline stories in the chapters that follow draw on contemporary empirical studies from different service fields and perspectives – practitioners, managers, development workers, and service recipients – and were undertaken by a range of practitioner-researchers, whose research contributed outstanding work for their postgraduate degrees. For some time, as tutors, we had been aware of the exceptional quality of academic research from our practitioner-students, and in realizing this book, we have been able to give the best of that work a public voice. The work of these contributing authors has allowed the book privileged access to insider stories and detailed perspectives from diverse organizations across a breadth of contemporary welfare settings.

Structure of the book to follow

The book adopts a thematic approach, organized into three parts, with each theme contributing to the bigger picture. Before turning to these, chapter

2 first examines political ideology and the ideas of civil society further, considering the recasting of relationships between civil society, the state, and markets, with consequent limitations on the roles of civil society and voluntary service organizations and actors.

Part One: The state of welfare and the new service industry

In Part One, three chapters explore the ongoing remodelling of welfare services, each considering the changing roles of voluntary services from the perspective of a different service field. Together, the chapters illustrate a new, increasingly privatized service industry with scaled-up and homogenized contracts, in which many large charities and voluntary organizations have become compliant participants. The chapters demonstrate the resulting erosion and frailty of badly needed services in some fields and the loss of specialist local services. All three chapters raise questions about the quality of services that can be maintained amid this onslaught of changes in welfare work.

Chapter 3 examines rapid changes and a growing privatization of social housing provision, with the emergence of huge, multi-service housing associations leading to serious consequences for poorer tenants and the supply of homes. Chapter 4 focuses on children's services in the context of an apparent crisis and impending reforms in statutory social work. It compares the experiences of professionals who have moved from local authority social work to charities, illustrating both the benefits and drawbacks of their current positions. The award of public service contracts to corporate contractors and predatory behaviours among large charities competing for contracts are well illustrated in chapter 5, which examines the involvement of voluntary organizations in criminal justice and probation services, further service fields undergoing major reforms.

Part Two: Power: Independence and grassroots organizing

Part Two considers organizations that have sought to retain autonomy and alternative models, in particular those working with specific groups in the population and focusing on grassroots approaches. The chapters question whether the goals, advocacy roles, and more participatory service approaches of small, often specialist local organizations can be sustained within the current climate. The black and minority ethnic voluntary organizations discussed in chapter 6 were established to offer alternatives to mainstream service failures and to combat racism. The chapter examines the survival of, and continuing needs for, specialist African Caribbean services provision in mental health provision.

The recent proliferation of faith-based food banks has highlighted serious inadequacies in public services. While other grassroots organizations are struggling to survive, faith-based organizations, such as those allied to the Black Majority Churches in chapter 7, are thriving, with growing incomes and membership, raising questions about potential collaboration between faith-based provision and the state in a secular society. Chapter 8 considers grassroots and local infrastructure organizations (Councils for Voluntary Services – CVS) in three local authority areas, where, in contrast to recent trends, local CVS support work retains some public funding. Questions about whether appropriate support can be sustained against the tide of external pressures and budget cuts demonstrate the ways in which grassroots and volunteer-led work is being recast. All three chapters highlight myths around the localism mantra, as burdens for unmet social needs but little power or resource devolve to small local groups, raising questions about the power they have to operate differently.

Part Three: Shadow conversations of workers

In Part Three, the three chapters highlight issues largely hidden from dominant narratives, exploring the experiences of workers facing rapidly changing conditions in emotionally demanding but ostensibly depoliticized settings. Chapter 9 highlights frontline workers' experiences. Despite worsening conditions, low pay, and excessive working hours, reflection that places organizational roles within a wider political context is mainly absent from dominant professional discussions, leaving workers feeling frustrated and disempowered.

Chapter 10, focusing on the implementation of the personalization programme in adult social care, explores workers' shadow conversations. These discussions are hidden from dominant organizational discourse, demonstrating the effectiveness of prevailing cultures in suppressing rational criticisms of changes, despite the visibly damaging impacts emerging both for services and workers. Chapter 11 similarly addresses concealed narratives, framing its research within ideas of collective well-being. It illustrates the lack of well-being now permeating voluntary service practice, with spaces for genuine meaning-making now displaced by competitive cultures and associated language and arrangements. It contrasts practitioners' narratives of their previous experiences, offering insights into the importance of alternative models.

Thus all three chapters confront assumptions about voluntary service work, the well-being of workers, and the value of provision under current conditions. They also provoke reflection on why mainstream narratives are allowed to dominate and, through past stories and hidden conversations, demonstrate that dissent persists. These reflections are central to our concluding chapter, which draws together ideas and issues raised in the different chapters, discussing the dangerous web that many voluntary organizations have been drawn into and the dilemmas that they now confront. This final chapter examines what it means to be a voluntary service organization, with rapidly vanishing spaces for alternatives and for voicing criticism and explores ways to reclaim civil society's independence and the spaces for dissent that are crucial to a healthy local democracy.

References

Baines, S., Hardill, I., and Wilson, R. (2011) 'Remixing the economy of welfare? Changing roles and relationships between the state and the voluntary and community sector'. *Social Policy and Society,* 10 (3), 337–9.

Baring Foundation (2015) *An Independent Mission: The voluntary sector in 2015.* London: Baring Foundation.

Barnes, M., Gell, C., and Thomas, P. (2010) 'Participation and social justice'. *Social Policy Review,* 22 (3), 253–74.

Barnes, M. and Prior, D. (eds) (2009) *Subversive Citizens: Power, agency and resistance in public services.* Bristol: Policy Press.

Brenton, M. (1985) *The Voluntary Sector in British Social Services.* Harlow: Longman.

Brown, P. and Calnan, M. (2010) 'The risks of managing uncertainty: The limitations of governance and choice, and the potential for trust'. *Social Policy and Society,* 9 (1), 13–24.

Buckingham, H. (2011) 'Hybridity, diversity and the division of labour in the third sector: What can we learn from homelessness organisations in the UK?'. *Voluntary Sector Review,* 2 (2), 157–75.

Cabinet Office (2011) *Open Public Services White Paper,* 11 July. Online. www.gov.uk/government/uploads/system/uploads/attachment_data/file/255288/OpenPublicServices-WhitePaper.pdf (accessed 26 August 2013).

— (2014a) *Transparency of Lobbying, Non-Party Campaigning and Trade Union Administration Act 2014.* Online. www.legislation.gov.uk/ukpga/2014/4/pdfs/ukpga_20140004_en.pdf (accessed December 2016).

— (2014b) *Open Public Services.* Online. www.gov.uk/government/uploads/system/uploads/attachment_data/file/291854/Open_Public_Services_Progress_Report_2014.pdf (accessed December 2016).

Cairns, B. (2009) 'The Independence of the Voluntary Sector from Government in England'. In M. Smerdon (ed.), *The first principle of voluntary action: Essays on the independence of the voluntary sector from government.* London: Baring Foundation, 35–50.

Carmel, E. and Harlock, J. (2008) 'Instituting the "Third Sector" as a governable terrain: Partnership, procurement and performance in the UK'. *Policy & Politics,* 36 (2), 155–71.

Challis, L., Fuller, S., Henwood, M., Klein, R., Plowden, W., Webb, A., Whittingham, P., and Wistow, G. (1988) *Joint Approaches to Social Policy: Rationality and practice*. Cambridge: Cambridge University Press.

Civil Exchange (2016) *Independence in Question: The voluntary sector in 2016*. London: Civil Exchange.

Clarke, J. and Newman, J. (1997) *The Managerial State: Power, politics and ideology in the remaking of social welfare*. London: Sage.

Clegg, S. (1989) *Frameworks of Power*. London: Sage.

Cooper, A. and Lousada, J. (2005) *Borderline Welfare: Feeling and fear of feeling in modern welfare* (The Tavistock Clinic Series). London: Karnac.

CSJ (2013) *Something's Got to Give: The state of Britain's voluntary sector*. London: Centre for Social Justice.

Hills, J., Obolenskaya, C.J.P., and Karagiannaki, E. (2015) *Falling Behind, Getting Ahead: The changing structure of inequality in the UK 2007–2013* (Social Policy in a Cold Climate Research Report 5). London: CASE & London School of Economics.

HM Treasury (2015) *Spending Review and Autumn Statement 2015: Key announcments*. Online. www.gov.uk/government/news/spending-review-and-autumn-statement-2015-key-announcements (accessed December 2016).

Hoggett, P. (2000) 'Social policy and the emotions'. In G. Lewis, S. Gewirtz, and J. Clarke (eds), *Rethinking Social Policy*. London: Sage, 141–55.

Holloway, J. (2005) '*Change the World without Taking Power. The meaning of revolution today. 2nd ed*. London: Pluto Press.

Jones, K., Brown, J., and Bradshaw, J. (1983) *Issues in Social Policy*. London: Routledge and Kegan Paul.

JRF (2016) *Destitution in the UK*. Joseph Rowntree Foundation. Online. www.jrf.org.uk/report/destitution-uk (accessed December 2016).

Keen, R. (2015) *Charities and the Voluntary Sector: Statistics* (House of Commons Library Briefing Paper Number SN05428). Online. researchbriefings.files.parliament.uk/documents/SN05428/SN05428.pdf (accessed December 2016).

Kendall, J. (2010) 'Bringing ideology back in: The erosion of political innocence in English third sector policy'. *Journal of Political Ideologies,* 15 (3), 241–58.

— and Knapp, M. (1996) *The Voluntary Sector in the UK*. Manchester: Manchester University Press.

LeBaron, G. and Dauvergne, P. (2014) 'Not just about the money: Corporatization is weakening activism and empowering big business'. *Open Democracy,* 14 March. Online. www.opendemocracy.net/author/peter-dauvergne (accessed May 2014).

Maguire, M. and Ball, S.J. (1994) 'Discourses of educational reform in the United Kingdom and the USA and the work of teachers'. *British Journal of In-Service Education,* 20 (1), 5–16.

Marquand, D. (2015) 'Can social democracy rise to the challenge of the far right across Europe?'. *New Statesman,* 8 December.

Mason, P. (2015) *Post Capitalism: A guide to our future*. London: Allen Lane.

McKie, R. (2016) 'Scientists attack their "muzzling" by government'. *The Guardian,* 20 February. Online. www.theguardian.com/science/2016/feb/20/scientists-attack-muzzling-government-state-funded-cabinet-office (accessed December 2016).

Milbourne, L. (2013) *Voluntary Sector in Transition: Hard times or new opportunities?* Bristol: Policy Press.

— and Cushman, M. (2015) 'Complying, transforming or resisting in the new austerity? Realigning social welfare and independent action among English voluntary organisations'. *Journal of Social Policy,* 44 (3), 463–86.

Murray, U. (2012) 'Local government and the meaning of publicness'. In J. Manson, (ed.), *Public Service on the Brink.* Exeter: Imprint Academic, 41–66.

— (2013) 'To what extent is the voluntary sector colonised by neo-liberal thinking?' Paper presented at the 8th International Critical Management Conference, *Extending the Limits of Neo-liberal Capitalism,* Manchester, 1–12 July. Online. www.independentaction.net/wp-content/uploads/2013/09/Voluntary-Sector-Neo-Liberal-thinking-Ursula-Murray.pdf (accessed December 2016).

NCIA (2015) *Fight or fright: Voluntary services in 2015* (NCIA Inquiry into the Future of Voluntary Services Summary and Discussion of the Inquiry Findings). London: National Coalition for Independent Action. Online. www.independentaction.net/wp-content/uploads/2015/02/NCIA-Inquiry-summary-report-final.pdf (accessed December 2016).

NCVO (2016) 'Fast Facts'. In *UK Civil Society Almanac 2016.* London: National Council for Voluntary Organisations. Online. https://data.ncvo.org.uk/a/almanac16/fast-facts-5 (accessed December 2016).

Padley, M. (2013) 'Delivering localism: The critical role of trust and collaboration'. *Social Policy and Society,* 12 (3), 343–54.

Perry, J., Williams, M., Sefton, T., and Haddad, M. (2014) *Emergency Use Only: Understanding and reducing the use of food banks in the UK.* Oxfam GB. Online. www.cpag.org.uk/sites/default/files/Foodbank%20Report_web.pdf (accessed December 2016).

Pfeffer, J. and Salancik, G.R. (2003) *The External Control of Organizations.* Stanford: Stanford University Press.

Powell, W.W. and Di Maggio, P. (eds) (1991) *The New Institutionalism in Organizational Analysis.* Chicago: University of Chicago Press.

Prochaska, F. (2014) 'The state of charity'. Lecture given at the Charity Commission Annual Public Meeting, 17 September. Online. www.gov.uk/government/news/the-state-of-charity (accessed December 2016).

Rees, J., Taylor, R., and Damm, C. (2013) 'Does Sector Matter? Understanding the experiences of providers in the Work Programme' (Third Sector Research Centre Working paper 92). Online. www.birmingham.ac.uk/generic/tsrc/documents/tsrc/working-papers/working-paper-92.pdf (accessed December 2016).

Taylor, M. and Kendall, J. (1996) 'History of the voluntary sector'. In J. Kendall, and M. Knapp, (eds), *The Voluntary Sector in the UK.* Manchester: Manchester University Press, 28–60.

UK Parliament (2016) *Charities (Protection and Social Investment) Act 2016.* London: Cabinet Office. Online. http://services.parliament.uk/bills/2015-16/charitiesprotectionandsocialinvestment.html (accessed 20 August 2016).

Walker, D. (2015) 'David Cameron's love affair with the voluntary sector is over'. *The Guardian*, 30 September. Online. www.theguardian.com/society/2015/sep/30/david-camerons-love-affair-voluntary-sector-over (accessed 4 August 2016).

Chapter 2
Civil society and neo-liberalism
Ursula Murray and Linda Milbourne

Chapter 1 has mapped the political, policy, and historical trajectories leading to the turbulent times in which voluntary organizations now find themselves. However, little in conventional theory has adequately explained their political entrapment and the dilemmas that they currently face. Two key ideological discourses emerged in the previous chapter that offer a frame for interpreting the experiences of voluntary service organizations discussed in later chapters. First, we argue that neo-liberal ideology has permeated the roles and purposes of many voluntary service organizations, resulting in a culture of compliance and survivalism, gradually displacing the ethical and moral roots of voluntary action. Second, the contested meanings of civil society are often underplayed; a clearer understanding is needed if we are to distinguish between its role as a form of consensual glue in maintaining social order and that of a promoter of independent critical voices.

Two key questions emerge. First, what is the rationale for voluntary service organizations if critical alternatives, as chapter 1 illustrates, are being marginalized? Second, what is the potential for civil society organizations and movements to rekindle critical voices and reclaim local democracy?

Neo-liberal ideology: Realigning public, private, and third sectors

The present malaise among voluntary services described in chapter 1 did not arise in isolation, and the explanation lies in a better understanding of the political economy and associated ideology reshaping the state, voluntary organizations, and civil society over the past four decades. This ideology is defined as 'neo-liberalism' and stands in opposition to the Keynesian rational economics that held sway in the post-war era until the end of the 1970s. In simple terms:

> Neo-liberalism sees competition as the defining characteristic of human relations. It redefines citizens as consumers, whose democratic choices are best exercised by buying and selling, a process that rewards merit and punishes inefficiency. It maintains

that the 'market' delivers benefits that could never be achieved by planning.

Monbiot, 2016a

It is not just an economic policy but also encompasses the social, cultural, and political, which valorize the individual and oppose collective welfare and public sector provision. Monbiot points out how this ideology is now so pervasive that few people even recognize it as ideology, such that it remained nameless for many years. Both Judt (2010) and Monbiot (2016b) describe how this transition to neo-liberalism came about at the end of the 1970s and how in different forms it has come to dominate politics and economics ever since. Neo-liberal market thinking has shaped consumer capitalism and corporate globalization in a lethal combination (Fraser, 2017). It has enabled the dominance of financial services, the digital revolution, and an omnipresent contract culture, also producing a housing crisis and rising levels of social inequality not seen since the 1930s.

Trade union powers to resist such changes and the socially protective value of public sector bureaucracies (du Gay, 2005) have both been undermined. A slow recovery from the global financial implosion of 2008 has reinforced a politics of austerity, allied to a smaller-state ideology. A marketized state (Bobbitt, 2002) is now transforming into a fully fledged market society where being human means becoming commodified. 'Hatred of dependency' (Hoggett, 2000: 159) and denying the importance of human interdependence are also pervasive. As Cooper and Lousada (2016) note, whereas the post-war settlement aspired to be humane and socially inclusive, albeit tainted by 'professional paternalism, institutional racism and vested interest, we now face a retreat from the idea of universal services towards the industrialization of social care itself'.

Whitfield (2012) has meticulously documented the way in which public sector modernization has mutated into four interrelated processes: financialization, personalization, marketization, and privatization. The neo-liberal policies of governments since 1979 have enabled corporates to enter newly created markets for public services and to profit from social and welfare services that were publicly owned. With government outsourcing providing an easy route to short-term profits, the corporate sector has lacked incentives for longer-term development. Instead, it has facilitated a huge growth in low-wage, low-quality jobs with reduced social protection for employees. There is a compelling case for arguing that neo-liberal economics is no longer sustainable and that it cannot respond either to recent global challenges such as climate change, ageing societies, and migration

(Mason, 2015) or to the marked class- and age-related cultural divides in the UK revealed in the outcome of the EU Referendum (Elliott, 2016).

Davies (2016) explains this illogical adherence to contemporary neo-liberalism by distinguishing different phases. Despite underlying economic applications or techniques remaining similar, he argues that ethical and philosophical stances have shifted and mutated. In particular, since 2008, he recognizes a punitive phase of neo-liberalism characterized by vindictive policymaking towards vulnerable populations that largely defies rational argument or evidence. The (irrational) necessity of austerity policies has been used to justify a smaller state but this is primarily about reducing the size and scope of the social state. Essentially, this means cutting local authority expenditure, and in turn, local voluntary services (especially medium and small organizations), which have relied on local government for half their funding. Public expenditure cuts of some 40 per cent to local government departments between 2010 and 2015 (IFS, 2015; *The Guardian*, 2015) will be replicated by 2020. With community centres, Sure Start provision, day centres, and libraries already closing, a quarter of local councils are now considering the closure and sale of public parks. Housing estates are being sold, driving social housing residents into private rented accommodation. Whereas 80 per cent of local authority funding currently comes directly from central government, by 2020 this will have fallen to 0 per cent, when it is due to be replaced by the retention of local business rates. While devolution is a potentially positive development, it could also prove to be a highly regressive change for localities with rapidly rising social care costs, proportionally high residential areas, and low business investment.

The private and voluntary sectors

The rapid growth of state funding for voluntary organizations and associated cross-sector partnerships between 1997 and 2008 emerged from a context of expanding public services. But after 2010, this reversed with rapid public policy changes under the Coalition and the Conservative governments, which reflected a sharp shift to an explicitly neo-liberal response to economic recession. The emphasis was on privatizing public services and extending the role of the corporate sector in UK services. New centrally driven government programmes emerged, such as the Work Programme in 2011 (Damm, 2014). Primary contracts were largely awarded to corporations, such as Ingeus, A4e, and Serco, but hundreds of voluntary organizations were engaged as sub-contractors to the private sector for the first time. By 2015, when the Probation Service was privatized, voluntary organizations were widely involved as bid partners and sub-contractors to corporate suppliers, despite negative experiences of the Work Programme.

As Ishkanian (2012: 177) observes, 'neo-liberal reforms are not benign'. Yet there was little criticism or expression of misgivings. From 2010 onwards, voluntary service infrastructure bodies, such as the National Council for Voluntary Organisations (NCVO) and the National Association for Voluntary and Community Action (NAVCA) encouraged voluntary organizations to bid for public service contracts nationally and locally, and policy and research discussions typically focused on the sector's role in 'scaling up to meet the challenge' (TSRC, 2012). ACEVO, the professional association of CEOs for voluntary organizations, consistently presented voluntary services as able to replace public sector delivery. These bodies adopted ostensibly neutral political positions, but were effectively promoting the incorporation of voluntary services into these neo-liberal reforms. Yet debates around the damaging impacts of privatization on services and the independent roles and purposes of voluntary action were strikingly absent (Benson, 2015).

The communitarian thrust of the Conservatives' Big Society agenda (Cabinet Office, 2011) was equally infused with neo-liberal principles. Lewis (2012) argues that its overriding purpose was always to drive through massive public spending cuts, implement marketization, new managerialist partnerships, and individualization in welfare through 'choice' and 'personalization' agendas. In effect, the aim was to realize a smaller, marketized state, locating responsibility for local burdens with individuals and groups whose voluntaristic merits were contrasted with negative state dependency.

A culture of compliance and survivalism

The silencing of voluntary organizations is a more complicated story than just their fear of losing funding; it is also a narrative of complicity in failing to publicly defend ideas of welfare, public service, and social justice. As chapter 1 describes, this has taken place over several eras of political and policy change, with voluntary service providers being increasingly harnessed to accede to government agendas.

Between 2010 and 2012, the absence among voluntary organizations of any co-ordinated or critical voice against the Welfare Reform Bill (2010–11), which ushered in a punitive Act, erasing many principles of the welfare state, was particularly telling. It was indicative of a loss of voice and capacity for dissent among many organizations, and this failure to challenge the neo-liberal agendas of the Coalition and Conservative governments after 2010 reflects a culture of fear subsequently reinforced by the confidentiality and gagging clauses in contracts. However, it does not explain an apparently self-serving attitude to the privatization of public services or misplaced aspirations that voluntary providers could replace public providers. Nor why voluntary organizations believed they could become partners with for-profit corporations without ethical or moral cost. Public debate on the wider ethical and moral meaning of public services and civic life has been eroded (Murray, 2012) and the complicity of voluntary organizations in this needs recognition.

From the early 1990s onwards, driven by business principles (Hood, 1991), New Public Management thinking was used to 'modernize' and discipline local government (Power, 1994; Hoggett, 1996). These ideas subsequently permeated voluntary organizations through contract culture, cross-sector partnerships, quality management systems, and audit systems. Enticed by a flow of funding, contracts, and special projects, much time and effort was expended in professionalizing voluntary organizations. The embrace of a new language and culture in seemingly benign new management systems incrementally changed the ethos of voluntary organizations. By the late 1990s, close links between leadership figures in the voluntary sector and senior politicians in the New Labour government secured a consensus, which marginalized criticisms. As many organizations remodelled, refocusing activities around a competitive business model, it reshaped thinking about organizational forms, purposes, and governance. The business model brought with it an obsession with a culture of measurement – targets and outputs – and echoes of the perverse ethics of the corporate world (Long, 2008). The widespread loss of a relational ethos (Miller *et al.*, 2006) has induced passivity and a culture of compliance rather than one encompassing dissent.

The pressures of open competition, which intensified after 2010, have also undermined the autonomy of smaller local organizations within federated national structures, such as Age UK. Competition from larger charities and housing associations has encouraged them to emulate top-down, corporate structures and operate centralized tendering. However, the overall picture is complex and varied. Local voluntary service organizations have generally remained more accountable to their local memberships, and many social movements exist outside the contract culture or are entirely reliant on voluntary action.

Civil society: Contested meanings

Chapter 1 highlighted how normative concepts of civil society serve the dominant ideology and negate more oppositional models that might encourage independent and critical voices. These contested meanings of civil society need a more explicit understanding in charting a path forward.

Civil society is a term that re-entered the political vocabulary in the UK in the 1980s, following the rise of radical social movements and political change in Eastern Europe. In the UK, its association is largely apolitical, and civil society has often been mistakenly equated with formal voluntary organizations. However, Edwards (2009) emphasizes civil society's vital role in the public sphere, highlighting the constrasting political ideas about civil society, while Howell and Pearce (2001) problematize the concept, identifying a consensus versus conflictual framework. Kaldor (2003: 10) likewise distinguishes between an activist civil society represented by social movements and a neo-liberal one, in which she locates charities. She distinguishes five different ways of understanding civil society, which offer further helpful distinctions: *societas civilis* – based on the rule of law and civility; *bürgerliche Gesellschaft* – encompassing all organized social life beyond the state and the family; *activist* – represented by social movements and civic activists; *neo-liberal* – in which she includes formal third sector organizations, including charities and voluntary services; and finally, the *postmodern* – which she associates with nationalist and fundamentalist movements. Civil society is therefore not intrinsically benign, philanthropic, or concerned with furthering social justice. Indeed, the strong associational life in 1930s Italy is recognized as having facilitated the development of fascism (Paxton, 2012).

Powell's (2007) explanation of current political tensions arising from the different historical roots of civil society is also helpful. First, the idea of civil society as social capital is grounded in neo-Tocquevillian associational and communitarian thinking (for example, Etzioni, 1993; Putnam, 2000). Ultimately inspired by market capitalism, this thinking underpins social policies allied with compassionate conservatism, in which the welfare gaps left by a smaller state will be plugged by small platoons of volunteers. Second, the idea of civil society engaged in social partnership conserves a corporatist model of social policy based on co-operative consensus between government, market, and civil society. Perspectives split between those who see the risks of co-option as suffocating civil society and generating new forms of governance and social control, and those who regard co-operation with the state, primarily at a local level, as potentially offering tangible forms of democratic inclusion: the state as enabler not enforcer. Third, a more recent social policy movement has sought to influence democratic representation and public service provision through promoting citizen co-production in welfare, a reworking of earlier forms of mutual associations.

There are concerns about each of these ways of understanding civil society, since most deny the importance of alternative political perspectives that might constitute a 'social left' (Powell, 2009: 50). Drawing on Bourdieu (1998), de Sousa Santos (2007; 2008), and others, Powell (2007) strongly critiques advocates of dominant liberal models of civil society, such as Etzioni (1993), Fukuyama (1995), and Putnam (2000). This criticism is reinforced by three examples from the past four decades discussed below, when the state has intervened directly to influence civil society in radically different ways: instituting the contract culture, introducing compassionate conservatism alongside restrictive legislation, and, earlier, some local governments promoting radical social-left policies in the 1980s.

Contract culture and civil society

Much has already been said in chapter 1 about New Labour's policies from 1997 onwards as a part of its Third Way political strategy, identifying a third sector between state and private sector to address state and market failures. Policymakers and academics effectively revived the concept and profile of 'civil society', and new funding streams reshaped voluntary organizations both as service providers in contractual partnerships with the state and in generating innovative community-based projects to tackle social problems. Thus, via rhetoric, policymaking, and funding patronage, New Labour instituted and extended a contract culture initiated by the previous Conservative government, harnessing the energies of many voluntary organizations into a state-defined agenda.

Compassionate conservatism

Civil society has also been redefined by Conservative politicians through compassionate conservatism, specifically in the Big Society agenda (Blond, 2010; Cabinet Office, 2010). A popular discourse emerged about the virtue of voluntary groups addressing locally understood needs within a leaner, more efficient and permanently smaller state (Cabinet Office, 2013). While this offered an attractive mobilizing metaphor around community empowerment and generated wide interest, it ultimately lacked coherence as a programme for change and fragmented when voluntary organizations encountered the lack of funding. The public investment necessary to achieve the localism strategies intended was absent. Despite a wave of criticism (Ellison, 2011) and the marginalization of Big Society as a political project, the community empowerment rhetoric has continued to resonate, whether in the efforts of volunteers running food banks and homeless shelters, faith-based organizations providing safety nets for people facing destitution (Taylor-Goodby, 2015; Trussell Trust, 2016), or in volunteers running libraries or local parks as in areas of London or Liverpool.

These examples raise questions about whether this is genuine voluntary action and community empowerment, or emergency responses to desperate needs and attempts to salvage loss of public services (Whitfield, 2016; Harris, 2014; Munby, 2015). Compassionate conservatism as a political ideology has ensured that voluntary efforts are increasingly being channelled into such community-based first aid to tackle growing welfare needs, curbing aspirations and activities more aligned to advocacy, campaigning, or dissenting civil society roles. Gaps in services and facilities, unmet needs, mechanisms directly suppressing dissent and criticism, and recent restrictive legislation are all examples noted previously of securing a seemingly new consensus about voluntary action.

Support for a social left?

The social left in civil society (Powell, 2007), which emerged in the UK voluntary sector in the late 1970s, stands in sharp contrast to the transitions illustrated above. Wainwright (2003) captures the lived history and impact of roughly a decade, when social movements, communities, trade unions, and the local state combined around devolved political power and developed radical alternatives. These addressed inequalities but also alternative local economic development and initiated far-sighted action research, such as around food policy. In summary, this social-left period demonstrated a fundamentally different role for civil society organizations, supported by a small number of left-leaning local authorities.

Following deep public expenditure cuts and the demise of these key public funders, especially the GLC and the metropolitan authorities (Mets), this upsurge of activity was marginalized by 1986 and gradually expunged from mainstream voluntary sector discourse. Yet the 1990s briefly saw radical social activism return around care in the community and domestic violence, with both translating into funded projects. The lessons of these times, especially those arising from reflections around 'in and against the state' (LEWRG, 1980), are a source of renewed interest as diverse new social movements once again emerge outside mainstream voluntary services. The Climate Psychology Alliance, Black Lives Matter, and Sisters Uncut represent a few among many new activist movements, discussion of which is largely absent from the discourse of voluntary services.

The rationale for voluntary service organizations

Where are formally organized charities and voluntary organizations located in these competing meanings of civil society? From distinctions explored above, it is clear that they can largely be identified with a consensual, neo-liberal understanding of civil society, co-opted into contracts, social partnerships, and social capital building projects, aiding state and markets. It is worth interrogating further the reasons for the existence of a distinct third sector and the ideological value to governments of distinguishing and co-opting this part of civil society. What is the rationale for voluntary service organizations if independent approaches are marginalized and critical dissent is not tolerated?

The growth and forms of voluntary service organizations have been rationalized at various times as responding to both state and market failures to adequately address social welfare problems by offering alternatives (Harris and Rochester, 2001). However, this reasoning hardly holds true for the present when alternative models have been significantly restricted by contractualism. Allied theory also highlights the comparative advantages of voluntary organizations working outside mainstream services, especially with marginal groups of people (Billis and Glennerster, 1998), as reasons for maintaining specialist voluntary service activities independently of public services. However, the proactive mainstreaming of voluntary providers into state services (Kendall, 2000) and now their incorporation into privatized contracts has lured voluntary services away from their previously more distinct or complementary service roles, undermining these apparent benefits. Thus, while these ideas make sense historically, they fail to explain recent transitions, with many charities competing and heavily engaged in a growing procurement market – no longer autonomous or specialist, but corporate partners or sub-contractors, unable to voice criticism or influence.

A Weberian organizational analysis, which identifies mutual and voluntary organizations as inevitably degenerating, gradually relinquishing social values in favour of growth, formal organization, and for-profit motives (Morgan, 1988), seems to offer some validity. Together with resource dependency theory (Pfeffer and Salancik, 2003), it assumes that pressures to survive successfully invariably produce organizations that seek to maximize their advantages through growth and increased income. In other words, all organizations are essentially competitive, driven by growth and survival needs. This may explain the actions of voluntary organizations heavily engaged in contractualism and the success of neo-liberal ideology in harnessing them, but fails to account for the many smaller local organizations that appear torn between social missions and financial viability. Nor does it account for widespread compliance with the constraints imposed in a corporate services market or the mainly uncritical acceptance of the ideological emphasis on voluntarism as a substitute for funded services.

The concept of institutional isomorphism in new institutional theory (Di Maggio and Powell, 1983) has been applied widely in voluntary sector research, to explain how smaller, less powerful organizations assume the features and arrangements of larger, more dominant organizations. Di Maggio and Powell (1983) point to the likelihood of organizations mimicking high-status agencies in similar fields of operation, showing how this begins as a rhetorical or expedient process or is used instrumentally to secure advantage (Aiken, 2010). Isomorphism can also be coercive, such as when small organizations are pressured to adopt uncomfortable terms in contracts because of their survival needs. As new arrangements slowly become the accepted way of doing things, the organizational environment gradually transforms, as individual organizations comply with dominant cultures and practices that have thus become normative, exerting further pressure on outsiders or resisters. Where cross-sector working is prevalent, it spreads expectations, discourse, and arrangements, fostering normative isomorphism and effectively achieving a dominant consensus about how things are done.

While this describes processes that often happen, isomorphism largely fails to analyse the power embedded in dominant organizational cultures, which determines these contextual rules of play (Clegg, 1989). As later chapters illustrate in varied settings, the models of more powerful actors and organizations legitimize and control discourse and behaviours, devaluing and marginalizing alternatives. Differential power in contractual relationships is overt and largely positional (Lukes, 1974), and contracts and sub-contracts are increasingly controlled at a distance through detailed specification and regulation: 'rituals of verification' (Power, 1997). Thus, small voluntary organizations especially have almost no opportunity to negotiate terms or use relational means to rebalance differential levels of power and influence the resulting exclusions and constraints.

Much voluntary sector research has thus focused on descriptive features or processes and has often stopped short of drawing on wider social, political, or organizational theory to seek explanations. Later chapters employ different theoretical perspectives to examine recent changes, and we argue that applying ideas of Foucauldian governmentality offers a valuable lens through which to examine the seemingly consensual spaces and normative arrangements that surround civil society and voluntary organizations. Communications and systemic changes are reinforced by technical and apparently neutral planning, management, and monitoring mechanisms to create powerful forces for embedding ideology, expectations, and actions. Accordingly, these become legitimized, reshaping organizational behaviours and discourse, ensuring their dominance and inevitability.

Concepts drawn from governmentality add to an understanding of the tools underpinning neo-liberalism and provide an insight into how the dominance of a particular ideology and associated arrangements is achieved and sustained. The increased prevalence of voluntary services adopting entrepreneurial models, partnering with corporate services (Dauvergne and LeBaron, 2014), and depending on private finance, together with a government utilizing behavioural sciences to shape welfare perceptions and behaviours and advance volunteerism, highlight further examples of governmentality at work, remodelling organizations, expectations, and also individual citizens' behaviours in wider civil society.

What is the potential for civil society to reclaim local democracy?

The result of the 2016 EU referendum has revealed deep geographical and class divides across the UK. This moment of heightened political change has also given rise to an upsurge of racism, xenophobia, and incivility. The rise of populist movements is linking a reactionary politics of identity with failures in social and economic policies (Malik, 2017). As de Sousa Santos (2007: xvi) points out, societies can be 'politically democratic but socially fascist'. In response to such growing forces of conservatism, Powell (2009) argues that democracy needs to reinvent itself from the bottom up. A current challenge for civil society is thus the renewal of local democracy: one in which 'there is no rigorous distinction between politics and ethics' (Eagleton, 2003: 178).

A progressive framework of local democracy is critical if the particularism of voluntary action is to connect with the broader political and welfare demands reshaping the role of the state. Yet local democracy has been hollowed out by decades of cuts to local government and erosion of its powers. Small-scale participatory governance has been privileged over representative forms of local democracy, when both are essential to any movement seeking to reclaim local democracy (Newman, 2014). Szreter (2012) argues that a robust UK civil society has always relied on effective and well-resourced public institutions, and that, historically, increased local government investment and local democratic accountability has been the surest way to promote strong civic engagement.

Devolution in England

Governments have turned to regional policy and renewed state intervention (Mazzucato, 2016) as the UK shows signs of recession and deficit reduction is now perceived as a failed economic policy (Wren-Lewis, 2016). The Prime Minister, Theresa May (Goodall, 2016), has specifically referred to Joseph Chamberlain, the late Victorian municipal activist and his 'civic gospel' (Szreter, 2002) as a model. The current devolution of powers from central government intended to promote economic growth and rebalance the UK economy has moved centre stage, but it also presents an opportunity for civil society to reclaim local democracy.

The UK is 'one of the most centralized countries in the OECD' (BBC News, 2014), with increasing dependence on London for creating jobs and for a third of all tax revenue (McGough, 2016). A growing demand from core cities to be allowed to make their own decisions and promote their own local economies has finally been heeded in the recent devolution of Whitehall powers and budgets to new English sub-regional Combined Authorities (CAs). Following in the wake of greater powers devolved to Scotland in 2014, the Cities and Local Government Devolution Act 2016 is bringing about fast-tracked devolution in England. Yet devolution remains a high-risk strategy with an unresolved contradiction at its core. If austerity, requiring budget cuts of 40 per cent by 2020 in the most deprived areas of the north, continues, the benefits of any devolved control may well be negated.

The scale of the new devolved powers is well illustrated by the Greater Manchester Combined Authority with its 10 local authorities, 12 Clinical Commissioning Groups, 15 NHS Trusts, joint ownership of the Local Enterprise Partnership, and 100,000 employees serving a population of 2.5 million people. In 2016, an NHS budget of £6 billion was devolved from Whitehall to promote integrated social care and health. The CA's role thus spans local economic growth, skills development, transport, housing, and health.

Greater Manchester CA leadership consists of the leaders of the ten councils each casting one vote. These local councils have a long experience of joint working on a voluntary basis, following the abolition of the Mets in 1986; they share powers, statutory duties, and, most importantly, politics. However, devolution deals require new metro-Mayors to be elected in 2017, and power struggles are anticipated. National politicians are already putting themselves forward to stand in Greater Manchester, Liverpool City Region, West Yorkshire, West Midlands, and others. In the south, devolution has been a more contentious process, with strong political resistance to mayoral governance.

The role of civil society

Civil society matters in reshaping any new settlement, yet devolution has been criticized as opaque, technocratic, and undemocratic with public debate largely absent. It has neglected 'who people feel they are and how they will be able to influence' (Carr-West, 2016). From the point of view of a small voluntary organization, 'what appears like devolution from a Whitehall perspective looks a lot like re-centralization' (Corry, 2015), generating concern that sub-regional authorities will favour contracts with private corporations or larger voluntary organizations with minimal accountability to local communities. A more positive view (Locality/NAVCA, 2016) is that devolution is an opportunity to revive local economies and to use economic growth to support social justice. This would allow ordinary people the agency and power to transform their public services.

Greater Manchester's 15,000 voluntary organizations have a £1 billion turnover (Dayson *et al.*, 2013), with half reporting at least one funding source from public funds, of which three-quarters were local authorities. New sub-regional provision involving voluntary services is already reported as improving mental health services, with commissioners collaborating across the old boundaries (Slawson, 2016), with small-scale, community-based organizations able to identify new needs or demonstrate how links with their communities can enhance services (Gamsu, 2011: 8). Devolved health and social care budgets could potentially lead to all commissioning being undertaken in this way, enabling innovatory rethinking.

Resolving differences and conflicts between particular interests and wider social and strategic demands is central to achieving such improvements. Yet current research by Hunter and Longlands (2016) into understanding and redefining civil society in the north of England speaks only of helping local communities to develop common goals or of the general relevance of locality, identity, and values. These emphasize associational life, boosting social capital, and transforming the feel of deprived neighbourhoods in the north of England. Is this neo-Tocquevillian associational and communitarian thinking sufficient at a time when regional inequalities, class, and social divisions have become so comprehensively exposed alongside growing impoverishment and serious welfare failures? Reclaiming local democracy is about a space where public values (Newman and Clarke, 2009) can be contested and where they can then become a focus for collective aspiration.

References

Aiken, M. (2010) 'Taking the Long View: Conceptualising the challenges facing UK third sector organizations in the social welfare field'. In A. Evers, and A. Zimmer (eds), *Third Sector Organizations in Turbulent Times: Sports, cultural and social services in five European countries*. Baden Baden: Nomos, 295–315.

BBC News (2014) 'UK "one of the most centralised OECD countries"'. *BBC News,* 12 January. Online. www.bbc.co.uk/news/business-25909238 (accessed 23 July 2016).

Benson, A. (2015) 'Voluntary action, the state and the market'. *Soundings: A Journal of Politics and Culture,* 60, Austerity and Dissent, 71–82.

Billis, D. and Glennerster, H. (1998) 'Human services and the voluntary sector: Towards a theory of comparative advantage'. *Journal of Social Policy,* 27 (1), 79–98.

Blond, P. (2010) *Red Tory: How the Left and Right have broken Britain and how we can fix it*. London: Faber & Faber.

Bobbitt, P. (2002) *The Shield of Achilles. War, peace and the course of history*. London: Penguin Books.

Bourdieu, P. (1998) *Acts of Resistance: Against the new myths of our times*. Cambridge: Polity Press.

Cabinet Office (2010) *Building the Big Society*, 18 May. Online. www.gov.uk/government/publications/building-the-big-society (accessed December 2016).

— (2011) *Open Public Services White Paper*, 11 July. Online. www.gov.uk/government/uploads/system/uploads/attachment_data/file/255288/OpenPublicServices-WhitePaper.pdf (accessed 26 August 2013).

— (2013) *Lord Mayor's Banquet 2013: Prime Minister's speech*. Online. www.gov.uk/government/speeches/lord-mayors-banquet-2013-prime-ministers-speech (accessed December 2016).

Carr-West, J. (2016) 'Lessons from the ballot box'. *The MJ,* 11 May. Online. www.themj.co.uk/Lessons-from-the-ballot-box/204228 (accessed December 2016).

Clegg, S. (1989) *Frameworks of Power*. London: Sage.

Cooper, A. and Lousada, J. (2016) 'What's our state of mind? Borderline welfare 10 years on'. Paper presented at the Tavistock Centre Seminar, London, 17 June.

Corry, D. (2015) 'Reach for a helpful partnership'. *The MJ,* 4 May. Online. www.themj.co.uk/Reach-for-a-helpful-partnership/204001 (acessed December 2016).

Damm, C. (2014) 'A mid-term review of third sector involvement in the Work Programme'. *Voluntary Sector Review,* 5 (1), 97–116.

Dauvergne, P. and LeBaron, G. (2014) *Protest Inc.: The corporatization of activism*. Cambridge: Polity Press.

Davies, W. (2016) 'The new neoliberalism'. *New Left Review,* 101 (September–October), 121–34.

Dayson, C., Eadson, W., Sanderson, E., and Wilson, I. (2013) *Greater Manchester: State of the voluntary sector 2013*. Sheffield: Centre for Regional Economic and Social Research.

De Sousa Santos, B. (ed.) (2007) *Democratizing Democracy. Beyond the liberal democratic canon*. London: Verso.

— (ed.) (2008) *Another Knowledge is Possible: Beyond northern epistemologies*. London: Verso: London.

Di Maggio, P. and Powell, W. (1983) 'The iron cage revisited: Institutional isomorphism and collective rationality in organizational fields'. *American Sociological Review,* 48, 147–60.

Du Gay, P. (ed.) (2005) *The Values of Bureaucracy.* Oxford: Oxford University Press.

Eagleton, T. (2003) *After Theory.* London: Allen Lane.

Edwards, M. (2009) *Civil Society.* Cambridge: Polity Press.

Elliott, L. (2016) 'The fragile UK economy has a chance to abandon failed policies post Brexit'. *The Guardian,* 17 July. Online. www.theguardian.com/business/2016/jul/17/uk-economy-brexit-failed-economic-policies (accessed December 2016).

Ellison, N. (2011) 'The Conservative Party and the "Big Society"'. In C. Holden, M. Kilkey, and G. Ramia (eds), *Social Policy Review 23: Analysis and debate in social policy, 2011.* Bristol: Policy Press, 45–62.

Etzioni, A. (1993) *The spirit of Community: Rights, responsibilities, and the communitarian agenda.* New York: Crown.

Fraser, N. (2017) 'The end of progressive neo liberalism'. *Dissent Magazine.* Online. www.dissentmagazine.org/online_articles/progressive-neoliberalism-reactionary-populism-nancy-fraser (accessed January 2017).

Fukuyama, F. (1995) *Trust: The social virtues and the creation of prosperity.* London: Hamish Hamilton.

Gamsu, M. (2011) *'Tell Us What the Problem Is and We'll Try to Help': Towards more effective commissioning of local voluntary sector organizations.* Manchester: Voluntary Sector North West.

Goodall, L. (2016) 'Who was Theresa May's political hero Joseph Chamberlain?'. *BBC News,* August 15. Online. www.bbc.co.uk/news/uk-politics-37053114 (accessed December 2016).

The Guardian (2015) Editorial: 'Osborne is creating a northern poorhouse'. 26 November. Online. www.theguardian.com/commentisfree/2015/nov/26/the-guardian-view-on-local-councils-osborne-is-creating-a-northern-poorhouse (accessed 23 July 2016).

Harris, J. (2014) 'Is saving Newcastle a mission impossible?'. *The Guardian,* 24 November. Online. www.theguardian.com/news/2014/nov/24/-sp-is-saving-newcastle-mission-impossible (accessed July 2016).

Harris, M. and Rochester, C. (2001) *Voluntary Organisations and Social Policy in Britain: Perspectives on change and choice.* Basingstoke: Palgrave.

Hoggett, P. (1996) 'New modes of control in public service'. *Public Administration,* 74 (Spring), 9–32.

— (2000), 'Social policy and the emotions'. In G. Lewis, S. Gewirtz, and J. Clarke (eds), *Rethinking Social Policy.* London: Sage, 141–55.

Hood, C. (1991) 'A public management for all seasons?'. *Public Administration,* 69 (1), 3–19.

Howell, J. and Pearce, J. (2001) *Civil Society and Development: A critical interrogation.* Boulder, CO: Lynne Reinner.

Hunter, J. and Longlands, S. (2016) 'Understanding and redefining civil society in the North: Laying the groundwork'. *IPPR North,* 21 April. Online. www.ippr.org/publications/understanding-and-redefining-civil-society-in-the-north-laying-the-groundwork (accessed December 2016).

IFS (2015) *Local Government and the Nations: A devolution revolution?* Institute for Fiscal Studies. Online. www.ifs.org.uk/uploads/publications/budgets/Budgets%202015/Autumn/Phillips_local_government_and_devolution.pdf (accessed December 2016).

Ishkanian, A. (2012) 'From shock therapy to Big Society: Lessons from the post-socialist transitions'. In A. Ishkanian, and S. Szreter (eds), *The Big Society Debate: A new agenda for social welfare?* Cheltenham: Edward Elgar, 168–78.

Judt, T. (2010) *Ill Fares the Land: A treatise on our present discontents*. London: Allen Lane.

Kaldor, M. (2003) *Global Civil Society: An answer to war*. Cambridge: Polity Press.

Kendall, J. (2000) 'The mainstreaming of the third sector into public policy in England in the late 1990s: Whys and wherefores'. *Policy and Politics,* 28 (4), 541–62.

Lewis, D. (2012) 'Conclusion: The Big Society and social policy'. In A. Ishkanian, and S. Szreter (eds), *The Big Society Debate: A new agenda for social welfare*. Cheltenham: Edward Elgar.

LEWRG (London-Edinburgh Weekend Return Group) (1980) *In and Against the State*. London: Pluto.

Locality/NAVCA (2016) *Devolution for People and Communities*. National Association for Voluntary and Community Action. Online. https://www.navca.org.uk/assets/000/000/121/Devolution_key_principles_FINAL_original.pdf (accessed December 2016).

Long, S. (2008) *The Perverse Organisation and Its Deadly Sins*. London: Karnac Books.

Lukes, S. (1974) *Power: A radical view*. London: Macmillan.

Malik, K. (2017) 'Liberalism is suffering but democracy is doing just fine'. *The Observer,* 1 January. Online. www.theguardian.com/commentisfree/2017/jan/01/liberalism-suffering-democracy-doing-just-fine (accessed 25 January 2017).

Mason, P. (2015) *Post Capitalism: A guide to our future*. London: Allen Lane.

Mazzucato, M. (2016) 'If Theresa May is serious about inequality she will ditch Osbornomics'. *The Guardian,* 19 July. Online. www.theguardian.com/commentisfree/2016/jul/19/theresa-may-industrial-inequality-osbornomics-austerity (accessed 23 July 2016).

McGough, L. (2016) '10 years of tax in combined authorities'. *Centre for Cities,* 25 July. Online. www.centreforcities.org/blog/ten-years-tax-combined-authorities/ (accessed December 2016).

Miller, C., Hoggett, P., and Mayo, M. (2006) 'The obsession with outputs: Over regulation and the impact on the emotional identities of public service professionals'. *International Journal of Work Organisation and Emotion,* 1 (4), 366–78.

Monbiot, G. (2016a) 'Neoliberalism: The ideology at the root of all our problems'. *The Guardian,* 15 April. Online. www.theguardian.com/books/2016/apr/15/neoliberalism-ideology-problem-george-monbiot (accessed 23 July 2016).

— (2016b) *How Did We Get into This Mess? Politics, equality, nature.* London: Verso.

Morgan, G. (1988) *Images of Organization*. London: Sage.

Munby, S. (2015) 'Miracles can happen'. *Soundings,* 61, 35–48.

Murray, U. (2012) 'Local government and the meaning of publicness'. In J. Manson (ed.), *Public Service on the Brink*. Exeter: Imprint Academic, 41–66.

Newman, I. (2014) *Reclaiming Local Democracy. A progressive future for local government*. Bristol: Policy Press.

Newman, J. and Clarke, J. (2009) *Publics, Politics and Power: Remaking the public in public services*. London: Sage.

Paxton, R. (2012) 'Pathways to fascism'. *New Left Review*, 74 (March–April).

Pfeffer, J. and Salancik, G.R. (2003) *The External Control of Organizations*. Stanford: Stanford University Press.

Powell, F.W. (2007) *The Politics of Civil Society: Neo-liberalism or social left*. Bristol: Policy Press.

— (2009) 'Civil society, social policy and participatory democracy: Past, present and future'. *Social Policy and Society*, 8 (1), 49–58.

Power, M. (1994) *The Audit Explosion*. London: Demos.

— (1997) *The Audit Society: Rituals of verification*. Oxford: Clarendon Press.

Putnam, R.D. (2000) *Bowling Alone: The collapse and revival of American community*. New York: Simon & Schuster.

Slawson, N. (2016) 'Nicky Lidbetter: My anxiety has been a motivator'. *The Guardian*, 24 May. Online. www.theguardian.com/society/2016/may/24/icky-lidbetter-my-anxiety-has-been-motivator-mental-health (accessed 23 July 2016).

Szreter, S. (2002) 'A central role for local government? The example of late Victorian Britain'. *History and Policy*, 2 May. Online. www.historyandpolicy.org/policy-papers/papers/a-central-role-for-local-government-the-example-of-late-victorian-britain (accessed December 2016).

— (2012) 'Britain's social welfare provision in the long run: The importance of accountable, well-financed local government'. In A. Ishkanian, and S. Szreter (eds), *The Big Society Debate: A new agenda for social welfare?* Cheltenham: Edward Elgar.

Taylor-Goodby, P. (2015) 'Making the case for the welfare state'. *Policy and Politics*, 43 (4), 597–614.

Trussell Trust (2016) *Food Bank Use Remains at a Record High*. Online. www.trusselltrust.org/2016/04/15/foodbank-use-remains-record-high/ (accessed December 2016).

TSRC (2012) 'Third sector service delivery – marrying scale and responsiveness?'. Third Sector Research Centre Seminar, Birmingham, 8 March.

Wainwright, H. (2003) *Reclaim the State: Experiments in popular democracy*. London: Verso.

Whitfield, D. (2012) 'UK social services: The mutation of privatisation. Online. http://tinyurl.com/hsf5t45 (accessed December 2016).

— (2016) 'Direct and collateral damage to the future of Barnet libraries'. Online. http://tinyurl.com/glupprn (accessed December 2016).

Wren-Lewis, S. (2016) 'The New Brexit economics'. *New Statesman*, 26 July, 34.

Part One

The state of welfare and the new service industry

1

Chapter 3

Is this the death of social housing?

Cate Evans

Rapidly changing government policies on housing and major concerns about housing shortages set the context for this chapter. Recent caps and reductions in housing benefit, fixed-term tenancies, and affordable (near market-rate) rents have compounded a wider crisis. The extension to housing associations of the right-to-buy augurs a future with limited social housing supply. While many smaller housing associations remain firmly committed to providing local services, procurement processes and huge, multi-service contracts have accelerated the migration of many larger associations towards corporate business models. These large housing associations are now perceived by many as big business in social clothing. This chapter therefore questions the point at which housing associations no longer belong in the third or charity sector and significantly, whether these transitions form part of a wider erosion of social housing. The idea of a distinct third sector, contributing to services as an organized part of wider civil society, has featured in policy since the 1970s but more recent cross-sector collaboration, contracting, and private investment have increased the complexity, blurring organizational identities (Billis, 2010).

The chapter draws on research examining the changing characteristics of housing associations carried out during the period of the Coalition government, locating this alongside subsequent policy developments and their impacts on social housing. The chapter starts by examining key moments in the history of housing associations, alongside the changing political and policy context. The research study findings are then discussed in the light of current research and highlight crucial questions about the future of social housing.

Key historical moments for housing associations

Housing associations have a long and varied history, with some tracing their roots back to medieval alms houses and others to nineteenth-century charitable trusts. Research has identified housing associations as forerunners in welfare provision and adaptive to shifting public welfare regimes (Holmes, 2006).

From the inter-war period to the 1960s, social housing comprised mainly large-scale, low-rise public provision (Mullins and Pawson, 2010). However, the 1960s, as chapter 1 describes, saw a renewed focus on poverty and social injustice, with social housing needs becoming prominent following the documentary *Cathy Come Home* (Loach, 1966) and the foundation of campaign organizations, such as Shelter. New forms of housing associations developed, often through local churches renovating run-down, inner-city properties for local low-income families (Holmes, 2006). By contrast, local authorities were concentrating on large-scale, system built, high-rise developments shaped by Conservative policy around housing subsidies. However, policies shifted sharply towards rehabilitating low-rise housing stock after 1966, with the return of a Labour government (HM Ministry of Housing and Local Government, 1966).

Disillusionment with public and private sector landlords alongside growing interest in the third sector (Mullins and Pawson, 2010) converged under a Labour government with the 1974 Housing Act (UK Parliament) establishing Housing Action Areas as priorities for urban regeneration. This released generous funding to bodies capable of renovating decaying inner-city housing, and housing associations that had already demonstrated this ability in urban regeneration gained a key role (Holmes, 2006). This funding generated significant growth in housing associations' provision, increasing their share of social housing from 5 per cent in 1974 to 11 per cent in 1988 (Mullins, 2010), but their roles were still largely complementary to local authority provision. New regulations followed requirements to register for grant funding, raising concerns about reduced independence and being drawn away from their philanthropic roots (Mullins, 2010).

With the return of a Conservative government in 1979, goals to reduce local state powers saw considerable devolution of social housing stock to housing associations (Holmes, 2006). The subsequent 1988 Housing Act (UK Parliament) facilitated two key changes: local authority transfer of all or part of their housing stock to housing associations and the classification of housing associations as non-public bodies, allowing them to seek private sector investment. Large Scale Voluntary Transfer Associations (LSVTs) were established from the transfer of large sections of council housing to association ownership and management, often accompanied by staff and other resources. The size of the English housing association stock tripled: by 1997, housing associations held 22 per cent of social housing stock, and by

2007, some 50 per cent (Mullins, 2010). They also supplied nearly all of the new-build social housing (DCLG, 2010).

Thus, in under two decades, housing associations had moved from a supplementary role into a mainstream social housing provider. Their increased reliance on private finance rather than government subsidy forced organizations to review their positions. Many moved away from identification with a voluntary or non-profit label, preferring to be seen as social entrepreneurial bodies with increasingly corporate cultures (Mullins and Riseborough, 2001).

Policy and politics: The Coalition years

When the Coalition government took power in 2010, it instigated one of the most controversial upheavals in welfare provision. Among these changes, the future of social housing was threatened through the 2011 Localism Act, which introduced flexible tenure (Mullins, 2011). These were time-limited tenancies, as short as two years, replacing the previous lifetime-assured tenancies. Shorter tenancies could free up social housing for people in need (DCLG, 2011), but guidance on criteria for curtailing, allocating, or re-allocating tenancies was absent, and organizations had to develop individual strategies.

Adding to the increasing uncertainties, a new framework for funding social housing was introduced, promoting affordable rents (Homes and Communities Agency, 2011). 'Affordable' was defined as 'up to 80% of market rents', applicable to both newly developed and existing homes to help fund new developments. Although the Charity Commission challenged this rent framework (Tickell, 2011) as potentially threatening the charitable status of housing associations through accruing commercial income, the financial complexity meant that the case was unproved.

The Welfare Reform Act (Cabinet Office, 2012) launched a new universal credit, effectively capping benefits for those out of work, reforming housing benefit, and imposing the bedroom tax. While reforms were ostensibly intended to simplify the complex benefits system and to promote employment over benefit dependency, significant criticism ensued, as housing support for the unemployed would be severely limited (Birch, 2011). These changes have disproportionately affected those living in social housing: some 70 per cent of the 500,000 people affected. They also conflicted with the affordable rents' policy, leaving the largest groups of people in social housing unable to afford the higher rents. A media broadcast (BBC, 2011) alluded to 'social cleansing', identifying how poorer families would be forced out of high-cost areas such as London, creating ghettos and segregation among rich and poor, with other commentators also highlighting the growth in far-right political parties as linked to such policy reforms (Riddell, 2010).

Policy and politics: The 2015 Conservative government

Since the original research for this chapter was undertaken, significant policy changes affecting housing associations have followed, and the national crisis around housing supply has deepened. In 2015, a total of 17 per cent of households (10 per cent renting from housing associations) lived in social housing, compared to 42 per cent in 1979 (Wiles, 2015). These figures underline the scale of transformation. The recent Housing and Planning Act (UK Parliament, 2016) heralds further erosion, undermining the rationale for social housing. The Act has extended the right-to-buy to housing association tenants. To fund discounts offered under the scheme, local authorities face selling their most valuable housing stock. This reduces social housing held overall by housing associations and local authorities, as properties transfer into private ownership. The original right-to-buy policy generated a loss of nearly 1.5 million local authority homes following its introduction in 1980, destabilizing and fracturing existing communities (Harris, 2008; 2016).

The 1 per cent reduction in social rents over four years proposed in the 2015 budget will also lead to roughly 4 per cent in lost income for housing associations because previous rent calculations were based on annual increases above inflation. This precedent of central government intervention combined with the income lost has also undermined the ability of housing associations to raise private funding (Apps, 2015), with serious consequences for building new homes or maintaining existing ones. The 2016 Housing and Planning Act brings an end to lifetime tenancies, so that all new social housing tenants must now be offered time-limited tenancies. Additionally, the Act's pay-to-stay policy requires social tenants with incomes over £40,000 in London and £30,000 elsewhere to pay market rents, although the government has recently proposed withdrawing the compulsory nature of this policy. However, if social landlords opt to implement such rent rises because of pressures on social housing and finance, many tenants will be unable to afford to stay in their existing homes and equally unable to afford the rapidly rising private sector rents. This will aggravate the exclusion of ordinary working residents from some areas, while enabling gentrification.

These changes have already caused some housing associations to signal their departure from social housing. In August 2015, one of the largest

London housing associations, Genesis, announced its withdrawal from building new properties for social tenancies, and several others are likely to follow (Murtha, 2015). Even associations fully committed to delivering social housing have indicated a need to diversify services to safeguard their incomes, risking mission creep towards a private rental market.

Although government policies have opened new opportunities, the overall levels of uncertainty are hindering any clear strategies. For some of the housing practitioners faced with making tough decisions in a rapidly changing environment, identification with the third sector has offered an important reference point. However, that identity is clearly in transition, and regulation of housing associations has recently led to their reclassification as non-financial public corporations for statistical purposes (Wiles, 2015). This may be short-lived, as private sector investment in housing associations is increasing, while the government, seeking to reduce public debts, is reluctant to classify housing association debt within its figures. Associations are now being advised to assume a new status of 'social benefit' organizations, replacing their charitable status.

Changing characteristics of housing associations: Primary study

In order to examine the changing characteristics and identities of housing associations, a primary study involving a mixed-methods approach was conducted. Information was gathered via an online survey and through semi-structured interviews. The survey included both closed and open-ended questions and was distributed via LinkedIn and through direct mailings. The 47 respondents to the online survey all worked within the social housing sector: 55 per cent were directly employed by housing associations, 26 per cent were self-employed, and 13 per cent were board members. They also represented a wide range of organizational types (see Appendix, Table 1). Feedback from representatives of small and medium-sized associations was limited, but should be placed in the context of 90 per cent of all housing association stock owned by only 272 organizations (17 per cent of registered providers), while 952 smaller housing associations (61 per cent) account for only 1 per cent of the social housing stock (Tenant Services Authority, 2011). Thus, while the research lacks feedback from many relevant organizations, it represents the views of large organizations controlling the majority of homes.

Six semi-structured interviews enriched the survey information, with participants selected to represent a range of experience across social housing organizations. They included senior managers from large scale voluntary transfer associations (LSVTs), a large group structure housing association, and consultants working for a specialist national housing body.

From the information gathered, recurring themes emerged that were raised by a variety of respondents; these broadly fell into three key areas, as described below.

Changing characteristics of housing associations

The first theme concerned the overall shift in the position of housing associations, with a move away from a public sector ethos towards the private sector. The second was the significant impact of government policy on housing associations and anxiety that this was increasingly eroding social housing. The third element was the divergent or polarized experiences among housing associations of different types and sizes, which respondents saw echoed in wider society, with a growing ghettoization of the poor and those on middle incomes becoming proportionately larger among social housing tenants.

Predictions made on trends in social housing provision and their related effects on wider society were surprisingly accurate. Respondents identified a division between those (often smaller) associations serving the poorest tenants, effectively becoming marginalized but firmly rooted within a third sector identity, and those focusing on middle income (affordable rent) residents, migrating towards private sector characteristics. The sections that follow initially present views on these themes from the numerical information. Subsequent sections elaborate on this analysis, drawing on the open-ended survey comments and interview material.

Sector allegiance and identity

Respondents were asked to identify the sector in which they viewed their organization as located: first when it was established, second in the present and third in three years' time. Overall, there was a clear perception of movement away from a public sector ethos and towards the private sector, with 40 per cent identifying themselves as within the private sector or moving towards it, and away from the third sector in future years. However, a third of respondents still regarded themselves as within the third sector in the foreseeable future (See Appendix, Table 2).

When these perceptions were analysed by type of housing association (see Appendix, Table 3), over half of the LSVTs placed themselves within the public sector when established, reflecting their local authority origins, but located themselves within the third sector when the research was conducted, reflecting declining state housing responsibilities.

By contrast, a majority of large housing associations and group structures (together the largest group of respondents) positioned themselves between the public and third sectors at foundation, but over half identified a shift towards the private sector since. There were mixed views on their future positions, with several indicating a move towards the private sector, while others identified a hybrid model between private and third sectors. Although views varied, this group of large associations indicated that migration towards private sector characteristics was most likely.

The comparisons above reflect the increasing heterogeneity among housing associations in values and associated arrangements. However, in parallel, there was a visible trend overall of shifting away from public towards private sector characteristics, as associations responded to changing policies, funding regimes, and dominant expectations around operational models.

Response to new housing policies
SEE APPENDIX, TABLE 4

Questions aimed to map the likely take-up of different initiatives. In summary, most respondents (90 per cent) expected their organizations to implement affordable rents but only two-thirds expected to implement flexible or shorter-term tenancies, despite these two policies being commonly associated. Some organizations therefore seemed to be planning to continue tenancies for life but within the new rent structures, apparently conflicting with policy recommendations. There was also significant interest in community engagement and support, and associations appeared keen to involve residents and support tenants' and community organizations.

Nearly a fifth of respondents anticipated that their organizations would seek changes in their legal status within three years, and one respondent expected to float on the stock market. These reflected the group of associations that indicated a probable transition towards the private sector.

Changing profile of housing residents?
SEE APPENDIX, TABLE 5

The majority of respondents predicted a change in the profile of their tenants, expecting to house more vulnerable residents but also more in full employment, echoing perceptions of the growing social polarization discussed further below. Many anticipated two distinct client groups for social housing: the vulnerable (generally without employment and with the highest support needs) and those in full-time employment (often identified as 'middle-income'), squeezing out those on low income or in low-paid, often part-time work and the unemployed.

A slow death for social housing associations or a more fragmented future?

The analysis above identifies significant changes predicted by professionals in the characteristics of housing associations even before the policy changes since 2015. Hybridity, from taking on features and arrangements commonly associated with other sectors, has led to shifting identities and values and may slowly change core purposes (Billis, 2010). In parallel, funding and other policy pressures are both dividing and constructing different kinds of associations. The survey comments and interviews uncovered a wealth of complementary information, enabling insight into reasons for these apparent trends and adding to the emerging picture. The material below is organized thematically and includes illustrative quotes from survey respondents and interviewees.

Commercial orientation: Moving away from third and public sector features and values

Many of the detailed responses supported views of a definite trend among some organizations away from the public and third sectors and towards the private sector, demonstrating a noticeable commercial orientation. One respondent said 'associations will be forced to behave in more commercial ways in order to maintain their financial health'. Added to this, resentment was expressed towards the Coalition government, with many feeling that moves towards private sector behaviours would 'increase divergence' in organizational priorities and fragment housing associations as a sector.

The idea of a group of housing organizations increasingly identifying with the private sector or corporations recurred frequently. The language used often reflected this commercial orientation, such as: 'building the organizational brand', 'customer service penetration', 'greater purchasing power', and 'considering credit ratings'. Organizations keen to fully 'embrace opportunities to develop for affordable rents' doubted that their futures lay with the third sector. Echoing others, the following comment illustrates perceptions of how this was playing out:

> [Housing Associations] will increasingly have to self-fund through private finance, bond issue and so on. In future, because of this, will they genuinely be HAs in the sense they are, or just another form of [very large-scale] private landlord?

As they increasingly seek support through private finance, associations are enticed towards private sector characteristics and behaviours and away from values and missions more characteristic of social housing and the third sector. Effectively a boundary is crossed when pursuing financial survival starts to supersede the organization's original social values. The discussion above illustrates the emerging picture in the study, and more recent research corroborates these worrying trends (Milbourne and Murray, 2014a; Mullins *et al.*, 2014).

Finance and funding policies

Government grants and rent income, supplemented by private finance, have been the main funding sources for housing associations, but the changes outlined above, coupled with a rapid decline in public housing and local government resources, have forced greater dependency on raising alternative finance. Reflecting on earlier upheavals, many respondents believed that the recent government policies would cause pivotal changes in social housing, with one saying that they 'represent the biggest cultural shift since 1988'.

Some respondents highlighted the crippling impact of recent policies on supported housing, with the combination of welfare benefit reforms, severe cuts to local authority budgets, and the shift to funding individuals rather than services dramatically reducing and confusing the funding available. One interviewee confirmed an increasingly common picture that their organization proposed to 'sell off the social care section due to inviability', while many identified difficulties with sustaining specialist social support services amid current financial strictures.

Conflicting policies also generated major challenges, such as 'the demand to push rent levels up ['affordable' rents] while driving benefit bills down'. The 'widening gap between [real] affordability and rents charged' would, as many emphasized, increase rent arrears and the number of residents evicted. Any visible increase in levels of rent arrears triggered concerns about housing associations' reputational worth for continued private finance arrangements, since it would affect their ability to service debts and worsen the levels of risk perceived by lenders. As one interviewee highlighted, demonstrating 'financial viability is critical because we're funded to a significant degree by financial markets so we need to retain that confidence'. Alongside a looser regulatory framework, this 'could well, over time, impact on whether lenders are prepared to continue giving us preferential rates'. Ultimately, the effect would be to undermine the ability of housing associations to purchase and improve housing stock, producing a longer-term downward spiral in available and genuinely affordable social housing. The recently imposed rent reductions have further weakened housing association finances and exacerbated the risks perceived by investment institutions (Evans, 2015).

Other impacts of changing policies

Respondents were concerned about the uncertainties caused by rapidly changing and conflicting policies, all too frequently implemented with little regard for unanticipated consequences. The comments below summarize frequently voiced views:

> [T]here's a sense that they've thrown a lot of balls up into the air and they don't know where they're going to land, never mind anybody else ... a number of these policies are in conflict with one another.

The contradictions have worsened over time, producing a perception that the economic and political climate is making operating 'infinitely harder'. Traditionally, housing associations have entered into mergers and take-overs to solve policy challenges, creating some very large associations and group structures. However, these strategies may prove insufficient to address recent challenges, as one respondent explained: 'when you think you have a solution ... it gets pulled away from you because of another [problem] coming in somewhere else'. By 2012, many respondents already viewed policy changes as creating unsustainable conditions, generating comments like 'we'll do what we need and hope for better days to come'. However, rather than better days, the situation has worsened. While several respondents viewed the growing challenges as stimulating creative thinking around positive strategies, collaborative problem solving, and even a 'return to the original [social] focus for housing associations', others feared the trend towards privatization and commercialization. As the 2015 policies hit home, at least two large housing associations announced their withdrawal from social housing provision (Dudman, 2015).

Rationalizing the retreat of some large associations from social obligations, several respondents expressed the view that housing associations would be faced with 'fill[ing] the gaps in welfare' provision left by the state's withdrawal and other voluntary service closures. Some felt the pressures to address welfare needs were intensified because of the negative press that housing associations had received, with the government 'lambasting them as part of the problem'. By September 2015, critical comments were dominant, with housing associations censured for inefficiency by the prime minister in responding to questions in the House of Commons.

Triggered by pressures and financial challenges, an undercurrent of mistrust seemed to be dividing housing associations between those pursuing financial growth and competitive behaviours and those adhering to social missions. Respondents raised concerns about the behaviours of other associations adopting different strategies and their wider effects on reputations. Many felt keenly that significant commercial 'developments will probably be dominated by a handful of larger organizations', leaving 'those that choose not to play this game as anomalies' – effectively marginalized. However, there was considerable disparity, with the diverse market value of housing regionally a significant factor in enabling space for creative strategies. One respondent predicted a 'split even further into "welfare" housing providers versus … "market rent" providers', largely dependent on the feasibility of new rent policies in different geographic areas.

Thus, many respondents identified recent government policies as responsible for polarization among housing associations and, consequently, adding to polarization in wider society. As one commented, 'some will become more like property developers while others will be community-based'. Another reflected on the impacts, predicting that 'many will find it difficult … to build new homes and to adhere to founding principles'.

Solutions in growth and diversification?

New property development, a key priority for many housing associations, is directly affected by government policy. As discussed above, policies leading to diminished funding and housing stock are restricting the abilities of associations to meet growing social housing demands. Underlining the consequences, one respondent declared that 'as long as current government policies exist, there will be a gradual reduction of social housing', a prediction borne out in Hutton's (2015) assessment of the 2015 Conservative government's policies, although he concluded that the decline in social housing would be rapid.

Growth and diversification were strategies increasingly adopted by housing associations keen to survive financially. Several planned to bid for an extended range of services in order to win contracts. One LSVT association manager explained the need to develop other work streams, since diversifying services allowed them to gain greater overall resources. This meant they could 'hedge against things getting too scary' while potentially continuing to fill welfare gaps, also collaborating with specialist voluntary organizations. Ironically, as funding frameworks shift, this position contrasts with earlier plans to relinquish costly social care support. There were also warning voices, pointing to 'danger there as well, for associations to kind of become almost too diverse', suggesting that over-extending and lacking specialist knowledge might lead to deterioration in services and overall reputation. Milbourne and Murray (2014b) illustrate situations where this has subsequently occurred, undermining local voluntary organizations and threatening the financial viability of good, specialist services.

The increasingly finance-led, competitive culture, together with divisions between associations, also limits collective lobbying of government, silencing a previously powerful voice that could challenge the negative impacts of policies and their practical consequences. This limitation raises further questions about housing associations' continuing abilities to provide the mediating characteristics identified as important features of voluntary organizations (Marshall, 1996: 58).

Successive governments have advanced capacity building, growth, mergers, and entrepreneurialism as means of strengthening organizations against adverse economic conditions. Often, however, they echo approaches in policy priorities, and instead of achieving sustainability, result in organizations undertaking activities useful to governments and redirect independent goals (Milbourne, 2013). For example, entrepreneurialism and diversification can attract resources, replacing those lost from the public purse; but failure to adapt, grow, merge, or adopt policy priorities relocates blame from governments to apparently recalcitrant organizations. The myth is that all organizations can succeed despite scarce resources; and as Nevile (2010) highlights, organizations that lose sight of their core purposes can be seriously destabilized.

Community cohesion and social disparity

While community engagement recurred as a theme throughout this research, many respondents emphasized worsening community cohesion and that changes among housing associations were potentially contributing to a widening gap between affluent and poorer members of society. Several recent policies, including benefit caps and the bedroom tax, are exacerbating the socially divisive conditions (Dudman, 2015) that respondents predicted at the time of this research.

Respondents highlighted three main elements related to these concerns. First, that policy changes were likely to generate growing social inequality, expressing anxieties about the increased 'drift of poorer people away from more expensive areas towards poorer ghettoes'. One interviewee predicted that her large housing organization would 'build … more shared ownership, outright ownership – certainly in London, and transfer that money to buy sites and deliver "affordable" housing ... outside [London]'. Regional variations in types of accommodation were frequently underlined as indicative of the potential social polarization and area inequalities that were emerging.

Second, respondents identified social inequalities as growing because of unaffordable rents and failure to fulfil basic housing needs. As one interviewee summarized, 'I think there's the perfect storm coming ... where for the first time in a long time we will have a real under-class'. Others predicted a repeat of conditions portrayed in Loach's 1966 film, anticipating 'another *Cathy Come Home* story, as people are shifted out of London, and we see real people and the impact'. In parallel, others predicted increasing social disparities and homelessness arising from mounting rent arrears and ensuing evictions, with poorer households forced out of unaffordable accommodation.

Third, fixed tenancies were identified as undermining community cohesion, with one respondent predicting that restricting 'lifelong tenancies may mean stock increasingly ... used for transitional welfare housing'. This results in temporary tenancies and a high turnover of residents, aggravating social instability in neighbourhoods. It would generate a 'less sustainable mix of residents' and undermine the potential to build cohesion and community resources.

The demise of social housing?

The research discussed in this chapter has highlighted the shifting culture among housing associations, explored through sector characteristics and associated values and behaviours. The same research repeated in 2017 would almost certainly find many large housing associations regarded as no longer part of the third sector. More significantly, the growth of social housing needs, coupled with reduced benefits and successive cuts to other services, raises the crucial question of what is happening to residents who depend on these large housing associations for a roof over their heads as they withdraw from social provision.

Since the initial research, many changes anticipated by study participants have occurred, including growing social and housing disparities. Some large associations are withdrawing from social housing provision, and access to social housing has been progressively restricted, with families being rehoused away from familiar local areas to regions where housing is cheaper. There is also greater dependency on private finance, although investment is also shrinking due to uncertainties.

Recent governments have significantly remodelled policies, producing substantial risks and threats for different kinds of housing association. Many are being induced to scale up, commercialize, and diversify services and massively increase financial borrowing, while others are struggling to meet welfare commitments or are facing insolvency. Shifts in policy and restricted funding are damaging to housing organizations, but they are also destabilizing the core providers of social housing at a time when needs are growing.

Housing associations now face a significant loss of income through unanticipated rent controls and discounted right-to-buy policies extended to tenants. This undermines financial planning, assets and the ability to access investment when growth and improvement in housing stock are badly needed (Dudman, 2015). Social landlords built over a third of all new homes in England in 2014–15 (NHF, 2016), but reducing their housing stock and assets and forcing greater reliance on for-profit housing developers when genuinely affordable homes are needed makes little policy sense (Hutton, 2015). Moreover, there are now major questions related to government land disposal for building projects.

Hutton (2015) predicts 'an epidemic of housing distress,' and the serious erosion of social housing is becoming increasingly evident. Recent history offers lessons about the immorality of uncontrolled markets, especially financial markets, and it seems wise to heed these lessons, when even government supporters (Blond, 2010) recommend curbing market practices to increase fairness. There are few signs of this, however, and every signal that monopolistic practices and growing debts against housing investment will continue, while individual and area-based social disparities spread. As Ellison (2011) argues, such practices work to the disadvantage of the most deprived in society, exacerbating inequalities. The transitions in social housing discussed above provide visible indicators of the erosion of welfare and housing services. In the longer term, it leads us to speculate whether future access to adequate shelter will be limited to those who can pay.

References

Apps, P. (2015) 'Associations may step back from bond market'. *Inside Housing.* Online. www.insidehousing.co.uk/business/finance/funding/associations-may-step-back-from-bond-market/7011516.article (accessed 9 September 2015).

BBC (2011) 'Housing benefit changes: Who will be affected?'. BBC News. Online. www.bbc.co.uk/news/uk-12674409.

Billis, D. (2010) *Hybrid Organizations and the Third Sector: Challenges for practice, theory and policy*. London: Palgrave Macmillan.

Birch, J. (2011) 'Capsize warning'. *Inside Housing.* Online. www.insidehousing. co.uk/capsize-warning/6514950.blog (accessed 19 May 2011).

Blond, P. (2010) *Red Tory: How the Left and Right have broken Britain and how we can fix it*. London: Faber & Faber.

Cabinet Office (2012) *Welfare Reform Act 2012*. Department for Work and Pensions. Online. www.legislation.gov.uk/ukpga/2012/5/pdfs/ukpga_20120005_en.pdf (accessed December 2016).

DCLG (2010) *Housing and Planning Statistics 2010*. London: Department for Communities and Local Government. Online. www.gov.uk/government/uploads/system/uploads/attachment_data/file/6863/1785484.pdf (accessed December 2016).

— (2011) *Definition of General Housing Terms*. London: Department for Communities and Local Government. Online. www.gov.uk/guidance/definitions-of-general-housing-terms (accessed December 2016).

Dudman, J. (2015) 'Social landlords must be wondering how much longer they can survive'. *The Guardian,* 24 September. Online. www.theguardian.com/housing-network/2015/sep/24/social-landlords-survive-housing-associations-adapt-die (accessed December 2016).

Ellison, N. (2011) 'The Conservative Party and the "Big Society"'. In C. Holden, M. Kilkey, and G. Ramia (eds), *Social Policy Review 23: Analysis and debate in socil policy, 2011.* Bristol: Policy Press, 45–62.

Evans, J. (2015) 'Housing association change adds £60bn to government debt'. *Financial Times,* 30 October. Online. http://tinyurl.com/zv8xnmy (accessed 28 December 2015).

Harris, J. (2008) 'Safe as houses'. *The Guardian,* 30 September. Online. www.theguardian.com/society/2008/sep/30/housing.houseprices (accessed December 2016).

— (2016) 'The end of council housing'. *The Guardian,* 4 January. Online. www.theguardian.com/society/2016/jan/04/end-of-council-housing-bill-secure-tenancies-pay-to-stay (accessed December 2016).

HM Ministry of Housing and Local Government (1966) *The Deeplish Study: Improvement possibilities in a district of Rochdale*. London: HMSO.

Holmes, C. (2006) *A New Vision for Housing*. Oxon: Routledge.

Homes and Communities Agency (2011) *2011–2015 Affordable Homes Programme – Framework*. Online. www.gov.uk/government/uploads/system/uploads/attachment_data/file/371817/affordable-homes-framework.pdf (accessed 15 February 2016).

Hutton, W. (2015) 'The broadening of right-to-buy will inevitably worsen the housing crisis'. *The Guardian,* 20 September. Online. www.theguardian.com/commentisfree/2015/sep/20/right-to-buy-disastrous-for-housing-market (accessed December 2016).

Loach, K. (1966) *Cathy Come Home*. BBC.

Marshall, T.F. (1996) 'Can we define the voluntary sector?' In D. Billis, and M. Harris (eds), *Voluntary Agencies: Challenges of organisation and management*. Basingstoke: MacMillan, 45–60.

Milbourne, L. (2013) *Voluntary Sector in Transition: Hard times or new opportunities?* Bristol: Policy Press.

— and Murray, U. (2014a) '*The State of the Voluntary Sector: Does size matter? Paper 1* (NCIA Inquiry into the Future of Voluntary Services Working Paper 9). Online. www.independentaction.net/wp-content/uploads/sites/8/2014/07/Does-Size-Matter-paper-1-final.pdf (accessed December 2016).

— (2014b) *The State of the Voluntary Sector: Does size matter? Paper 2* (NCIA Inquiry into the Future of Voluntary Services Working Paper 10). Online. www.independentaction.net/wp-content/uploads/2014/07/Does-size-matter-paper-2-final.pdf (accessed December 2016).

Mullins, D. (2010) *Housing Associations* (Third Sector Research Centre Working paper 15). Online. www.birmingham.ac.uk/generic/tsrc/documents/tsrc/working-papers/working-paper-16.pdf (accessed December 2016).

— (2011) *Community Investment and Community Empowerment: The role of social housing providers in the context of 'Localism' and the 'Big Society'.* Birmingham: TSRC. Online. www.birmingham.ac.uk/generic/tsrc/documents/tsrc/reports/community-investment-community-empowerment-consultation-draft.pdf (accessed December 2016).

— and Pawson, H. (2010) 'Housing associations: Agents of policy or profits in disguise?' In D. Billis (ed.), *Hybrid Organizations and the Third Sector: Challenges for practice, theory and policy.* Basingstoke: Palgrave Macmillan, 197–218.

— and Riseborough, M. (2001) 'Non-profit housing agencies: "Reading" and shaping the policy agenda'. In M. Harris and C. Rochester (eds), *Voluntary Organisations and Social Policy in Britain: Perspectives on change and choice.* Basingstoke: Palgrave Macmillan, 154–70.

—, Czischke, D., and Van Bortel, G. (2014) *Hybridising Housing Organisations: Meanings, concepts and processes of social enterprise.* Abingdon: Routledge.

Murtha, T. (2015) 'The housing association that will no longer build homes for the poor'. *The Guardian,* 7 August. Online. www.theguardian.com/housing-network/2015/aug/07/housing-asssociation-no-longer-build-homes-poor-genesis (accessed 6 September 2015).

Nevile, A. (2010) 'Drifting or holding firm? Public funding and the values of third sector organisations'. *Policy & Politics,* 38 (4), 531–46.

NHF (2016) *Key Statistics Briefing: How many homes do housing associations build?* National Housing Federation. Online. http://s3-eu-west-1.amazonaws.com/pub.housing.org.uk/KSB1_How_many_homes_do_HAs_build.pdf (accessed January 2016).

Riddell, M. (2010) 'The coming housing crisis is bad news for everyone but the far Right'. *The Telegraph,* 1 November. Online. www.telegraph.co.uk/comment/columnists/maryriddell/8103068/The-coming-housing-crisis-is-bad-news-for-everyone-but-the-far-Right.html (accessed June 2012).

Tenant Services Authority (2011) *Regulatory and Statistical Return 2010–11.* London: Tenant Services Authority.

Tickell, J. (2011) 'Look both ways'. *Inside Housing,* 15 March. Online. www.insidehousing.co.uk/analysis/opinion/look-both-ways/6514060.article (accessed December 2016).

UK Parliament (1974) *Housing Act 1974.* Online. www.legislation.gov.uk/ukpga/1974/44/pdfs/ukpga_19740044_en.pdf (accessed December 2016).

— (1988) *Housing Act 1988.* Online. www.legislation.gov.uk/ukpga/1988/50/pdfs/ukpga_19880050_en.pdf (accessed December 2016).

— (2016) *Housing and Planning Act 2016.* The Stationery Office. Online. www.legislation.gov.uk/ukpga/2016/22/pdfs/ukpga_20160022_en.pdf (accessed December 2016).

Wiles, C. (2015) 'This move into the public sector could signal the end for housing associations'. *The Guardian,* 30 October. Online. www.theguardian.com/housing-network/2015/oct/30/end-housing-associations-ons-public-sector (accessed December 2016).

Chapter 4

Transitions from the statutory to the third sector: The experience of social workers

Antony Moore

It is frequently claimed that statutory social work in the United Kingdom is in crisis, with a national vacancy rate of 14 per cent for full-time qualified social worker posts in local authorities across the country and about one in seven social workers leaving employment in 2013 (DfE, 2014). Yet the demand for qualified social workers is likely to increase, particularly in national children's charities (Jones, 2014) as the current government extends the 2008 Children and Young Persons Act through a new Children and Social Work Bill (UK Parliament, 2008; 2016), enabling local authorities to outsource most current responsibilities for children's services. This already applies to looked-after children and care leavers' services, but the longer term promises wider deregulation and commercialization of social work services.

This chapter first considers the recent remodelling of statutory social work and its impact on both statutory and third sector social workers. It subsequently looks at the research exploring the experiences of social workers who have moved from the statutory to the third sector and concludes with a discussion of what this reveals about current changes and future potential in third sector social work.

Social policy and remodelling social work

Ferguson (2008) argued that the social work profession has suffered more than any other in statutory health or welfare from neo-liberal political and economic strategies during the past three decades, and these have intensified under recent governments since 2010, with an assault on public services. However, the welfare reforms under New Labour governments between 1997 and 2010 also saw business-led models of management reinforced and an expansion of market forces in social work. These trends combined with a distrust of the profession, leading to its exclusion from key welfare programmes, fragmenting both social work organizations and the social work task (Jordan and Jordan, 2000).

Indeed, the growth of the social care sector together with increasing individualization of services has contributed to a deprofessionalization of social work, and Spandler (2004: 195) argues that individualization policies undermine 'a healthy and vibrant public sector that collectively develops best practices' in provision and support. Peters (2012) takes this argument further, maintaining that concepts of welfare and empowerment no longer underpin social work delivery; instead, individualization, combined with an ethos of meeting performance-related targets, has resulted in coercive and punitive interventions that focus on the personal failings of service users rather than underlying structural inequalities. She questions therefore whether social workers have merely become agents of state control.

The ideal of socially responsible citizenship is also being eroded in favour of incentivizing employment and abolishing so-called welfare dependency. Highlighting increased expectations on those in need to become self-reliant or reliant upon family, friends or charity, Rogowski (2013a) identifies how forms of state social support, not least statutory social work, continue to be cut back. In parallel, those judged a risk to themselves or others are dealt with in increasingly authoritarian ways.

Social workers

Research (Bowyer and Roe, 2015) identifies that a social worker's average working life is now under eight years (compared to 16 for nurses and 25 for doctors), indicating a low return from investment in training and serious challenges for building and retaining professional expertise. This study also identified a 25 per cent permanent staff vacancy rate in 2013–14 in London boroughs and similar numbers of staff on agency contracts. An earlier study (Jones, 2005), exploring the frontline experiences of statutory social workers, reported high levels of stress, increasing bureaucracy, and endemic organizational change intended to improve service quality, while the time social workers spent with service users was considerably reduced. These issues were echoed in later reports (Scottish Executive, 2006; Lord Laming, 2009; Social Work Task Force, 2009), which all highlighted excessive workloads, cumbersome bureaucracy, inflexible IT systems, poor resources, low morale, and a shortage of qualified staff.

A British Association of Social Workers' survey (2012) identified that the cumulative effects of cuts in services led 88 per cent of social workers to believe that lives could be put at risk, while 77 per cent reported jobs being cut and vacancies unfilled, and 77 per cent described their caseloads as unmanageable. Similarly, Community Care's (2013) research found that 82 per cent of statutory social workers believed that the threshold for defining child protection cases had risen in the previous year, with 58 per cent concerned that pressure had been applied to reclassify cases to a less serious 'child in need' category. Some 72 per cent regarded this as resulting directly from budget cuts, while others attributed it to insufficient child protection social workers (59 per cent) or to high vacancy rates (43 per cent).

Rogowski (2013b) observes that 'social work policy and practice is dominated by managers (and in turn, managerialism) who shape the daily experience of social work. They control what social workers do ... and demand that social workers exercise control over resources and in turn users'. The outcome is a severely constrained social work profession, effectively unable to engage in radical or critical social work. As Rogowski goes on to argue, 'rather than engaging in relational work ... social workers are forced into being "people processors" or "e-technicians", inputting data onto computer templates'.

Exodus from the statutory sector

It is hardly surprising therefore that statutory social workers seek to leave such demoralizing conditions, and Wermeling's (2013) US study identified four significant reasons for this: caring responsibilities, dissatisfaction with social work education, discontentment with social work's perceived lack of effectiveness, and the poor value ascribed to the profession in society. The US National Association of Social Workers (2009) identified similar reasons for social workers leaving, including dissatisfaction with their education and their poor status compared with other healthcare professionals. This report also highlighted serious safety concerns, with some 70 per cent of frontline staff having been threatened or the victim of violence, with staff also leaving for better-paid employment in alternative professions. A Swedish study (Tham, 2007) found that nearly half the social workers planned to leave even though 54 per cent had been in their current workplace for only two years or less. They cited organizational culture, particularly the extent to which they felt undervalued and unsupported in their work, or felt managers were uninterested in their health and well-being, as the most significant factors for leaving.

These studies reflect many concerns expressed by UK statutory social workers, but some findings may be culturally specific. For example, in contrast to the UK, none directly cites stress, burnout, job satisfaction, or career commitment as factors for leaving. Balloch *et al.* (1999), however, found that UK social workers experienced more stress and violence than workers in other public health and welfare services, which directly correlated with low levels of job satisfaction. Nevertheless, other consistencies across international research provide significant insights into the social work profession. For example, poor retention is a recurrent finding, and Weaver and Chang's (2004: 7) study of California's public child welfare workers demonstrates voluntary turnover as 'so closely associated with burnout, job satisfaction and career commitment,' that they suggest the concepts 'are practically synonymous with intention to leave'.

The aftermath of the Baby P tragedy in 2007 (Cooper, 2008; Shoesmith, 2016) highlighted how UK statutory social work, specifically child protection, is repeatedly caught in a highly politicized and toxic blame culture, in which media and national politicians frequently castigate social workers and local authority agencies for supposed 'failure'. In 2011, the much-lauded Munro Review of Child Protection recommended that social workers be freed from excessive and demoralizing bureaucracy and tick-box exercises that had become the norm following this blame culture. However, Munro's recommendations remained implemented only in part. The combined working pressures and blame culture have resulted in statutory social workers rarely remaining in frontline posts beyond five years, with the majority then moving to managerial positions or finding employment within other sectors (Jones, 2005).

Social work in the third sector

Contrasting with these increasingly punitive conditions surrounding statutory social work, social work in the third sector has thrived. Voluntary organizations overall have grown exponentially over some 15 years, delivering roughly £15 billion of social services contracts (NCVO, 2016). While state income to the sector is now declining, large children's charities appear relatively stable and some have maintained growth, accessing new programmes and contracts, and attracting private sponsorship (Milbourne and Murray, 2014).

Gillen (2007) reports social workers as increasingly finding jobs with voluntary service providers, ranging from grassroots organizations to national charities, where their roles are generally less clearly defined, with greater flexibility in approach and more opportunities to develop services. Third sector work is also perceived as less bureaucratic, although access to training, pay, and working conditions and job security are regarded as better in the statutory sector. However, overall there is little research regarding social workers' experiences of employment in voluntary organizations, and the research described below set out to explore this gap.

Research with charity social workers

Based on a qualitative approach, the research utilized in-depth semi-structured interviews undertaken with six experienced social workers employed by a large national children's charity (NCC). All were qualified social workers with at least five years' experience in the third sector and had previously worked in the public sector for at least two years. All participants had worked for NCC for five years, except for one, who had recently left to work for the private sector. All the interviewees worked either in managerial or senior social work practitioner roles across London and South-East England, linked to asylum-seeking families, care leavers, young offenders, children with disabilities, and residential education for children with special educational needs. The sample thus captures social workers with diverse service perspectives, who were well established in their careers rather than junior staff.

The primary aim for the research was to understand the motivations for transitions to the third sector and the impacts on the social work role, as well as exploring any preconceived ideas on the benefits and challenges of moving. Participants were also invited to reflect on the experiences of changing sectors and on the effects of social policy changes on their third sector social work roles and on children's charities over the previous five years; they were also asked for their views on future conditions.

Becoming a social worker and leaving statutory social work

All of the participants interviewed had been motivated to seek a career in social work, in part for altruistic reasons. However, it was evident that none had naively entered into the social work profession solely on this basis and all cited ulterior motives for doing so, such as 'career progression', the professional authority to 'influence decision making', and financial remuneration.

Participants gave several reasons that influenced their subsequent decisions to leave statutory social work. The most significant of these were the constraints experienced in developing positive relationships and undertaking direct work with service users. Bureaucracy was a major contributory factor in this, as Annie (senior social worker) explained:

> I had reached the point where it became evident the demands of the job, the paperwork, did not allow you to do the work properly and I wasn't having space or time with young people.

Several interviewees also referred to the 'power imbalance' and increasingly authoritarian approach to the work they were undertaking, with Jane (deputy manager) also highlighting stress, workloads, and violence as significant:

> It started to feel like we were doing to and not working with families ... I was feeling quite tired and it was stressful with high caseloads, not just working with children and young people but their families too and the anger and violence directed at social workers.

Transition to the third sector

Most participants professed to having no preconceived ideas regarding the third sector prior to moving to NCC. However, this was not borne out by their comments. As Roxy (deputy manager) described:

> I knew nothing about the third sector really ... although I had friends who worked for other national children's charities and I knew they had a lot more autonomy and did much more hands-on work rather than fire-fighting all the time.

Jane anticipated 'a smaller caseload and greater chance to do more creative ... direct work'. Others, however, commented that colleagues in statutory social work regarded moving to the third sector as an 'easy' or 'soft' option, with those who had made the transition somehow perceived as 'less professional' by statutory sector colleagues, potentially 'shirking professional responsibilities' or 'not doing proper social work'. There were also observations about feeling sidelined and a definite hierarchy existing, such as CAMHS (Children and Adolescent Mental Health Services) social workers being taken more seriously. As Lauren (senior social worker), described, 'the perception is that the hard graft is done in a local authority team and being in the voluntary sector is the easy option, a cop-out'.

However, this was certainly not how participants perceived themselves, as Annie (senior social worker), observed: 'Yes, there was that feeling in statutory, but I certainly didn't see it as a soft option, for me it was about vital work that wasn't being done by the local authority.'

Key factors in choosing to work in the third sector

Decisions to leave the statutory sector and move to the third sector linked clearly to the desire for greater opportunities to undertake direct work with service users and operate more autonomously. Lauren contrasted this with her previous experience: 'The benefits for me are the autonomy ... that you would not get in a local authority post, but it's also about focus and time and not responding to crisis all the time.' Opportunities to undertake more 'specialized' work and the increased kudos arising from being recognized as an expert in a chosen field were also significant.

None of the participants cited poor pay within the statutory sector as an issue, and many had taken lower pay in joining NCC, either in real terms or compared to their respective grades in statutory services. As Jane explained, 'I was much better paid in the local authority, but you don't go into the voluntary sector to make money.'

This is not to suggest that participants were unconcerned about comparatively low salaries, and Annie, suggesting a less positive work environment emerging, named pay as one of a number of reasons for deciding to return to statutory social work: 'If I'm doing all this work, I might as well get a half-decent wage for it.'

Making the transition and the benefits of working for NCC

Experiences of making the transition indicated few difficulties. However, Roxy (deputy manager), commented on 'an overwhelming sense of being deskilled' and experiencing guilt for not feeling continually pressured.

It was also challenging for some to reconnect with reflective practice. In Lauren's words:

> It took time to get used to the less frenetic pace because it was about developing relationships ... rather than tasks that needed to be undertaken and initially I felt a bit guilty about that but it helped me to reflect on practice a lot more.

While low pay was accepted as a given, this was outweighed for most by the idea of having more time, as Jane described:

> If you wanted to make money you would go to H [London borough] as a locum manager; but with all the concomitant stresses? If you want a work–life balance you make choices.

Participants especially valued working for a national organization with a shared sense of purpose in contrast to the different criteria and thresholds in every local authority, as Luke (project manager) explained:

> Being in a national, recognized charity, I feel I belong to something worthwhile, there is a mutual loyalty, and I can visit a project in Lancashire or Scotland and there is a unity. Staff are immediately friendly and you have a shared sense of purpose, and I know it sounds clichéd, but almost like a family.

Jane echoed Luke's comments, describing her experience of working for another national children's charity:

> It is good working for a national organization. It's different from working in a local authority. I went to meetings in different parts of the country and felt a part of something bigger – you can really get involved so you don't feel like such a small cog in a big wheel.

The majority of participants also felt that they were genuinely valued personally and organizationally, that they were listened to and supported by management and had access to good supervision. As a consequence, staff turnover was low. Illustrating some of these experiences, Lauren explained how 'supervision was taken very seriously and was undertaken individually and at group level so you could really contribute and it was meaningful'. Roxy offered the example of a flexible and supportive manager: 'I have targets ... but if I put a case to my manager about how I approach the work I am listened to.'

Organizational change: Positive impacts

While participants were clear that NCC had adopted a more business-like stance recently, there seemed to be a dominant consensus that this was necessary and had been positive in terms of improving public recognition of the NCC's identity and purpose. Luke (project manager) explained the need to streamline and adapt in smart ways in order to improve services for users and 'become more efficient' as resources decline:

> I think it had lost its way ... ten or fifteen years ago if you asked the public, no one was sure what NCC was about but they refocused and developed new initiatives and put it back in people's minds.

Roxy also rationalized the need for changes:

> Given the climate, I think they needed to be more business-like. There was a lot of waste, almost frivolity ... and NCC needed to get up to speed with what was going on out there.

Paul (local manager) discussed both the challenges and benefits of changes, commenting:

> It's all based on output and outcomes and that can be limiting, but by demonstrating effective service delivery and positive outcomes it makes services and individuals attentive to how those services work; and it shouldn't ... mean losing a connection at grassroots level. A lot of tenders ... need to demonstrate how participation

is managed, how to engage with hard-to-reach individuals and communities.

Organizational change: Negative impacts

The negative impacts of change and the contract culture were also acknowledged, including increased bureaucracy, more paperwork, meeting budget requirements, conflicting priorities, and diminished control over the work, as Lauren outlined:

> The concern about meeting budgets is there pretty much all the time and becomes a massive anxiety for everybody ... each year the goal-posts move and it's very destabilizing for the team and could well have an impact on service users.

Jane highlighted loss of autonomy through contract compliance, describing:

> very little control over what we did. The local authority would specify its requirements and we were expected to comply ... they seemed to have the idea that because they had commissioned the work they had the right to manage us.

Paul added to these examples of changing experiences, explaining:

> The organization has changed massively, beyond all recognition and not always in positive ways. It can no longer support services through voluntary contributions and has moved into procurement of services. Greater attention is paid to compliance potentially at the risk of service delivery, and sometimes the mechanisms in place can be overly bureaucratic and time consuming and that puts parameters around innovation.

For Annie, the recent changes had been so significant as to influence her decision to leave the charity after 30 years:

> Things have become really difficult recently, which I feel has never really been acknowledged. I don't get out because I'm spending all my time doing safeguarding ... and I don't do any of the support work which is what I came here to do. The bureaucracy has become overwhelming. It's low pay and long hours and has taken over my life. I suppose I should tell you I am leaving to work as a [statutory] social worker. They have told me the case load is unmanageable [laughs] but I will take my chances.

Working with the statutory sector

A recurrent theme was the sense of increasingly undertaking work that participants regarded as once the responsibility of statutory social workers, as Roxy outlined:

> The nature of social work has changed in local authorities and I'm not blowing my own trumpet here but in terms of experience and enquiring nature; and often we have had to take on that role … asking questions that they are afraid to ask because we know the families and have developed good relationships with them. Often the [statutory] social worker will give them a package of care and they are gone, never to be seen again until there is a crisis or review.

Linked to this and consistent with other research, participants considered that thresholds for accepting referrals in statutory children's services had significantly increased, as Luke described:

> Clearly there is a heightening of thresholds, what [statutory] social workers will get involved in; and it has meant social workers in the organization are picking up more cases than they were before and stuff that may well have been picked up on a statutory basis previously, so we are dealing with more vulnerable and higher risk cases, and I think there is that expectation from local authorities.

The wider social policy context

Despite the negative changes outlined, only half the participants made direct links between changes and the wider social policy context. Only two commented on recent government proposals to outsource and effectively privatize the majority of children's services; both were critical. In Luke's words:

> I think children's services, child protection, should remain in the statutory sector. They have clearly defined procedures and structures, know how to respond and work closely with health and police and such. I can't see that happening with G4S and that will lead to more mistakes being made.

There was little recognition or reflection that these proposals could have potentially significant future implications for children's services and for NCC as a provider, beyond the issue of economic survival.

Remaining in employment with NCC

Finally, despite the impact of changes that participants identified, most intended to remain in their current posts rather than returning to the statutory sector or pursuing alternatives. None of the participants stated an intention to leave the social work profession.

Social work: A fragmenting profession?

Research described earlier in this chapter identified the low status of social work as a strong contributory factor for social workers leaving the statutory sector. In contrast, this study emphasizes that transfer to the third sector enabled opportunities for specialization which gave participants status. The idea of specialization appears at odds with assumptions about social work in the third sector having less clearly defined roles (Gillen, 2007), but these participants evidently felt that they were afforded sufficient autonomy and flexibility to develop the specialist skills that would best meet the needs of service users.

There has been criticism of large national third sector organizations for adopting business-like, managerial practices (Rochester, 2013), which leads to stifling flexibility and innovation (Carmel and Harlock, 2008), but the evidence from NCC is that those services not overly dependent upon statutory funding and contracts have encouraged positive innovation. While organizational change was also accompanied by negative experiences, the process of decentralization alongside devolution of power has encouraged services and workers to become more autonomous in making decisions at a local level. Alongside increased flexibility, autonomy and opportunities for innovation, the study also illustrated that third sector social workers could undertake focused, high-quality work with service users and had more time both personally and professionally compared with working in the statutory sector. However, this had begun to change.

Participants variously described being valued by NCC, being listened to by managers, and having access to good supervision, reflecting Smith and Shields's (2013) research, which suggests that work motivation levels and job satisfaction are strongly correlated with autonomy, variety, and opportunities for creativity alongside positive support. These findings also confirm Tham's (2007) work, which shows that organizations where social workers felt well taken care of and where managers were interested in their health and well-being were more likely to retain staff.

Barth (2003) argued that the desire of individuals to undertake socially valuable work prevails over their needs for a higher salary and that employers take advantage of this to underpay them. Wermeling (2013) challenged this assumption, suggesting that earning an above-average income was important to social workers in signalling status, and associated high salaries with retention. However, this study shows low pay as endemic in the third sector, but that other benefits outweighed low pay for most participants. Suggesting that participants were unconcerned with their comparatively low salaries would, however, be misleading. Most made references to low pay either overtly or covertly and one participant indicated this as a deciding factor in leaving NCC and returning to statutory social work. NCC's pay scales for social workers are weighted so that pay is capped at below the national average salary for the same post in the statutory sector (Lombard, 2009), but its practice of employing both paraprofessionals and professionals from a range of disciplines on the same pay scale complicates direct comparisons. Arguably, this enables any employee with the talent and experience to progress within the organization and negates professional elitism.

Ambiguities around the demarcation of the social work role may have contributed to facilitating the flexible approaches that participants welcomed being able to adopt in their work, but could also undermine professional credibility externally. This was a major concern reported in the research on statutory social work and a symbolic marker of status, as cross-sector and contractual work grows. Moreover, the findings illustrated that participants are increasingly undertaking more complex work that cannot be expected of paraprofessionals who lack social work qualifications. Overall, this reflects trends in the wider erosion of pay and conditions in the UK.

None of the participants expressed significant difficulties in transitions to the third sector although this clearly required a change of ethos and approach and gave some the sense of feeling deskilled. However, opportunities to reconnect with reflective practice and what one participant described as 'learning to be, not do' were evidence of positive experiences around their transitions, with participants feeling supported by third sector colleagues and line managers. However, given the length of time these participants had been employed in the third sector, it is possible that statutory social workers transferring currently or in the future might experience greater difficulties because of the extent of changes over the past decade.

All of the interviewees were well established in middle- and upper-echelon third sector careers and saw themselves and their statutory social work peers very differently. They were critical of the latter for adopting a disparaging attitude to third sector colleagues and also because of shifting boundaries and the gradual transfer of cases and roles from statutory services.

Competition and envy play a role in such conflicting attitudes, but they also highlight the gradual loss of shared purpose and cohesion across social work. The sense of identification engendered among participants was primarily with NCC, as opposed to with the social work profession.

When considering the impact of recent changes and contracting, participants pointed to the imposition of changes without consultation, increased bureaucracy, instability, anxiety in meeting budgets, and a shift away from social work roots. Despite this, none of the participants made reference to social work within NCC as being in crisis and they were largely supportive of drives to become more business-like. This may reflect a 'legitimate' (Stacey, 2003) organizational discourse among participants who had little or no experience of tendering for commissioned work. Responsibility for certain difficulties was also attributed to statutory children's services, rightly or wrongly, rather than to wider social policy shifts or internal reorganization. Some criticism of recent changes was quite explicit, highlighting overwhelming levels of bureaucracy, low pay, and long hours to the point that the job had 'taken over'. Notably, the participants described experiences very similar to those reported by statutory children's services social workers in research cited earlier (British Association of Social Workers, 2012; Community Care, 2013).

If the current pattern of outsourcing fostering and care-leavers' services is any future indicator, opportunities for third sector organizations to take a greater role in providing children's social services are likely to multiply and may well include frontline child protection services. Bold reforms, potentially threatening to the underlying principles of social work and children's rights, are being processed through Parliament in the 2016 Children and Social Work Bill. The changes proposed remove core children's services from local authority control and accountability, placing them in a commercial marketplace (Butler, 2016). With fast-track training, the ability of providers to sidestep legislation, and political powers directing standards, both Brindle (2016) and Butler (2016) speculate that this could lead to a deeper social work crisis and further fragmentation of social work to the detriment of public interests in meeting wider social needs.

The widespread outsourcing of statutory children's services generates increased risks, including confused accountability and complexities associated with independent organizations intruding into family life and sharing data across public, private, and third sector organizations (Munn, 2014). Jones (2014) also suggests that if charities increase their roles, it could produce a fragmented child protection system with statutory failures simply re-emerging among charities, with accountability further compounded when corporate contractors are involved. The current lighter regime around regulation, accountability, and transparency in the charity sector would need to be strengthened in the public interest, but this is already generating negative experiences from current contracts. Finally, a two-tier social work system could also emerge, with statutory workers transferred to the third sector with protection for better pay and conditions than third sector or private sector social workers, further dividing the profession.

This research identifies much that is positive about social work roles in a national charity such as NCC. However, if statutory children's services are further outsourced to national charities and private sector contractors, a very careful assessment is needed of how organizations like NCC could maintain what is good and valuable, and ensure they avoid inheriting the perennial crisis of statutory social work.

References

Balloch, S., McLean, R., and Fisher, M. (1999) *Social Services: Working under pressure*. Bristol: The Policy Press.

Barth, M.C. (2003) 'Social work labour market: A first look'. *Social Work*, 48, 9–19.

Bowyer, S. and Roe, A. (2015) 'Social work recruitment and retention'. *Research in Practice. Strategic Briefing*. Dartington. Online. www.rip.org.uk/resources/publications/strategic-briefings/social-work-recruitment-and-retention-strategic-briefing-open-access-download-2015 (accessed January 2016).

Brindle, D. (2016) 'Government's "bold reforms" are only for children's social workers'. *The Guardian*, 26 January. Online. www.theguardian.com/society/2016/jan/26/bold-reforms-childrens-social-workers-nicky-morgan (accessed January 2016).

British Association of Social Workers (2012) *The State of Social Work 2012*. London: British Association of Social Workers and Social Workers Union.

Butler, P. (2016) 'Ray Jones: "Social work is under real threat"'. *The Guardian*, 20 July. Online. www.theguardian.com/society/2016/jul/20/ray-jones-social-work-threat-childrens-services-privatisation (accessed 26 July 2016).

Carmel, E. and Harlock, J. (2008) 'Instituting the "Third Sector" as a governable terrain: Partnership, procurement and performance in the UK'. *Policy & Politics*, 36 (2), 155–71.

Community Care (2013) *Child Protection Survey Report*. Online. www.communitycare.co.uk/ child-protection-survey-report/#.U1J_LFeeaVM (accessed 31 March 2014).

Cooper, A. (2008) 'Misguided vengeance'. *The Guardian*, 2 December. Online. www.theguardian.com/commentisfree/2008/dec/02/baby-p-haringey-social-services-sackings (accessed 26 July, 2016).

DfE (2014) *Children's Social Work Workforce: Key numbers as at September 2013*. London: Department for Education.

Ferguson, I. (2008) *Reclaiming Social Work. Challenging neo-liberalism and promoting social justice*. London, Thousand Oaks, CA, and New Delhi: Sage.

Gillen, S. (2007) 'Staff tell us their contrasting tales of working in the voluntary sector viz a viz the statutory sector'. *Community Care*. Online. www.communitycare.co.uk/2007/04/11/staff-tell-us-their-contrasting-tales-of-working-in-the-voluntary-sector-viz-a-viz-the-statutory-sector/ (accessed December 2016).

Jones, C. (2005) 'The neo-liberal assault: Voices from the front-line of British social work'. In I. Ferguson, M. Lavalette, and E. Whitmore (eds), *Globalisation, Global Justice and Social Work*. London: Routledge.

Jones, R. (2014) 'U-turn on children's services privatisation hides underlying problems'. *The Guardian,* 24 June. Online. www.theguardian.com/social-care-network/2014/jun/24/u-turn-childrens-services-privatisation (accessed March 2017).

Jordan, B. and Jordan, C. (2000) *Social Work and the Third Way: Tough love as social policy*. London, Thousand Oaks, New Delhi: Sage.

Laming, Lord (2009) *The Protection of Children in England: A progress report*. London: The Stationery Office. Online. http://dera.ioe.ac.uk/8646/1/12_03_09_children.pdf (accessed December 2016).

Lombard, D. (2009) 'Senior social workers' pay falls short'. *Community Care,* 20 November. Online. www.communitycare.co.uk/2009/11/20/senior-social-workers-pay-falls-short/ (accessed 15 July 2014).

Milbourne, L. and Murray, U. (2014) '*The State of the Voluntary Sector: Does size matter? Paper 1* (NCIA Inquiry into the Future of Voluntary Services Working Paper 9). Online. www.independentaction.net/wp-content/uploads/sites/8/2014/07/Does-Size-Matter-paper-1-final.pdf (accessed December 2016).

Munn, M. (2014) 'Plans to allow outsourcing of child protection will put young people at risk'. *The Guardian,* 2 September. Online. www.theguardian.com/society/2014/sep/02/outsource-child-protection-young-people-risk-rotherham (accessed December 2016).

Munro, E. (2011) *The Munro Review of Child Protection: Final report. A child-centred approach*. London: Department for Education. Online. www.gov.uk/government/uploads/system/uploads/attachment_data/file/175391/Munro-Review.pdf (accessed December 2016).

National Association of Social Workers (2009) *Social Work Reinvestment: A national agenda for the profession of social work*. Washington, D.C.: National Association of Social Workers.

NCVO (2016) 'Fast Facts'. In *UK Civil Society Almanac 2016*. London: National Council for Voluntary Organisations. Online. https://data.ncvo.org.uk/a/almanac16/fast-facts-5 (accessed December 2016).

Peters, E. (2012) 'Social work and social control in the third sector: Re-educating parents in the voluntary sector'. *Practice: Social Work in Action,* 24 (4), 251–63.

Rochester, C. (2013) *Rediscovering Voluntary Action: The Beat of a Different Drum*. Basingstoke: Palgrave Macmillan.

Rogowski, S. (2013a) *Critical Social Work with Children and Families. Theory, context and practice*. Bristol: Policy Press.

— (2013b) 'Neo-liberalism and social work: Facing the challenges'. *Policy Press Blog,* 13 March. Online. https://policypress.wordpress.com/2013/03/13/neoliberalism-and-social-work-facing-the-challenges/ (accessed 2 July 2014).

Scottish Executive (2006) *Changing Lives: Report of the 21st century social work review*. Edinburgh: Scottish Executive.

Shoesmith, S. (2016) *Learning from Baby P.* London, Jessica Kingsley Publishers.

Smith, D.B. and Shields, J. (2013) 'Factors related to social service workers' job satisfaction: Revisiting Herzberg's motivation to work'. *Administration in Social Work,* 37 (2), 189–98.

Social Work Task Force (2009) *Building a Safe, Confident Future: The final report of the Social Work Task Force November 2009.* London: Department for Children, Schools and Families.

Spandler, H. (2004) 'Friend or foe? Towards a critical assessment of direct payments'. *Critical Social Policy,* 24 (2), 187–209.

Stacey, R.D. (2003) *Complexity and Group Processes: A radically social understanding of individuals.* New York: Brunner-Routledge.

Tham, P. (2007) 'Why are they leaving? Factors affecting intention to leave among social workers in child welfare'. *British Journal of Social Work,* 37 (7), 1225–46.

UK Parliament (2008) *Children and Young Persons [HL] Act 2008.* Online. http://services.parliament.uk/bills/2007-08/childrenandyoungpersonshl.html (accessed December 2016).

— (2016) *Children and Social Work Bill [HL] 2016–17.* Online. http://services.parliament.uk/bills/2016-17/childrenandsocialwork.html (accessed July 2016).

Weaver, D. and Chang, J. (2004) *The Retention of California's Public Child Welfare Worker.* Berkeley: California Social Work Education Center.

Wermeling, L. (2013) 'Why social workers leave the profession: Understanding the profession and workforce'. *Administration in Social Work,* 37(4), 329–39.

Chapter 5

Voluntary organizations and criminal justice: A misguided turn

Ursula Murray

Voluntary organizations have a long history of active involvement in prison reform, and 1,400 voluntary organizations regard themselves as linked in some way to recent criminal justice activities (Gojkovic, *et al.*, 2011). Some have enjoyed a national profile in service delivery, including Nacro and Catch 22, and others in advocacy and campaigning, such as the Prison Reform Trust and the Howard League. However, the majority are neither large nor national but small or medium-sized and often quite localized.

This chapter considers proposed government policy changes in the penal system, followed by a review of the different ethical choices that voluntary organizations have adopted in the implementation of these changes. The government's enrolment of voluntary organizations in prison management since 2010 and subsequently in implementing Transforming Rehabilitation in 2014, which part privatized the Probation Service, are both highly contentious. Voluntary organizations have been exemplary in reshaping policy discussion towards rehabilitation. However, their involvement in new forms of service delivery within the penal system can equally be understood as a misguided turn and even a systemic ethical failure by their leaders.

Prison: A massive and costly failure?

There are approximately 86,000 people in prison in the UK at any one time, which is double the level in 1995 and the second highest in the EU (Prison Reform Trust, 2016). Despite longstanding evidence of the costs and ineffectiveness of custodial sentences (Muncie and McLaughlin, 1996), prison remains a massive and costly failure in terms of rehabilitation (Clifton, 2016). The prison service costs £13 billion a year and yet nearly half of all prisoners reoffend within one year (Clifton, 2016: 8), with even higher levels for shorter sentences. Around 40 per cent of prisoners also have low levels of literacy and educational achievement, which impact on their capacity to enter the job market. In 2016, the retiring Chief Inspector of Prisons' verdict on the overall state of UK prisons was 'disgusting' (Hattenstone and Allison, 2016), and his report highlighted how purposeful activity had plummeted by nearly half (HM Inspectorate of Prisons, 2015: 8). Community sentences have also fallen markedly since 2009 (Clifton, 2016) in favour of prison sentencing. Meanwhile deaths in custody, self-harm, and suicide have risen sharply, particularly for women (MoJ, 2016); legal highs abound and diet is deemed poor, with the daily food allowance set at only £2.02 per person per day in 2015 (HMIP, 2016).

This is not to say there is no inspiring practice in prisons. New Hall has pioneered support for women with complex needs (James, 2016) and the Swaledale Open Academy enables access to higher education (Allison, 2016). However, these are exceptions. More generally, as a consequence of austerity policies, the prison service overall has seen staff cut by 30 per cent since 2010, greatly reducing time out of cells, with the prison education service cut by nearly a quarter. A4e terminated contracts for prison education in 12 London prisons in 2014 because they were unprofitable (Gentleman, 2014). Yet in late 2016, these cuts together with the growing crisis in prison suicides, drugs, violence, and riots have forced the government to recruit 2,500 more prison officers, including 400 immediately for the ten most critical prisons.

Social policies concerning the high levels of domestic violence, mental ill health, race, and poverty all intersect with the penal system, but remain largely out of sight. Prison has increasingly become the place where many people with mental ill health and homelessness problems end up. Women constitute 5 per cent of the prison population, yet account for 25 per cent of the cases of self-harm (Roberts, 2015), and the impact of prison on families is severe. It affects 200,000 children annually with a range of negative consequences on mental and physical health, and on children's education.

The Harris review in 2015 strongly emphasized that prison should be a place of rehabilitation. Along with a growing awareness that the present system is both failing and unsustainable, 2015–16 saw a welcome shift, if only in the political rhetoric towards prison reform. An agenda spanning two decades of 'tough on crime and tough on the causes of crime' (Blair, 1995) has been driven forward by four Minsters of Justice supported by both major political parties, accompanied by ever more stringent sentencing. Even Kenneth Clarke (replaced as Justice Minister in 2012 for pursuing reform) accepted unsustainable budget cuts. The earlier agenda has now given way to a public discussion about rehabilitation, with new proposals around localized support in the community seen as an important component of preventing reoffending (BBC News, 2016), together with the introduction of devolved budgets to prisons. However, without a wide-ranging joined-up strategy, the parallel cuts in public services, from Sure Start to social housing provision, may simply undermine any benefits of this shift. Since mid-2016, the Conservative government has been reviewing its policy position on prison reform, suggesting that it is considering the overall system.

Voluntary organizations and a privatized penal service

Voluntary organizations have a long history of penal reform and radically challenging the emphasis on prison as resolving wider social problems. They have also long provided essential support services to families and individuals affected by the impact of prison.

Since 2010, however, some larger charities have also become involved in prison management. For example, Turning Point and Catch 22 together won a 26-year £415 million contract in partnership with the multinational conglomerate Serco to run the new private prison of Belmarsh West (Ricketts, 2010). At the time, the Howard League and NAVCA met with the Charity Commission to challenge whether running a prison was a legitimate charitable undertaking. The Howard League argued in unequivocal terms that managing prisons was a 'contradiction of charitable purposes' (Crook, 2012), as it involved taking part in decisions involving punishment as a part of a profit-making business. Yet the Commission ruled 'that both charities are acting within their objectives' (Crook, 2012). However, for many groups there remains an important distinction between involvement in prison management, as above, and the support or education services within prisons or to former prisoners provided by local groups or charities, such as the voluntary support of, for example, the Samaritans or Alternatives to Violence (AVP).

The conflicting viewpoints on the involvement of charities in prison management can also be linked to the introduction of private prisons in the UK. Of 150 prisons, 14 are now run by either G4S Justice Services, Serco Custodial Services or Sodexo Justice Services (MoJ, 2014a). Nine new such prisons were announced as part of the sale of the prison estate in inner cities (Wintour, 2015), and new larger prisons are being built specifically to cut costs. However, these are now grappling with the impact of austerity cuts, a lack of profit, drug problems, suicidal inmates, and an inexperienced and demoralized staff (Gentleman, 2016). The specific failures of private prisons have been widely highlighted, not least by the alleged abuse at the G4S-run young offenders' centre in Medway in 2015. This private security firm has now withdrawn from children's services contracts, including the Medway facility (Travis, 2016a). The charity War on Want has also identified G4S as at the centre of a 'global mercenary industry' (Norton-Taylor, 2016), underlining how the legitimization of prison privatization through the involvement of voluntary organizations remains highly contentious.

In the USA, the growth of private prisons from 5 to 100 within a decade was interpreted as the emergence of a 'prison industrial complex' generating large returns and profit (Schlosser, 1998). US prisons now incarcerate 2 million people and 25 per cent of the world's prison population. The majority are non-violent offenders, leading Pelaez (2008) to question whether this is 'big business or a new form of slavery'. In the UK, Frances Crook of the Howard League also regards the criminal justice system as a highly profitable supply chain feeding corporate interests, with commercial companies, uninterested in reform and rehabilitation, sucking in charities. Crook (2012) considers that such charities are simply naive to think that they have any leverage in how prisons are run and considers that commercial companies use them as a veneer to divert criticisms. Others refer to charity roles in partnering with corporate providers in tendering as 'bid candy' (Kerr, 2013: 46), used simply to win contracts.

Under the Coalition government (2010–15), funding flowed towards larger national charities in a number of other ways, indicative of the multiple roles that certain major charities were starting to play in the government's new privatizing agenda. Garside *et al.* (2013) identified the award of £53.7 million in MoJ contracts between May 2010 and October 2012 to voluntary organizations involved in criminal justice. Direct funding to specific organizations included the drug Rehabilitation for Addicted Prisoners Trust (RAPT) project (£8.6m), Working Links (£6.4m), Nacro (£5.6m), Barnardos (£2.4m), the infrastructure body CLINKS (£1.5m), and the Salvation Army (£1m). Over the same period, G4S Care and Justice Services received £308.4 million and Serco received £287.3 million for the outsourced operation of prisons, detention centres, escort services, and electronic monitoring. The Cabinet Office's Rehabilitation Social Action Fund of £2.4 million also announced awards in 2014 to 12 ex-offender charities, including Crime Reduction Initiatives (CRI), St Giles Trust, and others (Cabinet Office, 2014).

Transforming rehabilitation: Privatizing probation

Despite criticism and calls for caution, 2014 saw voluntary organizations drawn ever more deeply into government plans for a newly privatized Probation Service, as new partners or sub-contractors to corporate providers. Although the Transforming Rehabilitation strategy announced in

2013 (MoJ, 2013) has progressive elements, it was also primarily devised as an ideological and cost-saving exercise that has now dramatically changed the ownership and management of probation services in England and Wales.

A public sector Probation Service has been replaced by 21 Community Rehabilitation Companies (CRCs) in England and Wales, now largely located in the private sector. Overall, just two companies (Sodexo and Interserve) now control more than half the former probation services. The Ministry of Justice awarded ten-year contracts to 17 private companies, each partnered with a national charity (including Nacro, Shelter, St Giles Trust, CRI, and P3). Three of the remaining CRCs are run by Working Links, a joint public, private, and voluntary sector venture, and just one new CRC is a mutual based on public and voluntary sector probation staff (MoJ, 2014b). Notably, G4S and Serco withdrew their bids after accusations of serious fraud in overcharging £100 million on electronic tagging (Travis, 2014). Of the 300 sub-contractors also named, 75 per cent were voluntary organizations expecting to secure contracts or grants as tier 2 and tier 3 sub-contractors to tier 1 private companies and their charity partners.

In summary, a select few large charities exist in tier 1 partnerships with private companies. Some, such as CGL (Change, Grow, Live), are largely dependent on service contracts, with little grassroots membership involvement or accountability and are social enterprises in all but name. Small to medium voluntary organizations, often with long-established, locally based connections, may have been named as potential tier 2 and 3 providers/sub-contractors, but many are now falling out of the system entirely.

Six new resettlement prisons are being built with an extended supervision role for probation involving some 45,000 additional offenders a year who will be released from short prison sentences (of less than 12 months). They will be subject to a new range of supervision and rehabilitation activities at the disposal of, and defined by, the Courts.

Unblocking radical reform

With nearly half of all prisoners on sentences of less than 12 months reoffending within a year, the costs and ineffectiveness of prison appear to have finally become politically unsustainable. A decade ago, the Social Exclusion Unit identified key social causes of crime and reoffending and recommended new initiatives in response (Lanning *et al.*, 2011). Since then, there have been attempts to develop whole-systems approaches to improve on the costly failures of custodial sentences. However, the results of a pilot project in post-prison support across seven London boroughs, based on the

Total Place approach (HM Treasury, 2010), ultimately proved disappointing. As Clifton (2016) explains, a key reason was that despite the local costs and efforts expended to prevent someone ending up in prison, any financial benefits ultimately accrued to the central budget of the Ministry of Justice.

Some of these tensions have been positively resolved in the Youth Justice Custody Pathfinders project in England, which created financial incentives for local authorities to focus on prevention and alternatives to custodial sentences. As a result, the number of young people in custody fell dramatically, from 3,000 in 2005 to 1,000 ten years later (Clifton, 2016: 14). Summarizing how this was achieved, Wong *et al.* (2015) describe how local authorities formed groups of five to maximize efficiencies in developing community services and supervision schemes in which voluntary organizations played an important part. In 2015, the then Minister of Justice visited Texas, where similar success had been achieved in projects with adult prisoners (Dart, 2015), following President Obama's efforts to reduce sentences for non-violent offenders in a penal system that disproportionately affects black Americans.

Driven by the need for reduced budgets following on from austerity politics, the political rhetoric around crime and prison prevention in the UK has begun to suggest a new potential to shift away from a punitive policy stance. While sentencing reform to reduce prison numbers remains fundamental to any real change, the other key challenge is how to unfreeze the resources locked up in a patently ineffective prison system and redirect them away from the control of the Ministry of Justice to incentivize crime prevention and rehabilitation for less serious crime at a local level. Good practice in Scotland has, for example, considered and addressed violence in society through an alternative lens of public health, prompting a significant fall in violent crime incidents, whereas they have risen sharply in England (ONS, 2016).

Such an approach chimes well with the wider devolution of budgets from central to local government in England. However, prior to the Transforming Rehabilitation strategy, custody and probation budgets could potentially have been combined, but the probation budgets are now locked into a set of rigid ten-year contracts with private companies and their charity partners. As Clifton (2016) argues, in the longer term the renewal of such contracts should pass to local government and new sub-regional city mayors, enabling the pooling of budgets and radically extending local capacity to invest in services and innovate. Agencies in a locality would then work collectively to avoid bearing the cost of sending someone to prison, encouraging them to keep low-level offenders, especially women, out of prison entirely.

The cost to small and medium-sized voluntary organizations

However, the present reality is now one in which potentially innovative, small and medium-sized voluntary organizations are threatened with closure as a consequence of Transforming Rehabilitation and the privatization process.

In 2013, the Criminal Justice Alliance (CJA) highlighted to an All-Party Parliamentary Penal Affairs Group the significant strengths that smaller organizations contributed in terms of innovation, quality of work, and localism (Helyar-Cardwell, 2013). A clear concern was that organizations working in the penal system that were not contracted as part of new supply chains defined by the CRCs and the Courts would find themselves excluded and their valued support for prisoners and their families would be marginalized. The CJA also warned against false expectations about the proportion of funding that would actually reach small organizations in the privatized Probation Service. It voiced disquiet, too, about the exclusion of local authorities, fearing that they might withdraw from established, too, local webs of activity, compounding the impact of wider public service cuts impacting on any effective rehabilitation strategy.

When the contracts and sub-contracts were awarded for the new Community Rehabilitation Companies, the infrastructure body for voluntary organizations, CLINKS, in association with NCVO and the Third Sector Research Centre (TSRC) jointly established a system to track and monitor the experiences of smaller voluntary organizations. Their initial report, *Early Doors* (CLINKS *et al.*, 2015), confirms wide-ranging concerns. It recorded disruption to established local partner relationships, albeit in the early stages of implementation, and that nearly half of the 150 organizations surveyed had been adversely affected by the changes, with anxieties about contracts or the absence of promised funding emerging from the CRCs. The report describes how many groups are 'watching, waiting and negotiating … in a state of limbo, unclear whether they would be funded to provide services' (CLINKS *et al.*, 2015: 6). There is also a perception that traditional funders are now unwilling to resource what have theoretically become central government-funded services.

Funding now follows Court recommendations, and previously relevant roles and services may be ignored. Some voluntary organizations reported a dramatic reduction in referrals and were unclear whether this was because there was now a lack of knowledge as to their existence.

Other voluntary organizations reported having to help the new CRCs understand a sector with which they had no previous relationship, while also negotiating prices or grappling with contracts shaped by payment by results, with all the attendant risks for small organizations of becoming over-stretched financially. The geographic boundaries of CRCs also differ from police or local authority boundaries, adding yet another layer of complexity and confusion to new systems. The findings from this research (CLINKS *et al.*, 2015) indicate that a long-established ecology of collaborative, multi-agency relationships and trust, built up locally between the former probation trusts, prisons and diverse stakeholders, alongside support roles from local authorities, has been seriously disrupted. A CLINKS follow-up report in 2016 confirms this pattern, and a recent assessment compiled by MPs confirms the extent to which such voluntary organizations have been squeezed out in criminal justice reforms (Kay, 2016).

The new CRC system is excluding rather than extending the range of community groups involved. It has particularly affected support for women. The director of Agenda (an alliance for women and girls at risk) has highlighted the much higher reoffending rates for women and how small, specialist women's centres can offer effective alternatives to custody and incarceration. This director argues, along with others, that such centres tackle the drivers of reoffending, including domestic violence, poor mental health, addiction, and the need for help with parenting. Budget cuts and the new model for delivering probation mean that these alternatives are increasingly under threat. As she points out, 'large private companies are now responsible for supervising most offenders, and those delivering specialist services for women are reporting significant funding cuts, with many worried they may be unable to continue to provide their vital services' (Sacks-Jones, 2016).

A further pattern emerging is that provision originating from grassroots voluntary movements, such as anti-trafficking or domestic violence, which have been widely lauded as innovative and have received government funding, then find themselves caught up in competitive tendering to renew their funding. At this point, many have lost their contracts, which have been awarded to large charities or private companies, such as the widely acclaimed Poppy Project, whose contract was awarded to the Salvation Army (Ishkanian, 2014). Likewise, few women's refuges, which are key structures in addressing domestic violence, continue to be run by Women's Aid in London, but have been outbid in competitive tenders by housing associations such as Hestia. Characteristically, costs are pared down by stripping out the specialist support services that are needed and reducing services to little more than hostel accommodation, often lacking emergency beds. This is in marked contrast to the ongoing specialist support provided by SOLACE, which has managed to retain refuge provision in six London boroughs.

Since 2012, the crime prevention charity Sova, employing 135 staff, now finds itself submerged as a wholly owned subsidiary of the major charity CGL (previously CRI) with its 2,400 staff. The latter doubled its turnover during the Coalition government years and this 'contract winning machine' (Brindle, 2016) anticipates a further 12 per cent rise in income in 2015–16 to £158 million. Like a for-profit corporate, CGL offers a widening menu of roles, extending from its traditional drug and alcohol and offender services, into mental health, social care, and public health. While providing staff with a well-being hour each week, the organization has held back staff pay rises over the previous five-year period. This highlights the downward pressure on the provision and shows that eliminating the costs of specialized skills is integral to successful tendering strategies.

Large charities, such as the CGL, Salvation Army, Hestia, and Barnardos, among many others, have all prompted the closure or takeover of smaller charities involved in support roles around the wider penal system. While vigorously pursuing its business model, CGL counters the claim that it is predatory and argues that it provides varied services supporting successful drug rehabilitation. It is also important to stress that not all large charities see themselves as business-driven or lack a membership base or wider accountability to an activist or grassroots base.

The perspective of smaller voluntary organizations on the role of large charities and outsourcing is inevitably more critical (Milbourne and Murray, 2014a). With some losing service contracts for which they had previously been applauded, such organizations experienced civil servants as managing the contracting process mainly to bring about competitive procurement. They reported that the potential to develop small, flexible alternatives was simply ignored. Civil servants, tasked by politicians primarily with demonstratinge enhanced competition, were perceived as largely uninterested in whether their decisions would result in poorer service outcomes. They also ignored more creative solutions such as through new kinds of partnerships. Smaller voluntary organizations that focused their tenders on improving the quality of existing provision simply misread how competition itself and destruction of a public sector had become the main purpose.

A failure of leadership?

Voluntary organizations faced a difficult dilemma from 2010 onwards in deciding how to respond to this intensified contract culture. A major plank of the Coalition government was to extend competition, and the dominant assumption was always that this would privilege corporate contractors. However, constant government references to the provider roles of the voluntary and private sector left unsaid that the key voluntary sector partners anticipated were the large national charities. The onward march of larger charities was the unavoidable consequence of government policies intent on extending competition, with many small and medium-sized voluntary organizations inevitably being sacrificed.

Did key infrastructure organizations, including CLINKS, NCVO and ACEVO, in their leadership roles for voluntary organizations misjudge the consequences of the government agenda in the privatization of the Probation Service? Prior to contracts being awarded, CLINKS questioned whether smaller charities would be squeezed out of provision and the risks this would pose to survival, but it also highlighted the opportunities for voluntary organizations. This, rather than the ethical question of the fundamental rights or wrongs of privatizing the Probation Service, dominated its debates. As an MoJ-funded organization, the position of CLINKS, perhaps inevitably, reflected the status quo of government policy.

Case studies: An alternative view?

Two case examples of small campaigning and advocacy organizations lying outside the mainstream contract culture provide a different lens through which to view this ethical dilemma of whether voluntary organizations should have participated in the privatization of the probation service. They are drawn from wider research of the experiences of small organizations (Milbourne and Murray, 2014a: 12–13; 2014b).

Former Prisoners

Mark, the director of Former Prisoners, described how they had positioned the charity as an advocacy group in the voluntary sector tradition of 'filling a gap'. He commented that as yet no market had been created and they were therefore not on the radar of larger charities. They had wrestled with how to differentiate themselves from the work that sub-contracting involves and find 'the right thing to do'. He considered that to become a sub-contractor would fundamentally change the nature of their work. They were now developing new roles and typically needing to develop new skills. It was a case of 'falling accidentally into these arrangements' – as could often happen when identifying and responding afresh to unmet needs.

Mark saw sub-contracting to the private sector 'as all about competing at minimal cost', with the result that 'the fundamental nature of what you do becomes different'. Asked why many voluntary organizations in the justice sector had supported privatization of the Probation Service and pursued sub-contracts with corporates as a route to survival, he thought that many of them had simply ignored the ethical price. In his view, people tended to believe that they 'do great work and know how to make it happen and so access to any finance to make more of this happen just seems deserved'. He added that during the New Labour era many projects had also got 'fatter and fatter and when the taps were turned off, there was a sense that they had a moral right to get hold of this source of money'. This had given rise to a sense of entitlement and wilful ignorance by parts of the voluntary sector, in which critical and political awareness had been sidelined.

Live Justice

Hugh, the CEO of Live Justice, described how they were a hub for developing good practice, information sharing and training. It was, he said, a very collaborative world and a 'safe space' to talk openly. However, there was no money to be made from it, and he commented that 'left to the market there would be no provision at all'. Live Justice had built excellent inter-agency relationships, including with local commissioners. Hugh described what was happening in the wider justice sector to the Probation Service as very depressing. In his view the relational culture that underpinned the best working practices was being destroyed.

He described how his organization had sought to remain outside the contract system and associated arrangements, wanting 'to clarify who we were'. As a result, the organization had taken a stance to remain independent of such constraints. He explained how people from other organizations working under contracts would say, 'we just wish we were now in your position'. In his view, very large and medium-sized charities now needed to ask genuine questions about 'what they want to be'. He thought that many charities that had made the decision to survive by competing for contracts were now struggling financially, finding that their primary 'customers' had shifted. He also pointed out that as soon as a contract was won, charitable grant funders tended to pull out. To go even further and become a sub-contractor to a corporate would in his view fundamentally change the nature of their work.

Asked about the role of the voluntary sector in facilitating or resisting this privatization, Hugh recalled a regular meeting of charities and public bodies in the criminal justice field where the chair had gone round the table asking each of them to comment. Only a handful of people had spoken out against privatizing the Probation Service and he added that the mainly small and medium-sized charities present 'seemed to be rubbing their hands with glee'. It was, he said, 'desperately sad' and represented 'naivety' in prevailing attitudes. He was especially critical of how Nacro – with a turnover of £80 million, 99 per cent of which came from government contracts, describing itself as 'a provider of choice' and shifting its stance 'with the politics of the day' – could define itself as a charity. He was adamant that 'these kinds of organizations should not now be allowed to be called charities … they should become straightforward non-profit social enterprises'.

A systemic ethical failure

The present government's criminal justice agenda is driven by the search for financial savings and by its ideological commitment to achieving a smaller state. By 2020, 'public expenditure outside health will fall to the lowest proportion of GDP since at least 1948', and projections show that Ministry of Justice spending will have nearly halved between 2010 and 2019 (Crawford *et al.*, 2016). In summary, it remains unclear how all the talk of reform marries up with the current and intended budget reductions and the long-term commitments already assigned in prison management and probation. Hutton (2015) concludes that it will produce 'the emasculation of innovation, of prison, probation, court and security systems, alongside an assault on local government'. By early 2017, the prison service is indeed coming close to collapse (Travis, 2016b) and privatizing the probation services has been branded a failure by two watchdog inspections (Merrick, 2016).

While the role of the voluntary organizations in pressing for rehabilitation over many years has been exemplary, their role in facilitating the change to a privatized probation system has been ill-judged. It has divided voluntary organizations and jeopardized the innovative contributions of smaller voluntary sector justice groups, with many now closed or under threat of closure, while benefitting large charities. The consequence is the loss – both current and future – of innovative ideas and development work in criminal justice, which smaller organizations have nurtured in localities and niches of activism over many years. Inevitably, locally responsive provision is now being lost to a new supply chain privileging larger organizations able and willing to work with multinational, corporate contractors.

Decisions about service suppliers are increasingly driven on finance and size, disregarding longstanding experience and quality of provision. This underlines why the role of charities effectively operating as social enterprises urgently needs clarifying.

In facilitating the privatization of the Probation Service, voluntary organizations have perversely helped to undermine the wider potential for radical penal reform. The absence of any collective voice of opposition to the privatization of the Probation Service from the voluntary sector was a serious misjudgement. The result is a probation system locked into ten-year contracts, almost totally transferred into the hands of private corporations and made politically palatable by the veneer of voluntary sector involvement. Collectively, these changes constitute a systemic ethical failure by the leadership of voluntary organizations – a failure driven by survivalism, hubris, and ambition, together with a fatal inability to think critically about the political economy underlying the moral dilemmas and sectional interests now so brutally exposed.

References

Allison, E. (2016) 'Prison no bar to higher education as university "campus" opens in Kent jail'. *The Guardian,* 22 February. Online. www.theguardian.com/education/2016/feb/22/prison-education-university-kent-jail-swaleside (accessed December 2016).

BBC News (2016) 'Prison's overhaul announced by David Cameron'. *BBC News*, 8 February. Online. www.bbc.co.uk/news/uk-35518477 (accessed December 2016).

Blair, T. (1995) Labour Party Leader's Speech, Brighton 1995. Online. www.britishpoliticalspeech.org/speech-archive.htm?speech=201 (accessed December 2016).

Brindle, D. (2016) 'What pisses people off is that we are very businesslike'. *The Guardian,* 13 July. Online. www.theguardian.com/society/2016/jul/13/david-biddle-change-grow-live-charity-pisses-people-off-we-are-very-businesslike (accessed December 2016).

Cabinet Office (2014) 'Funding boost for programmes that reduce re-offending: In Centre for Social Action Funding Streams (2013–15)'. www.gov.uk/government/news/funding-boost-for-programmes-that-reduce-reoffending (accessed December 2016).

Clifton, J. (2016) *Prisons and Prevention: Giving local areas the power to reduce offending.* IPPR. Online. http://tinyurl.com/z4422av (accessed December 2016).

CLINKS/NCVO/TSRC (2015) *Early Doors: The voluntary sector's role in transforming rehabilitation.* Online. www.clinks.org/resources-reports/early-doors-voluntary-sector's-role-transforming-rehabilitation (accessed December 2016).

Crawford, R., Emmerson, C., Pope, T., and Tetlow, G. (2016) *Risk to the Rules: Public spending.* London: Institute of Fiscal Studies. Online. www.ifs.org.uk/publications/8157 (accessed December 2016).

Crook, F. (2012) 'Charities involved in running prisons should have their charitable status revoked'. *Third Sector,* 24 August. Online. www.thirdsector.co.uk/frances-crook-charities-involved-running-prisons-charitable-status-revoked/management/article/1147160 (accessed December 2016).

Dart, T. (2015) 'Texas prison rehabilitation revolution catches eye of UK Justice Minister. *The Guardian,* 16 October. Online. www.theguardian.com/us-news/2015/oct/16/texas-prison-rehabilitation-revolution-michael-gove (accessed December 2016).

Garside, R., Silvestri, A., and Mills, H. (2013) 'Third Sector involvement in outsourcing'. In R. Garside, A. Silvestri, and H. Mills, *UK Justice Policy Review,* 3, 20–1. Online. www.crimeandjustice.org.uk/sites/crimeandjustice.org.uk/files/CCJS UKJPR 3.pdf (accessed December 2016).

Gentleman, A. (2014) 'A4e ends £17m prison education contract citing budget constraints'. *The Guardian,* 13 August. Online. www.theguardian.com/uk-news/2014/aug/13/a4e-terminates-prisoner-education-training-contract (accessed December 2016).

— (2016) 'Inside Oakwood prison: The private jail struggling to prove bigger is better'. *The Guardian,* 23 February. Online www.theguardian.com/society/2016/feb/23/inside-oakwood-prison-supersize-private-jail-g4s-profit (accessed December 2016).

Gojkovic, D., Meek, R., and Mills, A. (2011) *Offender Engagement with Third Sector Organisations: A national prison-based survey* (Third Sector Research Centre, Working Paper 61). Online. www.birmingham.ac.uk/generic/tsrc/documents/tsrc/working-papers/working-paper-61.pdf (accessed December 2016).

Hattenstone, S. and E. Allison (2016) 'Prisons inspector Nick Hardwick: "You shouldn't do this job for long because you get used to things you shouldn't"'. *The Guardian,* 29 January. Online. www.theguardian.com/society/2016/jan/29/prisons-inspector-nick-hardwick-interview (accessed December 2016).

Helyar-Cardwell, V. (2013) *Minutes of the All-Party Penal Affairs Parliamentary Group*. Online. www.clinks.org/sites/default/files/APPG on Penal Affairs Minutes 3.12.13.pdf (accessed December 2016).

HMIP (2015) *HM Chief Inspector of Prisons for England and Wales. Annual report 2015–16*. London: HM Inspectorate of Prisons. Online. www.justiceinspectorates.gov.uk/hmiprisons/wp-content/uploads/sites/4/2016/07/HMIP-AR_2015-16_web.pdf (accessed December 2016).

HMIP (2016) 'Life in prison. Food: A findings paper'. London: HM Inspectorate of Prisons. Online. https://www.justiceinspectorates.gov.uk/hmiprisons/wp-content/uploads/sites/4/2016/09/Life-in-prison-Food-Web-2016.pdf (accessed January 2017).

HM Treasury (2010) *Total Place: A whole area approach to public services*. Online. http://webarchive.nationalarchives.gov.uk/20130129110402/http:/www.hm-treasury.gov.uk/d/total_place_report.pdf (accessed December 2016).

Hutton, W. (2015) 'Michael Gove has a vision for reforming prisons – and justice'. *The Observer,* 19 July. Online. www.theguardian.com/commentisfree/2015/jul/19/michael-gove-justice-prison-system (accessed December 2016).

Ishkanian, A. (2014) 'Neoliberalism and violence: The Big Society and the changing politics of domestic violence in England'. *Critical Social Policy,* 34 (3), 333–53.

James, E. (2016) 'Inside the special prison unit where rehabilitation rules the roost'. *The Guardian,* 25 May. Online. www.theguardian.com/society/2016/may/24/special-prison-unit-where-rehabilitation-rules-hmp-new-hall (accessed December 2016).

Kay, L. (2016) 'Voluntary sector "squeezed out" in justice reforms, MPs conclude'. *Third Sector,* 26 September. Online. www.thirdsector.co.uk/voluntary-sector-squeezed-out-justice-reforms-mps-conclude/management/article/1410066 (accessed December 2016).

Kerr, S. (2013) Fair Chance to Work 2. Experiences from the first phase of Work Programme delivery in London. London: London Voluntary Service Council. Online. www.lvsc.org.uk/media/127586/fair%20chance%20to%20work%20 2%20-%20march%202013.pdf (accessed December 2016).

Lanning, T., Loader, I., and Muit, R. (2011) *Redesigning Justice: Reducing crime through justice reinvestment.* Institute for Public Policy Research. Online. www.ippr.org/files/images/media/files/publication/2011/07/redesigning-justice-reinvestment_July2011_7786.pdf?noredirect=1 (accessed December 2016).

Merrick, R. (2016) 'Privatisation of probation services branded a failure by two watchdog inspections'. *The Independent,* 4 October. Online. www.independent.co.uk/news/uk/politics/prison-privatisation-chris-grayling-probation-services-watchdog-criticism-government-failure-a7344361.html (accessed January 2017).

Milbourne, L. and Murray, U. (2014a) *The State of the Voluntary Sector: Does size matter? Paper 2* (NCIA Inquiry into the Future of Voluntary Services Working Paper 10). Online. www.independentaction.net/wp-content/uploads/2014/07/Does-size-matter-paper-2-final.pdf (accessed December 2016).

— (2014b) *The State of the Voluntary Sector: Does size matter? Paper 1* (NCIA Inquiry into the Future of Voluntary Services Working Paper 9). Online. www.independentaction.net/wp-content/uploads/sites/8/2014/07/Does-Size-Matter-paper-1-final.pdf (accessed December 2016).

MoJ (2013) *Transforming Rehabilitation: A strategy for reform.* London: Ministry of Justice. Online. https://consult.justice.gov.uk/digital-communications/transforming-rehabilitation/results/transforming-rehabilitation-response.pdf (accessed December 2016).

— (2014a) *Contracted-out Prisons.* Online. London: Ministry of Justice. www.justice.gov.uk/about/hmps/contracted-out (accessed December 2016).

— (2014b) *Table A: List of preferred bidders.* Online. London: Ministry of Justice . www.gov.uk/government/uploads/system/uploads/attachment_data/file/368266/table-of-preferred-bidders.pdf (accessed December 2016).

— (2016) *Safety in Custody: Statistics bulletin. England and Wales.* London: Ministry of Justice. Online. www.gov.uk/government/uploads/system/uploads/attachment_data/file/543284/safety-in-custody-bulletin.pdf (accessed December 2016).

Muncie, J. and McLaughlin, E. (1996) *The Problem of Crime.* London: Sage/OU.

Norton-Taylor, R. (2016) 'Britain is at centre of a global mercenary industry, says charity'. *The Guardian,* 3 February. Online. www.theguardian.com/business/2016/feb/03/britain-g4s-at-centre-of-global-mercenary-industry-says-charity (accessed December 2016).

ONS (2016) 'Crime and justice'. London: Office of National Statistics. Online. www.ons.gov.uk/peoplepopulationandcommunity/crimeandjustice (accessed December 2016).

Pelaez, V. (2008) 'The prison industry in the United States: Big business or a new form of slavery?' *Global Research*, 28 August. Online. www.globalresearch. ca/the-prison-industry-in-the-united-states-big-business-or-a-new-form-of-slavery/8289 (accessed December 2016).

Prison Reform Trust (2016) *Prison: The facts* (Bromley Briefings Summer 2016). Online. www.prisonreformtrust.org.uk/Portals/0/Documents/Bromley%20 Briefings/summer%202016%20briefing.pdf (accessed December 2016).

Ricketts, A. (2010) 'Consortium signs £415m deal to build and run prison'. *Third Sector*, 6 July. Online www.thirdsector.co.uk/consortium-signs-415m-deal-build-run-prison/policy-and-politics/article/1014234 (accessed December 2016).

Roberts, Y. (2015) 'Give our women prisoners the break they're long overdue'. *The Guardian*, 29 November. Online. www.theguardian.com/commentisfree/2015/ nov/29/give-women-prisoners-a-break (accessed December 2016).

Sacks-Jones, K. (2016) 'Prime Minister, if you want to keep mothers out of prison, don't cut the alternative'. *The Guardian*, 9 February. Online. www.theguardian. com/society/2016/feb/09/keep-mothers-out-of-prison-prime-minister (accessed December 2016).

Schlosser, E. (1998) 'The prison-industrial complex'. *The Atlantic*, December. Online. www.theatlantic.com/magazine/archive/1998/12/the-prison-industrial-complex/304669/ (accessed December 2016).

Travis, A. (2014) 'G4S agrees to repay £109m for overcharging on tagging contracts'. *The Guardian*, 12 March. Online. www.theguardian.com/ business/2014/mar/12/g4s-repay-overcharging-tagging-contracts (accessed December 2016).

— (2016a) 'Justice ministry to take over Medway child jail from G4S'. *The Guardian*, 5 May. Online. www.theguardian.com/business/2016/may/05/moj-to-take-over-medway-child-jail-from-g4s (accessed December 2016).

— (2016b) 'Prisons brought to the brink of collapse by Tory lord chancellors, says ex-boss'. *The Guardian*, 12 December. Online. www.theguardian.com/ society/2016/dec/12/prisons-brought-to-brink-of-collapse-by-tory-lord-chancellors-says-ex-boss (accessed January 2017).

Wintour, P. (2015) 'Nine new prisons to be built in England and Wales'. *The Guardian*, 9 November. Online. www.theguardian.com/society/2015/nov/09/ nine-new-prisons-england-and-wales (accessed December 2016).

Wong, K., Ellingworth, D., and Meadows, L. (2015) *Youth Justice Reinvestment Custody Pathfinder: Final process evaluation report* (Ministry of Justice Analytical Series). London: Ministry of Justice. Online. www.gov.uk/ government/uploads/system/uploads/attachment_data/file/414123/youth-justice-reinvestment-custody-pathfinder-final-evaluation-report.pdf (accessed December 2016).

Part Two

Power: Independence and
grassroots organizing

Marginalizing diverse voices? Working with minority interests against the tide of mainstreaming

Palmela Witter

This chapter explores the experiences of UK black and minority ethnic voluntary organizations in a climate of public services cuts, focusing on African Caribbean mental health services in different multicultural inner-city areas. It draws on findings from a study considering the extent to which voluntary organizations working specifically with these community populations are able to survive amid rapidly changing service cultures and in an environment where mainstreaming mental health services is increasingly becoming the norm.

UK black and minority ethnic communities are very diverse, including people of Black African, African Caribbean, South Asian, and Chinese heritage (Greene *et al.*, 2008). As the focus in this chapter is on a specific lived experience, it refers mainly to the African Caribbean or 'black' community, a descriptive term for people of African or mixed African heritage.

Black and minority ethnic organizations exist largely below the radar of the UK's voluntary sector (McCabe *et al.*, 2010). Many small-scale community organizations have gained a positive reputation for providing flexible service approaches, reaching people who might otherwise not access provision (Boateng, 2002). Recent governments have encouraged growth in local grassroots activities around health, anticipating reductions in public health and welfare spending (Phillimore and McCabe, 2015). However, government agendas and local community aspirations may well be at odds, and recent programmes in health and welfare services have generated contradictory political messages, threatening goals that many African Caribbean and other grassroots organizations were established to meet. As funding shrinks, together with the spaces for advocacy and campaigning, the future for such organizations seems increasingly fragile. Exploring these issues is therefore timely, and the chapter draws on research that seeks to capture the voices and experiences of voluntary organizations supporting black populations.

The chapter first describes how the research came about and then discusses definitions and the historical context of African Caribbean voluntary organizations, revisiting the reasons for their existence. Considering recent policy and political changes, it then examines dilemmas that they face, including around integrated or separate provision. The chapter subsequently explores examples from a primary study of black mental health organizations, analysing frontline experiences, and concludes by discussing the potential future of these organizations.

What sparked this research?

Two critical incidents prompted this study. First, a timely research article entitled, *Very Small, Very Quiet, a Whisper*, concerning the barely audible voices of black and minority ethnic voluntary organizations (Ware, 2013), launched a debate on their future, highlighting the lack of research in this area. Despite its importance, the absence of African Caribbean faces at this research event was marked. As Etienne (2016) notes, minority ethnic voices are seriously underrepresented among researchers and in policymaking settings, and even where they are invited or present, the result is invariably others taking views and making decisions for and about them.

The second critical incident that sparked this research involved my own role as a youth worker and mentor. I accompanied a 21-year-old black male to his GP for advice on his mental health status and, following assessment, the GP referred him to a generic mental health service provider, rather than to a local black-led mental health organization. This led to reflection on why the GP had made this referral and whether this was an informed clinical decision, a judgement about the provision, or a lack of awareness of the specialist black-led voluntary organization. As research discussed later in this chapter highlights, for this young man, mainstream mental health provision was likely to heighten levels of fear and mistrust that he had experienced already in encounters with similar services.

What is the black and minority ethnic voluntary sector?

Black and minority ethnic voluntary organizations have often been grouped as a separate sector, situated within, but at the periphery of, the wider voluntary sector (McLeod *et al.*, 2001): a 'visible' minority (Mayblin and Soteri-Proctor, 2011: 4), often little acknowledged for their achievements. More pejoratively, they have also been labelled 'an under-class to the mainstream voluntary sector' (Smith *et al.*, 1995: 109), inspiring little confidence in their reputation as service providers. However, like other voluntary organizations, minority ethnic organizations are diverse, fragmented as a sector, and therefore easier to define by their purposes and activities. Most African Caribbean voluntary organizations regard themselves as independent and operate informally (Paxton *et al.*, 2005), aiming to represent or provide support for groups of people from diverse ethnic backgrounds and heritage, including those from African, South Asian, and Chinese communities (Greene *et al.*, 2008). Inevitably, this diverse membership also adds to disparate features.

There are some 165,000 active small, medium, and large registered charities in the UK serving some 7 million beneficiaries (NCVO, 2015). However, these figures account only for registered charities, and McCabe *et al.* (2010) estimate there are a further 900,000 small, informal organizations, including many black-led groups. Surprisingly, among so many active under-the-radar organizations, official estimates suggest that African Caribbean organizations comprise less than 1 per cent of the total. Disparities in figures between different reports range between 5,000 (Voice4Change, 2007) and 12,400 organizations (NCVO, 2014), compounding doubts around their accuracy. As ROTA (2009) highlights, poor statistics on black and minority ethnic voluntary organizations further obscure public knowledge about their reach and achievements.

Historical transitions and survival

African Caribbean voluntary organizations developed in response to experiences of racism and unmet needs among diverse populations (Smith *et al.*, 1995). A politicized environment during the 1970s and 1980s saw a range of community action projects and radical professional groupings grow from both international and UK-based campaigns around social injustices. In parallel, anti-discriminatory legislation on race and gender was passed in the UK. As chapter 1 describes, many campaign and advocacy organizations developed alongside new models of activist and user-led service provision, critical of the failures of public services to seriously address the new legislation or meet the needs of specific groups.

New projects grew at local levels, including supplementary education, radical health and social work projects, and community rights centres, aiming to challenge the bureaucratized systems that appeared to perpetuate inequalities, whether related to race, class, gender, or disabilities. Despite these new community activist organizations breaking with traditional voluntary sector approaches, considerable diversity remained, with many large and national agencies still distanced from new developments (Harrison, 1987).

This depicts the context from which many African Caribbean voluntary organizations emerged. Many received support from urban local authorities with ethnically diverse populations that recognized their value as community-based organizations able to provide tailored, responsive, and participatory service models for specific or marginalized groups of people. Many of these organizations successfully secured grants from central and local government programmes, including urban development funds, and were frequently valued as preferred providers, able to speak on behalf of specific interest groups (Christie, 2003).

The list of once-thriving African Caribbean organizations is long and includes the Black Federation of Housing Associations (BFGA), the Council for Ethnic Minority Voluntary Organizations (CEMVO), and the 1990 Trust, giving credence to the worth of African Caribbean voluntary organizations in addressing inequality and challenging threats to specialist community services.

African Caribbean women played a key role in campaigning organizations around women's employment, setting up women's training centres for non-traditional skills, and in supporting women threatened with domestic violence. Southall Black Sisters, set up in 1979 to meet the needs of Black (Asian and African Caribbean) women, continues to provide culturally specific services for women affected by domestic violence (Christie, 2003) and has survived, often against the odds. In 2008, the organization won a landmark court challenge against Ealing Council, which planned to withdraw funding from specialist domestic violence services for minority ethnic women in favour of generic but inferior services, such as those taken over by housing associations (Milbourne and Murray, 2014). In this case, Southall Black Sisters succeeded because Ealing Council failed to take race legislation seriously in neglecting to conduct a race equality impact assessment (Whitfield, 2008), even though Southall Black Sisters had submitted ample evidence to prove the significant racial impact of its loss.

Ujima Housing Association, established in 1977, was the first black British housing organization. It flourished with funding from local government and the Greater London Council (JRF, 2001). Once a vibrant success story (Chouhan and Lusane, 2004), it was established to address the housing and related needs of black communities. From 1977 to the mid-1980s, it offered a 'shining example of black enterprise' (Hetherington, 2008). However, with the Greater London Council's demise in 1986, subsequent budget reductions, and the 1992 Conservative legislation forcing a shift from grants to competitive tendering, Ujima and numerous other organizations heavily dependent on public resources faced decline. A sequence of events, also including apparent mismanagement, poor leadership and governance, led the organization to struggle and fail. It was subsequently absorbed by a mainstream housing association – further evidence of a trend in African Caribbean voluntary organizations being progressively taken over (Rai-Atkins, 2002).

Policy and discourse

The demise of the Commission for Racial Equality and Race Relations in 2010 also marked a significant shift for African Caribbean voluntary organizations, as race was assimilated into an inclusive language of 'equality and diversity'. The harder-edged discourse of the 1970s and 1980s that focused on discrimination, racism, or sexism had already changed markedly with the Conservative government's promotion of new public management cultures. Through the 1990s, the language of quality, equality, and client choice gradually pervaded public service provision (Clarke and Newman, 1997), and 'race and ethnicity' were eroded from political and policy discourse (Hepple, 2010), obscuring needs for culturally specific services (Christie, 2003).

Under the Equality Act 2010, race discrimination was simply one among several categories, further transforming both language and dominant practices. Consequently, implementing racial equality could be subsumed under diversity and equality strategies, justifying the provision of all-inclusive and homogenized services, regardless of users' needs (Greene *et al.*, 2008). With scaled-up service contracts and diminishing welfare budgets, it is easy to see how rapidly specialist African Caribbean provision is disappearing from policy and funding priorities.

Some policymakers have continued to argue the importance of supporting small-scale, specialist organizations because they provide valuable approaches in reaching groups of people largely excluded from services (Boateng, 2002). Conversely, others maintain that specialist providers make a minimal contribution to services (Toepler, 2003) or are overly driven by ideological aspirations (Barnes *et al.*, 2006). Localism, coupled with austerity, has recently seen politicians pressing small community groups to expand their welfare roles, but Phillimore and McCabe (2015: 138) question how far they can mitigate the impact of inadequate welfare without 'the resources and capacity to respond to rising levels of need'. They may also be reluctant to bow to policymakers' agendas. Additionally, reliance on volunteers and activists, when these resources are invariably sparse where they are most needed (Mohan, 2011), means that sustaining activities is an ongoing challenge for grassroots groups.

Ware (2013) argues that black and minority ethnic voluntary organizations have been unique in reaching out to diverse communities, achieving remarkable outcomes. Over some 30 years, they have especially served as a 'beacon and voice' for many marginalized African Caribbean communities facing discrimination in housing, education, employment, healthcare, and the judicial system (Voice4Change, 2007). Successful organizations have been well documented (ROTA, 2009), but following the unhelpful transitions in legislation and political ideology outlined above, many longstanding organizations now face threats of closure. This includes former trailblazers (Hetherington, 2008), such as the CEMVO and the 1990 Trust.

The chapter now turns to current African Caribbean voluntary organizations, examining questions about their survival and future roles. Exploring historical perspectives, however, provokes questions about whether the reasons for which these voluntary organizations were initially established are equally important today, and these are discussed further in the concluding paragraphs.

Mainstreaming: A positive or a destructive way forward?

Solutions advanced in mainstream policy to promote resilience and survival among small and specialist voluntary organizations have included mergers, capacity building, and entrepreneurialism (Home Office, 2004; OCS, 2010). It is assumed, often mistakenly, that growth and diversifying services will be protective. However, as Milbourne (2013) highlights, these strategies chime well with policy, but can threaten core goals and ultimately destabilize organizations. Earlier policy commitments to cross-sector partnerships and state-led contracts offer salutary lessons. African Caribbean and other grassroots organizations were often pressured to adapt and professionalize so as to access resources in situations more suited to large, well-established organizations. However, as Harris and Young (2010) illustrate, many resisted growth and formalization in favour of retaining trust and close connections with local stakeholders. In the current austere climate, pressures towards mainstreaming and compliance with dominant arrangements are even greater, and scaled-up contracts, homogenized services and aggressive competition are – as earlier chapters show – eroding much of the specialist, local provision.

This chapter raises doubts about whether mainstreaming services can secure a continued role for African Caribbean voluntary organizations or may prove a destructive way forward. Put simply, mainstreaming services underlines their wide public availability rather than being restricted to a particular group or sub-set of society. While mainstream provision therefore reflects the aims of universal services, it does little to address the specific needs of African Caribbean (or other) populations. Additionally, as welfare is increasingly rationed, relatively few services remain universally available and, under pressure, have increasingly adopted a one-size-fits-all approach.

Healthcare and mental health services

Tilki *et al.* (2015) have few doubts about the drawbacks of African Caribbean voluntary organizations being drawn into mainstream healthcare arrangements, highlighting the negative impacts of recent service reforms. Their study points to increased marginalization of these organizations and the ways in which contracting arrangements have disadvantaged even the biggest alliances of organizations. The authors demonstrate how large mainstream charities have used partnership work to profit from African Caribbean knowledge and expertise and then abandoned any pretence of continued collaboration. They also report 'partnerships' where 'the promised share of resources has failed to materialise' (Tilki *at al.*, 2015: 97). The study also describes incorporation into contracts with larger organizations, diluting cultural specificity and eliminating the added value of African Caribbean organizations in meeting specific needs. Worse than these experiences, the authors conclude that a widespread political and policy context is emerging where concerns about African Caribbean health inequalities are rapidly vanishing.

The substantial failures of mainstream provision to adequately address such needs reinforce the continued case for specialist services. This may not apply equally to all services, but in the context of mental health, the evidence is compelling. A recent MIND report (2013: 8) identified that:

> … mainstream services are often experienced as inhumane, unhelpful and inappropriate. Black service users are not treated with respect and their voices are not heard. Services are not accessible, welcoming or well integrated with the community. Black people come too late, they are already in crisis, reinforcing circles of fear.

MIND's report, highlighting a crisis in mental health services, is a damning assessment of generic provision that is failing to address African Caribbean mental health needs. Similarly, the Mental Health Foundation's (2015) recent research identifies people from black, Asian and minority ethnic groups as twice as likely as the white population to be diagnosed with severe mental illness involving hospital admission. The same research reports that people from these communities are more likely to experience poor outcomes from treatment and to disengage from mainstream services because their needs are misunderstood and services are neither acceptable nor accessible. Many are therefore not registered with mainstream mental health services, producing a recognized gap in statistical information.

Further research from the Race Equality Foundation (Jerai, 2015) reveals a similar picture of failures, highlighting growing numbers of cases of black women who are reluctant to engage with services or acknowledge mental illness (Ferguson, 2016), becoming seriously unwell before they do. Jerai emphasizes the importance of alternatives to mainstream provision, as lifelines. All of these studies identified people as generally happier with voluntary services.

The MIND (2013) report is critical of current commissioning practice, arguing that the value of African Caribbean providers in mental health services needs better recognition and a better contractual environment to ensure their proper inclusion. However, engaging with the health commissioning process currently commits African Caribbean organizations to demanding mainstream arrangements in bidding, competing, and contract management, while also seeking to retain different goals and approaches. This reflects the problems that Tilki *et al.* (2015) describe. Not engaging, however, carries risks of increased marginalization, declining resources, and lack of influence on wider services, alongside growing dependence on volunteers in a challenging service field.

Black-led voluntary organizations in mental health

The chapter now turns to primary research, exploring longstanding, black-led voluntary organizations involved in mental health and their experiences of surviving recent pressures. The organizations studied are located in different parts of an English multicultural metropolitan city that has disproportionately high percentages of African Caribbean populations accessing mental health services (Bradley Commission, 2013).

The following sections of the chapter draw on findings from the author's studies of four African Caribbean mental health organizations, including interviews with one male and three female participants (Winston, Jenny, Michelle, and Samantha). Each identified themselves as of black British or black Caribbean heritage, with between 10 and 25 years' experience of working in African Caribbean mental health organizations. Two were managers, one a project development worker, and the fourth a volunteer. Their four organizations are described briefly below. All names of people, organizations, and places are pseudonyms.

Set up in 1980, The Cavern is a grassroots voluntary organization. Its management structure comprises professionals, doctors, and nurses who work with teams of 10–18 volunteers. The management team, staff, and volunteers identified themselves as 'non-white' and The Cavern has a distinctive development history as one of the first black-led organizations to address inequalities in mental health provision in the south-east of the city. It had successfully secured funding from the local NHS trust, the local authority, and the regional NHS mental health trust.

Organization South East, another black-led voluntary organization established in an adjacent area in 1986, is smaller than The Cavern, with fewer management committee members, staff, and volunteers. Overall, it aims to address the broad mental health needs of the area's African Caribbean communities and to provide advice and guidance on related issues. Key stakeholders, including the local NHS trust and local authority, provide funding and support. A particular strength is in the organization's location, close to a principal mental health institution and two prisons. Consequently, it offers a unique service to the high proportion of African Caribbean men admitted to hospital, mental institutions, and prisons.

Organization Umbrella, based in the north-east of the city, was regarded as a pioneer among local African Caribbean voluntary organizations. Set up in 1985, it is a firmly established infrastructure organization and is well-placed to support and offer a collaborative base for many smaller community-oriented organizations. Organization Umbrella acts as a spokesperson, representing 12 local African Caribbean voluntary organizations, and seeks to influence local policymaking and funding.

The Grove, located centrally in the city, was established in 1986 to provide an inclusive mental health service working with more generic provision. It has several bases across the city and in other centres nationally. Although The Grove is not a black-led mental health organization, it aims to prioritize specific service needs, including those of African Caribbean communities. The senior black practitioner based at The Grove expressed his views, in which he compared his previous experience in black-led mental health voluntary organizations both as a practitioner and in community-based work.

The findings from these cases are organized thematically. They include illustrative quotes from participants, offering insights into key issues raised above related to the challenges facing African Caribbean mental health organizations.

Perspectives from frontline staff
Confidence or demoralization?

Jenny (The Cavern) identified her organization as heavily reliant on local authority funding. This had generated tensions among management committee members, who would have preferred more diverse funders. Jenny highlighted issues where she felt the management committee could have supported staff and volunteers better, given that financial constraints, commissioning, and fund-raising, alongside the do-more-for-less culture, had all significantly affected the organization's morale. She felt she was now experiencing potential burnout through not being valued for her efforts, and was, 'seriously considering leaving the organization'. Reflecting on the level of anxiety and the struggles around staff and organizational experiences that Jenny conveyed, it seemed as if she was being positioned as a receptacle for 'containing' these emotions (Hoggett, 2006) because few other outlets existed.

Despite the difficulties Jenny described facing, she believed that she and other staff were resilient, and concluded of African Caribbean organizations that, 'our biggest value is our resilience ... the African Caribbean voluntary sector has strength despite everything'. This view emerged as a common thread among all the participants: the 'resounding strength' radiating from the heart of African Caribbean voluntary organizations.

Black leadership: Community-oriented or entrepreneurial?

A theme that emerged from several interviews was the lack of black leadership, including the powerful voices lost because of earlier closures among African Caribbean infrastructure organizations. There were implicit criticisms about the quality of current leaders, and while participants identified leaders among small groups of individuals and organizations, their perception was that they rarely came together to offer a coherent message when needed. Referring to his previous work in a black-led organization, Winston (The Grove) emphasized the general level of fatigue, but also criticized a lack of engagement with technology and entrepreneurial ideas:

> there needs to be new blood and fresh perspectives ... this is a new era and the landscape is changing ... some people have been on the Management Board for 20 years and we have to move away from the old ways of doing things.

He contrasted the marked difference between The Grove and black-led management committee structures, suggesting that 'grassroots African

Caribbean voluntary organizations need an injection of ... social media, the internet; the younger generation have that entrepreneurial skill'.

However, Winston recognized that entrepreneurialism could be at the cost of community expertise and that it was essential not to neglect the knowledge and expertise of key staff and volunteers who 'know their community so well', which 'comes from a wealth of hands-on experience within African Caribbean communities'. Winston identified a fine balance between entrepreneurial skills – exploring new approaches – and long-standing experience, and concluded that 'one cannot survive without the other', voicing the challenge facing many voluntary organizations of how best to marry these ideas.

Winston also referred to a neighbouring local authority that provided capacity-building training for African Caribbean voluntary organizations to improve skills and retain strong leaders. However, few workers seemed attracted to attend, and he questioned what feedback had been received about the value of the courses.

Commenting on the same courses, Samantha from Organization South East highlighted the absence of spokespersons to represent African Caribbean groups, which meant that despite good intentions, such initiatives were superimposed by mainstream organizations. Michelle from Organization Umbrella, voicing similar concerns, proposed the need for an advocate for change to represent African Caribbean voluntary organizations and promote a bottom-up approach, raising awareness on policy issues and enabling organizations to influence changes. Without such representatives, the 'whisper' (Ware, 2013) of African Caribbean voluntary organizations remains unheard.

Networks, trust, and integrity

Collaboration and issues of integrity and trust also emerged as prominent themes from interviews, often coupled with concerns about organizational identity, values, and strengths. In order to maintain integrity, Samantha (Organization South East) explained the importance of 'not selling your soul ... to survive'. However, Michelle (Organization Umbrella) felt that 'partnership and collaboration' were 'the only way to survive', while also stressing that 'partnership must be based on equality' – seemingly a tall order in current times. Michelle adopted more entrepreneurial language, suggesting that 'investment is key', but despite this, reflected others' views about needing to 'maintain integrity and not sell your soul', defining 'lines I won't cross'. She went on to emphasize the importance of valuing 'our knowledge and experience – we know a hell of a lot and have been doing it for so long ... We should have written the book by now!' Thus for Michelle, allegiance to the values, knowledge, and identity associated with African Caribbean organizations apparently overrode external collaboration and defined the kinds of initiatives or actions that were acceptable.

Reference was frequently made to trust. Mistrust was seen as hindering African Caribbean voluntary organizations from developing strong networks. Participants clearly wished their organizations to be prominent in service delivery, able to meet the needs of African Caribbean groups failed by mainstream provision. However, mistrust often surfaced, weakening governance and leadership within organizations and their ability to access funding and engage effectively in collaborative networks. In effect, the 'lines I won't cross' and 'not selling your soul', while important statements about values and identity, were also indicative of entrenched feelings and the potential for mistrust pervading these voluntary organizations.

Evidence from the demise of some organizations discussed earlier suggests that intra-organizational mistrust has often played a part in weakening governance and in closures, alongside failures among organizations to be mutually supportive. In an increasingly fragmented and hostile environment, the approaches that participants highlighted as important, such as finding ways to discuss new strategies and to develop a collective voice and collaborative activities, appear crucial in strengthening African Caribbean organizations and overcoming the problems identified.

What future for the African Caribbean voluntary sector?

The earlier discussion and the examples illustrated above offer insights into the dilemmas facing African Caribbean voluntary organizations: the conflicted views and unclear strategy on how to address the future. Craig (2011: 381) asks 'who is to blame' for this often pessimistic picture: politicians, policymakers, NHS agencies, community stakeholders, or the organizations themselves? Central government and policymakers clearly carry responsibility for ideological and concrete changes in how public services are conceived and constructed; they are also gatekeepers for local government resources – and their decline and redirection. However, a less welcome observation emerging from the research was that internal feelings and anxieties (Hoggett, 2006) in African Caribbean organizations – the burnout, demoralization, and mistrust that participants described – were undermining reflective and creative strategies and the ability to act collectively to face challenges.

Arguably, by not moving with the times, by not becoming more market-facing and contract-ready, African Caribbean organizations are separated from the concerns of many other voluntary service organizations. Resisting mainstreaming and maintaining an independent stance could be regarded as ways in which many African Caribbean organizations are segregating themselves (Craig, 2011). However, the process of being defined by others – whether through the types of services deemed appropriate or approaches to organizing – has exacerbated a sense of alienation amid recent changes. Equally, stripping resources from specialist local services, despite overwhelming evidence of mainstream failures in providing black mental health support, has added to beliefs that wider society is heedless of the reasons why African Caribbean organizations are needed. Remaining separate may retain important specialist provision and avoid it being swamped in generic services; but failing to develop the creative strategies needed to survive with integrity in the current environment – the soul of African Caribbean organizations that study participants wanted to preserve – could simply generate counter-productive resistance.

The examples above highlight the diverse, fragmented, yet distinctive nature of African Caribbean voluntary organizations, which have remained little explored in research to date. As Tilki *et al.* (2015) demonstrate, research undertaken from the perspective of African Caribbean organizations offers vital insights into the disproportionate impacts of recent service reforms on already disadvantaged populations. The need for meaningful research on African Caribbean mental health services and on wider provision is more pressing now than when Craig (2011) argued for studies that could both be valued among African Caribbean organizations and influence policy and mainstream practice.

When McLeod *et al.* (2001) conducted their research on the sustainability of African Caribbean voluntary organizations, resources were greater and organizations could go some way to meeting their communities' needs. However, since then, the roles of voluntary organizations in influencing and criticizing policy directions have become increasingly compromised, restricting the expression of dissent. With dramatic changes in the socio-economic and political landscape since 2010, funding for activities associated with racial discrimination and specific needs has largely disappeared, adding to the frailty of African Caribbean voluntary organizations and weakening their voices and visibility (Ware, 2013). Specialist services, such as in mental health, alongside small advocacy groups, have suffered disproportionately. Overall, African Caribbean voluntary organizations have lost considerable political ground and presence.

Crisis or uncertain future?

In concluding, the chapter therefore asks: is this a crisis point for the future of African Caribbean voluntary organizations? The research discussed here suggests few easy paths for creating an effective future role and leaves open the question of whether engaging in commissioning can offer a solution despite all its drawbacks or whether severely limited resources means groups should prioritize advocacy alone. These are ongoing dilemmas for such organizations.

A particular difficulty when writing this chapter has been to highlight the positive benefits and values of African Caribbean voluntary organizations at a time when their struggles and shortcomings have become far more acute. The distinctiveness and enduring strengths of these organizations are recurring themes that emerge from this study and are echoed in other research (Craig, 2011; Ware, 2013) that highlights the unique qualities of these organizations in providing specific services to marginalized communities. A crisis? Perhaps. African Caribbean voluntary organizations, like many other small voluntary organizations, are experiencing serious hardships in an austere and turbulent world, but they have also demonstrated resilience, surviving with committed local people, despite scarce resources and a harsher climate of cultural challenges than many community groups have experienced.

What does the future herald? Study participants argued for an important ongoing role for African Caribbean voluntary organizations in providing specialist and tailored services, and most believed that their organizations could survive outside mainstream provision, but might need to develop different approaches. Mainstream involvement may offer inclusion and influence, but can also jeopardize goals, leading to disempowerment and alienation because outsiders fail to value their specialist concerns. As Ellison (2011) stresses, expecting small community groups to engage in mainstream provision to resolve the fallout from social inequalities and welfare cuts while policies ensure rewards for large corporations in the contract race is blatantly unjust and a road that many African Caribbean voluntary organizations may choose not to tread. If sustaining services proves impossible, the priorities may instead be to prioritize campaigning to influence the shape of mainstream services.

Despite fears that many African Caribbean voluntary organizations might be engulfed in generic provision, unmet needs and the failures and prejudices of mainstream services illustrated in this chapter continue to drive the need for their separate existence, certainly in mental health. For those trying to sustain alternatives, a future is clearly vital, but its form has still to emerge amid the present strictures. This survival, as Tilki *et al.* (2015: 100) admit, may mean losing some 'innovative, cost-effective … accessible and culturally sensitive services'. However, neglecting to work with and benefit from the creativity of African Caribbean voluntary organizations signals little policy commitment to the health of all members of society, especially to those most in need.

References

Barnes, M., Newman, J., and Sullivan, H. (2006) 'Discursive Arenas: Deliberation and the constitution of identity in public participation at local level'. *Social Movement Studies*, 5 (3), 193–207.

Boateng, P. (2002) *The Role of the Voluntary and Community Sector in Service Delivery. A cross cutting review*. London: HM Treasury.

Bradley Commission (2013) *Black and Minority Ethnic Communities, Mental Health and Criminal Justice* (Briefing 1). Centre for Mental Health.

Chouhan, K. and Lusane, C. (2004) 'Black voluntary and community sector funding: Impacts on civic engagement and capacity building'. York: Joseph Rowntree Foundation.

Christie, Y. (2003) *The Black Spaces Project*. The Mental Health Foundation, 4 (20).

Clarke, J. and Newman, J. (1997) *The Managerial State: Power, politics and ideology in the remaking of social welfare*. London: Sage.

Craig, G. (2011) 'Forward to the past: Can the UK black and minority ethnic third sector survive?'. *Voluntary Sector Review*, 2 (3), 367–89.

Ellison, N. (2011) 'The Conservative Party and the "Big Society"'. In C. Holden, M. Kilkey, and G. Ramia (eds), *Social Policy Review 23: Analysis and debate in socil policy, 2011*. Bristol: Policy Press, 45–62.

Etienne, J. (2016) *Learning in Womanist Ways. Narratives of first-generation African Caribbean Women* (Trentham Books). London: UCL IOE Press.

Ferguson, A. (2016) '"The lowest of the stack": Why black women are struggling with mental health'. *The Guardian*, 8 February. Online. www.theguardian.com/lifeandstyle/2016/feb/08/black-women-mental-health-high-rates-depression-anxiety (accessed December 2016).

Greene, R., Pugh, R., and Roberts, D. (2008) *SCIE Research Briefing 29: Black and minority ethnic parents with mental health problems and their children*. Online. www.scie.org.uk/publications/briefings/briefing29/ (accessed December 2016).

Harris, M. and Young, P. (2010) 'Building bridges: The third sector responding locally to diversity'. *Voluntary Sector Review*, 1 (1), 41–58.

Harrison, B. (1987) 'Historical perspectives'. In NCVO (ed.), *Voluntary Organisations and Democracy*. London: National Council for Voluntary Organisations.

Hepple, B. (2010) 'The new single equality act in Britain'. *The Equal Rights Review*, 5, 11–24.

Hetherington, P. (2008) 'In Ruins'. *The Guardian,* 16 January. Online. www. theguardian.com/society/2008/jan/16/housing.communities (accessed 14 May 2014).

Hoggett, P. (2006) 'Conflict, ambivalence and the contested purpose of public organizations'. *Human Relations,* 59 (2), London: Sage, 175–94.

Home Office (2004) *ChangeUp: Capacity building and infrastructure framework for the voluntary and community sector.* Online. www.surreycvsnetwork.org. uk/_Files/_OTH/ChangeUpFullFile.pdf (accessed December 2016).

Jerai, S. (2015) 'Black and minority ethnic people are shortchanged by mental health services'. *The Guardian,* 25 June. Online. www.theguardian.com/ healthcare-network/2015/jun/25/black-minority-ethnic-people-shortchanged-mental-health-services (accessed December 2016).

JRF (2001) *The Role and Future Development of Black and Minority Ethnic Organisations.* York: Joseph Rowntree Foundation.

Mayblin, L. and Soteri-Proctor, A. (2011) *The Black Minority Ethnic Third Sector: A resource paper* (Third Sector Research Centre Working Paper 56). Online. www.birmingham.ac.uk/generic/tsrc/documents/tsrc/working-papers/working-paper-58.pdf (accessed December 2016).

McCabe, A., Phillimore, J., and Mayblin, L. (2010) *'Below the Radar' Activities and Organisations in the Third Sector (Third Sector* Research Centre Working Paper 29). Online. www.birmingham.ac.uk/generic/tsrc/documents/tsrc/ working-papers/working-paper-29.pdf (accessed December 2016).

McLeod, M., Owen, D., and Khamis, C. (2001) *Black and Minority Ethnic Voluntary and Community Organisations: Their role and future development in England and Wales.* London: Public Studies Institute.

Mental Health Foundation (2015) *Fundamental Facts about Mental Health.* Online. www.mentalhealth.org.uk/publications/fundamental-facts-about-mental-health-2015 (accessed December 2016).

Milbourne, L. (2013) *Voluntary Sector in Transition: Hard times or new opportunities?* Bristol: Policy Press.

— and Murray, U. (2014) *The State of the Voluntary Sector: Does size matter? Paper 2* (NCIA Inquiry into the Future of Voluntary Services Working Paper 10). Online. www.independentaction.net/wp-content/uploads/2014/07/Does-size-matter-paper-2-final.pdf (accessed December 2016).

MIND (2013) Mental Health Crisis Care: Commissioning excellence for BME groups. Online. www.mind.org.uk/media/494422/bme-commissioning-excellence-briefing.pdf (accessed December 2016).

Mohan, J. (2011) *Mapping the Big Society: Perspectives from the Third Sector Research Centre* (Third Sector Research Centre Working Paper 62). Online www.birmingham.ac.uk/generic/tsrc/documents/tsrc/working-papers/working-paper-62.pdf (accessed December 2016).

NCVO (2014) *UK Civil Society Almanac 2014.* London: National Council for Voluntary Organisations. Online. https://data.ncvo.org.uk/almanac14/ (accessed December 2016).

— (2015) 'Workforce'. In *UK Civil Society Almanac 2015.* London: National Council for Voluntary Organisations. Online. https://data.ncvo.org.uk/a/ almanac15/workforce/ (accessed December 2016).

OCS (2010) *Supporting a Stronger Civil Society: An Office for Civil Society consultation on improving support for frontline civil society organisations.* London: Cabinet Office, Office for Civil Society. Online. www.gov.uk/government/uploads/system/uploads/attachment_data/file/78926/support-stronger-civil-society_0.pdf (accessed December 2016).

Paxton, W., Pearce, N., Unwin, J., and Molyneux, P. (2005) *The Voluntary Sector Delivering Public Services: Transfer or transformation?* York: Joseph Rowntree Foundation.

Phillimore, J. and McCabe, A. (2015) 'Small-scale civil society and social policy: The importance of experiential learning, insider knowledge and diverse motivations in shaping community action'. *Voluntary Sector Review,* 6 (2), 135–51.

Rai-Atkins, A. (2002) *Best Practice in Mental Health: Advocacy for African, Caribbean, and South Asian communities.* Bristol: The Policy Press.

ROTA (2009) *The Economic Downturn and the Black, Asian and Minority Ethnic (BAME) Third Sector.* London: Race on The Agenda. Online. www.rota.org.uk/webfm_send/25 (accessed December 2016).

Smith, D.J., Rochester, C., and Hedley, R. (1995) *An Introduction to the Voluntary Sector.* London: Routledge.

Tilki, M., Thompson, R., Robinson, L., Bruce, J., Chan, E., Lewis, O., Chinegwundoh, F., and Nelson, H. (2015) 'The BME third sector: Marginalised and exploited'. *Voluntary Sector Review,* 6 (1), 93–101.

Toepler, S. (2003) 'Grassroots associations versus larger nonprofits: New evidence from a community case study in arts and culture'. *Nonprofit and Voluntary Sector Quarterly,* 32 (2), 236–51.

Voice4Change (2007) 'Bridge the gap: What is known about the BME third sector in England'. England: Voice 4Change. Online. www.voice4change-england.co.uk/webfm_send/6 (accessed December 2016).

Ware, P. (2013) '*Very Small, Very Quiet, a Whisper …': Black and minority ethnic groups, voice and influence* (Third Sector Research Centre Working Paper 103). Online. www.birmingham.ac.uk/generic/tsrc/documents/tsrc/working-papers/working-paper-103.pdf (accessed December 2016).

Whitfield, L. (2008) *Southall Black Sisters: The case against Ealing R (Kaur & Shah) v London Borough of Ealing.* London: Public Law Project. Online. www.voice4change-england.co.uk/index.php?q=webfm_send/23 (accessed December 2016).

Chapter 7

The role of faith-based organizations in welfare delivery

Wale Olulana

Many voluntary organizations in the UK were established through mainstream religious organizations or closely associated individuals. Currently, faith-based charities have a combined income of £16.3 billion, representing a quarter of all charity income (Bull *et al.*, 2016). Four in ten charities are faith-based and nearly half the organizations protecting human rights and overseas development have religious roots. Alliances between secular and faith-based groups are generally seen to have contributed positively to changes in social policy (Deakin, 2010), although any universally positive association has also been contested (Lynch, 2014).

Following the 2008 financial crisis – and the ensuing politics of austerity – poverty and destitution in UK society (JRF, 2016) have become normalized. Food banks, homeless night shelters, and refugee centres supported by local faith communities often provide the only safety net as the state withdraws (Trussell Trust, 2016). Some faith-based campaigning organizations, such as Church Action on Poverty and Justice and Peace, as well as Quaker-sponsored campaigns across diverse policy issues, adopt a political stance, emphasizing justice over charity, which involves both speaking up for the voiceless and a radical critique of capitalism. A new generation of faith-based community activists has also emerged in recent years. London Citizens (Bretherton, 2015) has a membership widely drawn from churches, mosques, trade unions, schools, and universities and has campaigned effectively for the London Living Wage for cleaners, demanded reform of financial institutions, and challenged failures in recent government housing policy.

Within this overall scenario, the growth of evangelical and Black Majority Churches (BMCs) providing a wide range of welfare services is the primary focus of this chapter. It first considers the growth of BMCs and then the wider question of the role of faith-based voluntary organizations in social welfare, drawing on research undertaken in the London Borough of Barking and Dagenham, which investigates the desire for partnership between black African-majority churches and the local council in providing much-needed public services. A critical aspect to emerge is the slippage between the aspirations and conflicting needs of both the BMCs and the council.

The growth of evangelical and Black Majority Churches

During the 1950s and 1960s, migrants from the Caribbean brought their skills, hopes, and unique expression of the Christian faith to the UK (Francis, 1998). While there is now a black presence in mainstream churches, migrants initially experienced cold treatment from the established, predominantly white churches. Deakin (2010) identifies how the initial failure of the mainstream Christian churches to accommodate black Christian migrants from the West Indies and West Africa and the arrival of Hindus, Muslims, and Sikhs from the Asian sub-continent created a new religious diversity, in which ethnic and religious differences combined in a variety of different constellations. Caribbean migrants established social action projects to support community members, leading to the emergence of black-led churches, which subsequently became social havens for growing immigrant communities based on their faith, identity, and cultural affiliations.

Since the 1980s, BMCs have grown rapidly (Evangelical Alliance, 2006) following the arrival of many African migrants to the UK and London in particular. This new, extroverted Christian community differs significantly from the more traditional, reserved forms of religious expression. Its business-friendly orientation, messages of economic empowerment, professional achievements, and political engagement and advocacy all offer solutions to prejudices, opposition, and racial injustice. The BMCs attract a large following among young, politically minded, middle-class ethnic minorities. An urban explosion of BMCs in Britain is something of a paradox, as official statistics point to declining church attendance; but the past 20 years have seen a major shift in the landscape (Cartledge, 2012).

A strong history of welfare delivery and good governance among established mainstream churches has made it difficult for BMCs to compete for public service contracts. Instances of mission drift or projects becoming casualties of hybridization have also led BMCs to emphasize the use of self-generated funds and to reposition themselves as relevant groups able to provide solutions to community problems (Adedibu, 2012). Another noticeable recent change is the greater utilization of skilled professional volunteers from congregations for social action projects, together with increased acceptance of the need for separate charitable bodies distinct from the faith community. Adedibu notes that both strategies have helped to minimize mission drift.

With cuts to local government funding and welfare benefits, the question of how local faith communities can take a stronger role in ameliorating the impact on vulnerable and disadvantaged communities is a very live one. Twentieth-century voluntary action has characteristically emphasized motivation that comes from 'love of one's fellow man' and action 'which promotes the well-being of others' (Prochaska, 1988: 7). Community engagement has also featured centrally in the theological values of faith communities (Loewenberg, 1995). However, there are many members of faith communities who consider wider welfare engagement as imprudent, fearing compromise, misunderstood motivations, or a secularization of their faith. Faith groups may not want to adhere to government monitoring requirements (Cairns *et al.*, 2007) and can be hostile to the wholesale adoption of secular bureaucratic practices (Jeavons, 1994).

Faith-based voluntary organizations and social welfare

Policymakers identify faith-based organizations as driven by values and commitment, with an important contribution to make in building cohesive communities and renewing civil society (LGA, 2002: 3). Projects often arise from the normal activities of faith congregations, with members giving and receiving care through informal relationships. These then develop into a separate charity as awareness of wider social needs grows. Knowledge of local needs, access to large meeting places, and leadership in organizing community activities are among the many reasons why the faith sector has been seen as valuable in contributing to social policy at different times.

In 2010, the then leader of the Conservative Party, David Cameron, spoke of a Big Society, of rolling back state control, and of a society where people come together to solve problems and improve life for themselves and their communities. These ideological themes were reiterated in the 2010 Conservative Party Manifesto (Conservative Party, 2010). The stress on moral breakdown and a discourse highlighting 'broken Britain' (Blond, 2010) with solutions located in Big Society was particularly persuasive for faith-based organizations, since it emphasized community responsibility and their role in remedying the state's failures and withdrawal. Once it became clear that little or no funding was attached to the Big Society agenda to support new roles, its attraction for voluntary organizations waned but did not entirely disappear.

For public authority funders, partnering with faith-based organizations remains attractive. Local communities are seen as having much tacit knowledge to bring to partnerships (Wilkinson and Appelbee, 1999), but this needs to be validated and respected by power-holders, and recognized as a basis for community empowerment. In practice, community partners invariably have to react to predetermined agendas, and pervasive contractual cultures and arrangements place small organizations at a disadvantage. There are also concerns around the roles of faith-based social action groups in securing public funding, focused on whether the service is accessible to all and whether there is an intention to proselytize. Conflict can arise over particular policies and doctrines, for example a charity's attitudes on issues such as divorce, homosexuality, and abortion (Ryan, 2016: 11).

Johnsen (2014) argues that boundaries are now generally clearly drawn between the faith community or congregation and their service-delivery organizations. This division appears to have become widely embedded as good practice, with public and independent funders requiring separate constitutions and lines of accountability so that faith affiliation or heritage may be much less visible. While recognizing the importance of faith to the motivations of many service providers, Johnsen (2014: 5) concludes that differences between faith-based and secular provision 'should not be exaggerated'. Rochester and Torry (2010: 130) similarly saw no discernible element of evangelism among organizations studied, despite 'a theological imperative of giving service'; and Noyes and Blond (2013: 4) also reported claims of proselytizing as 'ill-founded'.

However, the research referenced above has largely focused on publicly funded, faith-based social action (Cairns *et al.*, 2007) or the activities of large faith-based organizations that are independent of local congregations (Birdwell, 2013). A growing number of congregations among charismatic-evangelical churches view evangelism and social action as mutually inclusive and adopt a holistic approach to social action projects, such as debt advice or food banks, providing 'a more subtle form of relational service, with fewer strings attached' (Cloke *et al.*, 2013: 7). This approach is regarded as ambiguous by critics since boundaries are unclear, and some argue that this 'passive faith' model corresponds to proselytism (Sider and Unruh, 2004). Others, however, view it as a difference that needs better understanding.

There are also distinct evangelical traditions. Some have strong links to US-based institutions and a close association with the development of 'compassionate conservatism', an ideology that arose in response to the charge of selfishness generated through the espousal of neo-liberal, free-market economic policies. This ideology enabled George W. Bush to present himself to the US electorate as a 'compassionate conservative' (Powell, 2007: 167) and underlay the 2010 Conservative Party's Big Society agenda in the UK. The latter was widely embraced by religious leaders because it seemed to address the growing loss of humanitarianism in society, leading to a political vacuum of purpose and meaning.

Faith-based welfare organizations have become particularly significant in London, where the number of churches has risen by about 50 per cent since 1979 and church attendance by 16 per cent between 2005 and 2012 (British Religion in Numbers [BRIN], 2013). London has also grown rapidly, by 2 million people over some 25 years, and of the 8.6 million people recorded in the 2011 Census, over a third were born outside the UK (ONS, 2011), creating a city with the second largest immigrant population in the world. These rapid changes raise important questions about social cohesion, alongside the emergence of new kinds of exclusions and racism. These concerns are reflected in the political rhetoric and policy positions of governments and political parties; and the role of religion in civic life is provoking broader questions about faith versus secularism in Western modernity.

While many politicians and policymakers utilize 'faith-based organization' (FBO) inappropriately as a generic term (Harris, 2010), in practice, not only religion, but worship style, theological emphasis, cultural differences, and leadership vary widely – features that policymakers often overlook. Additionally, internal metamorphosis has always been a phenomenon within different faith groups, including Christian churches, leading to the emergence of new groups and denominations, a further factor that policymakers tend to neglect.

Case study: BMC organizations in the London Borough of Barking and Dagenham (LBBD)

Barking and Dagenham's socio-economic role in the transformation of London is significant. Demographically, the borough has been radically reshaped by housing policy since the 1980s, with the 1979 right-to-buy housing legislation transforming this once stable working-class area, largely comprised of council housing estates. Far from becoming a home ownership community, some 40 per cent of the new homeowners then sold to developers, generating a new private rental market (Boffey, 2014) and enabling growth in exploitative landlordism. Demographic change has followed, with the white British population decreasing by nearly a third since 2001 and projected to fall to 44 per cent of the population by 2020. It has been replaced mainly by a black African population that trebled between 2001 and 2011 (LBBD, 2013b). New patterns of multi-occupation, high household turnover and dependence on benefits have inevitably produced a more impoverished, transient, and fractured population subject to significant discrimination (Harris, 2008). Compounded by the impact of the 2008 economic recession, the borough's communities are acutely in need of support structures to navigate change (LBBD, 2016). It is now the second most deprived borough in London, with the highest unemployment level at nearly 10 per cent (Trust for London, 2014), as its long-standing source of employment in the car industry has largely disappeared. Barking and Dagenham now has the second highest level of homelessness in London and a high rate of evictions. A quarter of all residents are low paid and the borough does poorly on all four indicators of health compared with London overall.

The borough's draft Community Strategy 2013–16 (LBBD, 2013a) identifies the many challenging issues facing the area, defining voluntary and community organizations as potentially key partners in processes of change and development. In 2014, the newly elected council leader drew attention to the 363 Christian churches now registered in a borough of 203,000 people, and underlined the potential for collaborative community development (Mayhew, 2014).

Research study

Set within the context outlined above, a research study was undertaken that aimed to investigate the potential opportunities and barriers to effective collaboration between the local borough agencies and BMC faith-based organizations.

In selecting organizations in the area for study, attention was paid to the range of different BMC congregations in terms of culture, size, income, and activities. The study adopted qualitative methods, and the discussion below draws on examples from semi-structured interviews with five BMC project leaders (mainly appointed and paid through the BMC community), three council officers, and one Council for Voluntary Services representative. The sample of organizations comprised ten faith-based organizations with a turnover greater than £400,000 and over ten years' experience of providing services in this area of high deprivation. The high income levels indicated the organizations' financial independence and viability in taking on autonomous community projects. Among services provided were health clinics with free health checks, including cardiovascular disease checks, women's health services, crisis pregnancy support, baby clothing, debt advice, food banks, tuition in Maths and English, youth work, homework clubs, homeless shelters, support for job seekers, and liaison with the police around crime. The information from council officers and projects leaders is presented separately, highlighting different viewpoints.

The council officers

The council officers' response to BMCs seeking to collaborate was broadly that 'the recession provides a necessity to do that'. They regarded faith communities as a potentially important partner to the local authority in providing services that would reach their communities, and recalled how the churches had quickly rallied their constituencies during the 2011 riots. They also recognized the breadth and depth of local knowledge among BMCs. The impact of austerity made it 'a necessity' to explore partnerships, and officers emphasized the council's intention to tackle the structural causes of exclusions that kept communities 'swimming against the tide' (O'Connor, 2007).

Council officers reported that the local authority position on partnerships emphasized that values were important:

> Any future collaboration should be assessed on the specific values people bring to the borough that help joint working between departments and individual organizations, supported by policies and a process which is free of inequality and allows accountability of all parties.
>
> Council officer

Those council officers with direct experience of funding faith-based organizations commended the lack of proselytism in most schemes that they had supervised. While they generally identified no record of proselytism, they did, however, consider that more clarity was needed about the use of faith symbols or religious objects, which often accompanied the use of religious buildings. Such a dialogue would serve to remove ambiguities in any partnership and any covert suspicions.

Officers also explained that the spontaneous and perhaps make-shift arrangements that some projects had provided to meet the needs of desperate community members gave 'insufficient consideration to service users' dignity, morale and safety'. They stressed that even though projects might appear professionally established, they regarded a publicly funded project as needing to convince partners of the quality of care: in other words, to carry the burden of proof for its quality.

The council officers also acknowledged that there could have been better support provided to projects and that there had been missed opportunities to build appropriate relationships with newly emerging communities including BMCs. They recognized that more work was needed around equalities and community cohesion and accepted that the power imbalances experienced by BMCs were undermining these goals, echoing research on regeneration and community development processes (Hoggett *et al.*, 2008). Greater understanding of the different strengths that BMCs brought would clear the way for better, more sustainable partnerships. Officers appreciated the role of faith-based organizations and wanted to maintain their involvement, not least because the council lacked the resources to provide these badly needed services. However, an absence of resources to fund the groups involved was not the only barrier.

The project leaders

The project leaders (PLs) interviewed came from organizations established by the BMCs, and received a large proportion of their funding from the churches. Few workers or volunteers involved came from the local neighbourhoods, since the BMCs drew their congregations from a wide geographic area.

Four key themes emerged from the information gathered:

- service to the local community
- funding and partnership difficulties
- sustainability of projects
- organizational relationships and leadership.

Service to the local community

There was a great deal of frustration about addressing unmet needs. Services were significantly oversubscribed for some projects, and a lack of funding meant that project leaders faced needy communities but were unable to train and mobilize volunteers. However, project leaders were motivated by a strong sense of duty or privilege in serving people, as one explained:

> You walk the streets, and you see people, you hear their stories, their pleas. You see people sleeping on the streets; you just want to do something.
>
> PL 2

Another project leader described her motivation more fully:

> It's about giving people a voice, speaking to authorities on behalf of the locals, enabling change through organizational and administrative support for local team work, promoting opportunities for cohesion in order to build a healthy and safe community.
>
> PL 5

Project leaders believed that growing churches and a motivated volunteer base made BMCs good partners:

> There's no shying away from saying that the black majority churches since the early 90s are seeing increasing attendance in numbers. What some people called mushroom churches are now 'much room' churches. It means more volunteers and donations to provide a basic level of service independently. People have settled here now and are being trained in churches to be part of community solutions not part of its problems.
>
> PL 4

Project leaders also spoke of a sense of cultural solidarity and cohesion within the African communities in addressing problems such as rising gun and knife crimes among black and minority ethnic young people. As one explained, 'There is an ideology of the African people that believes in taking care of its community and the vulnerable' (PL 2).

A common response from interviewees was that their organization was socio-economically and politically part of a community, not apart from it. However, although the services were very well utilized by people from the local area, this had not translated into locally based volunteers coming forward or becoming involved with church meetings. There was no evidence of real bonding between local service users on the one hand and providers and volunteers on the other, and most BMC volunteers lived significant distances away.

Funding and partnership difficulties

There was widespread dissatisfaction among the project leaders about funding competition. Failed attempts to secure adequate funding, competitive funding undermining potential collaboration, and inflexible regulations all contributed to difficulties arising, as described in the following examples.

A youth project had merged with a larger organization that 'manages the pot' and the project leader complained about them keeping back 'the major chunk of the grant'. A health centre leader believed that the centre's endeavours to anticipate priorities had been disregarded and failed to result in buy-in by public funders. Instead, funding had been awarded to a more established but less productive centre. Although the centre's statistics were impressive, it was not a fully registered GP service, and could generate Primary Care Trust partnership income only for local residents using the service, whereas it offered open access to all. A homeless project had been forced to close because of inadequate financial support to meet mounting utility bills and cleaning costs. Closure of other projects also arose because of unfunded costs. For example, a night shelter providing food shut because the regulators insisted on the installation of an on-site commercial kitchen, rather than allowing it to continue supplying meals that volunteers had prepared off-site for over a year.

Some project leaders were resistant to inflexible external requirements, believing that they had established their projects professionally and therefore should not bear the full burden for proving their service quality and standards. They felt that 'not just what we do, but how' was important, and that this was sufficient, albeit at odds with public bodies. They wanted to make funding partnerships work, but could also be defensive about their approaches. Maintaining boundaries between evangelism and the service projects was, however, generally understood as good practice, reflecting findings from the research discussed above.

Sustainability of projects

While the capacity of the church to provide services might be increased through participating in various partnerships, project leaders also recognized that these required organizational resources to be sustainable. They identified the importance of avoiding expanding too quickly beyond their capacity or without the necessary support to manage increased overheads and administrative processes. They also acknowledged that all parties needed to be realistic about the levels of expectation on those who volunteered. There was an acute awareness of ongoing welfare cuts and their impacts on the need to source more food for the food banks and increase support for growing numbers of job seekers and homeless people. Project leaders were also wary of what they identified as 'the major hazard' of potentially losing their focus by becoming burdened with statutory duties offloaded by a shrinking welfare state.

Some projects employed core administrative staff, while others were heavily dependent on volunteers whose commitment was seen as a strength and defining feature of several of the projects studied. Volunteers who were trained professionals were happy to serve freely, seeing their service as an integral part of their faith. However, volunteers can also lack skills or rewards, thereby posing capacity problems in sustaining expansion or ensuring compliance with service or monitoring requirements. In the longer term, PLs acknowledged that people might need incentives to participate if projects were to develop further.

Projects running daily or weekly had not succeeded in involving local people to contribute as volunteers. This was a concern, as many of the church member volunteers lived far away and, although happy to travel for the present, could experience a change in personal circumstances with an impact on the project. Typically, projects ran at fixed times, allowing volunteers to maintain work commitments, while a few paid staff handled ongoing administration. PLs considered that more attention was needed to support volunteers and to adequately remunerate increasingly overstretched staff, highlighting divergent interests in managing paid and unpaid staff working alongside each other. The recruitment of key staff was also based on availability and, inevitably, those available were not always the most suitable for specialist roles, such as licensing or work permit issues, which could often pose difficulties in projects.

Overall, the project leaders cautiously supported the idea of increased partnership work, citing the ongoing welfare cuts anticipated and the growing pressures these were likely to place on food banks and projects supporting job seekers and homeless people. Most believed that partnership could work but only if there was:

> ... a paradigm shift between parties, with a greater awareness of shared or negotiated power, prejudice replaced with more open policies, and judgement based on a partner's impact and performance rather than history.
>
> PL 3

However, what PLs often experienced were imposed changes, such as limitations around staff vetting or hygiene certificates, whereas what they sought was a more comprehensive revision of service delivery policy to address the issues of power and prejudice raised.

Organizational relationships and leadership

Although there was a strong desire for funding to increase public service delivery, the research also revealed poor co-operation for joint ventures between different BMCs. There was a self-interested determination to succeed as separate entities, echoing the competitive culture engulfing many voluntary organizations, which was generating deep fractures among BMC organizations. Those enticed deeper into this contractual culture indicated a certain excitement around becoming insiders, but their newly adopted entrepreneurial identities proved alienating to others. A collective narrative around managing this combination of insider and outsider roles, recognizing the dilemmas involved, was plainly needed.

Some PLs thought that most BMC faith communities would not want to lose their voice or their 'total grip' over their projects despite the consequences of 'standing alone or staying small'. They were concerned with retaining their outsider autonomy and were sceptical about systems that had previously let them down. Others indicated that they would take a principled stand against participation or simply resist changes. In other words, there were divisions among members of the BMC groups wanting to test new possibilities, potentially posing barriers to proceeding.

Leadership and structures of BMC organizations also emerged as key issues. Although the service projects were organized separately from the faith community, the operations, workforce, and often the leadership structures overlapped. This ensured that religious values remained firmly at the centre of decision making and underpinned the primary purposes of any philanthropic work, guarding against mission drift. The crossover of leadership and influence between the churches and their social action projects clearly provided advantages in developing a project initially. Support from the wider faith community enabled shared involvement in initiating grassroots changes and eased burdens, including for projects inundated with demands, also averting individual burnout. However, the crossover of involvement could also hinder funding bids that required a less partisan approach, posing an obstacle to partnering with public funders.

BMC leadership structures are typically a hierarchy or pyramid. The inherent constraint is that the core leaders become indispensable, with top-down decision making stifling initiatives, threatening creativity and generating a prevalent blame culture (Gibbs and Coffey, 2001). Some project leaders identified a wider, more diverse pool of leaders as necessary for different purposes, suggesting that leaders who inspire and connect people are often as important as those who assume formal positions.

Ongoing dilemmas of faith and welfare

This chapter highlights the role of black African-majority churches in establishing a strong presence in a locality through identifying local welfare needs and seeking to support these by securing public partnerships. They have endeavoured to become recognized advocates for a local community, reflecting an emphasis on economic empowerment and political engagement. However, the term 'community' was often used ambiguously by study participants, eliding meanings between local geographic and faith communities, and raises questions as to how 'community' is being understood. As Brent (2009) has argued, 'community' as a concept encompasses considerable ambiguity and is owned in different ways by different groups of people.

The ideological rationale of the Big Society continued to resonate strongly in the study, counterbalancing perceptions of an amoral and individualistic society; but ideas underpinning the projects more closely resembled compassionate conservatism (Powell, 2007: 173), with little evident critique advocating a more emancipatory approach. Economic recession was seen as providing opportunities for BMCs to expand social action projects to address a Big Society gap, despite the recognition that declining state welfare services and social infrastructure could result in faith-based organizations being used as substitutes. Additionally, there was little critical linkage to the role of wider market forces in dismantling state infrastructure or to the inherent contradictions in engaging with competitive funding cultures.

The research revealed tensions between empowerment and disempowerment and showed the acute imbalances of power experienced by relatively new migrant populations, experiencing a sense of ostracization as newly emerging communities. The contract culture presents dilemmas and trust issues for peoples who have historically not been heard, in offering both opportunities and threats to independent actions. The study illustrated the strengths of a charismatic, hands-on culture, displaying volubility and visibility of expression, and volunteers with a clear spiritual motivation pervading both the faith community and their work in local services.

BMC projects are clearly successful within their own faith communities. However, while the BMC leadership structures appear to work well for matters of faith, they can present barriers to productive working partnerships locally and with funders. Projects failed to engage local volunteers, and state funders, particularly are unwilling to fund ventures judged as religious or partisan. Any collaboration requires changes from the organizations and individuals involved, including changes in use of language or religious symbols in any services provided. While the study showed no evidence to support claims of evangelical proselytizing by the projects studied, the democratic norm in a predominately secular society such as the UK demands a non-evangelical, non-zealous demonstration of religious views outside the immediate faith community.

While most BMCs incorporate a separate non-religious, charitable organization alongside the church community, there were also dilemmas in managing this relationship. It was evident from this research that many BMCs are still reluctant to relinquish control of their charitable projects and allow greater distance, and further research exploring the extent of separateness would be valuable. Public funders regard such separation as a prerequisite in commissioning services, and without this, a key conclusion must be that barriers to any substantial partnership developing with public bodies will remain. A significant barrier to creating successful partnerships with public funders and councils therefore lies within the structures of the BMC world.

From a local authority perspective, a lack of collaboration between the diverse BMCs is also unhelpful in moving forward their aspirations for partnership. While the overlap between the church leadership structures and their social action projects currently forms a major obstacle to potential partnerships, this research also highlights the complexity of issues involved, including the inflexible conditions and loss of autonomous approaches that frequently accompany contract compliance. Thus there is no simple solution to the question of whether effective partnership with public funders over services is feasible, and inherent power imbalances and prejudices remain. Dialogue (Hoggett, 2004) and creativity around new middle ground are needed. With growing faith-based movements emerging, as this chapter illustrates, neglecting the wealth of human resources available makes little political sense, but it also raises new dilemmas. Oppositions and tensions clearly exist between secular and religious thinking, which, as Sandel (2010) argues, highlight the need to take society's moral and religious dimensions more seriously. However, as Taylor (2007) suggests, it may call for a different conversation, which reframes the discussion and moves it away from what often becomes a polarized debate around the sacred and the secular.

References

Adedibu, B. (2012) *Coat of Many Colours: The origin, growth, distinctiveness and contributions of majority black churches to British Christianity.* Gloucester: The Choir Press.

Birdwell, J. (2013) *Faithful Providers.* London: Demos.

Blond, P. (2010) *Red Tory: How the Left and Right have broken Britain and how we can fix it.* London: Faber & Faber.

Boffey, D. (2014) 'Private landlords cash in on right-to-buy and send rents soaring for poorest tenants'. *The Guardian*, 12 January. Online. www.theguardian.com/uk-news/2014/jan/12/right-to-buy-housing-scandal (accessed 1 August 2016).

Brent, J. (2009) *Searching for Community: Representation, power and action on an urban estate.* Bristol: Policy Press.

Bretherton, L. (2015) *Resurrecting Democracy: Faith, citizenship, and the politics of a common life* (Cambridge Studies in Social Theory, Religion and Politics). Cambridge: Cambridge University Press.

BRIN (2013) *British Religion in Numbers*. Online. www.brin.ac.uk/2013/london-churchgoing-and-other-news/ (accessed December 2016).

Bull, D., de Las Casas, L., and Wharton, R. (2016) *Faith Matters*. London: New Philanthropy Capital.

Cairns, B., Harris, M., and Hutchison, R. (2007) 'Sharing God's love or meeting government goals? Local churches and public policy implementation'. *Policy and Politics*, 35 (3), 413–32.

Cartledge, M.J. (2012) 'Pentecostalism'. In B.J. Miller-McLemore (ed.), *The Wiley Blackwell Companion to Practical Theology*. Oxford: Wiley Blackwell.

Cloke, P., Thomas, S., and Williams, A. (2013) 'Faith in action: Faith-based organisations, welfare and politics in the contemporary city'. In P. Cloke, J. Beamont, and A. Williams (eds), *Working Faith: Faith-based organisations and urban social justice*. Milton Keynes: Paternoster.

Conservative Party (2010) *Conservative Party Manifesto 2010*. London: Conservative Party. Online. http://conservativehome.blogs.com/files/conservative-manifesto-2010.pdf (accessed December 2016).

Deakin, N. (2010) 'Religion, state and third sector in England'. *Journal of Political Ideologies*, 15 (3), 305–15.

Evangelical Alliance (2006) *English Church Census 2005*. London: Evangelical Alliance. Online. www.eauk.org/church/research-and-statistics/english-church-census.cfm (accessed December 2016).

Francis, V. (1998) *With Hope in their Eyes: Compelling stories of the Windrush generation*. Nia.

Gibbs, E. and Coffey, I. (2001) *Church Next: Quantum changes in Christian Ministry*. Downers Grove: Inter-Varsity Press.

Harris, J. (2008) 'Safe as houses'. *The Guardian,* 30 September. Online. www.theguardian.com/society/2008/sep/30/housing.houseprices (accessed December 2016).

Harris, M. (2010) 'Social enterprise, the voluntary sector and mainstreaming faith'. Address given at the AHRC/ESRC conference *Faith and Policy: Where next for religion in the public sphere?*, 1 July. Online. http://margaretharris.org.uk/BritLib_june2010_d3.pdf (accessed 12 May 2016).

Hoggett, P. (2004) 'Overcoming the desire for misunderstanding through dialogue'. In S. Snape and P. Taylor (eds), *Partnerships between Health and Local Government*. London: Frank Cass, 118–26.

—, Mayo, M., and Miller, C. (2008) *The Dilemmas of Development Work: Ethical challenges in regeneration*. Bristol: Policy Press.

Jeavons, T.H. (1994) *When the Bottom Line is Faithfulness: Management of Christian service organizations*. Bloomington and Indianapolis: Indiana University Press.

Johnsen, S. (2014) 'Where's the "faith" in "faith-based" organisations? The evolution and practice of faith-based homelessness services in the UK'. *Journal of Social Policy,* 43 (2), 413–30.

JRF (2016) *Destitution in the UK*. Joseph Rowntree Foundation. Online. www.jrf.org.uk/report/destitution-uk (accessed December 2016).

LBBD (2013a) *Draft Community Strategy 2013–2016*. London: London Borough of Barking and Dagenham.

— (2013b) *Growth and Changes in Our Local Population*. London: London Borough of Barking and Dagenham. Online. www.lbbd.gov.uk/wp-content/uploads/2015/09/1.2-Growth-and-Changes-in-population.pdf (accessed 1 August 2016).

— (2016) *No-one Left Behind: In pursuit of growth for the benefit of* everyone. London: Barking and Dagenham Independent Growth Commission. Online. www.lbbd.gov.uk/business/growing-the-borough/our-strategy-for-growth/overview-2/ (accessed 1 August 2016).

LGA (2002) *Faith and Community: A good practice guide for local authorities.* London: Local Government Association.

Loewenberg, F.M. (1995) 'Financing philanthropic institutions in Biblical and Talmudic times'. *Non-Profit and Voluntary Sector Quarterly,* 24 (4), 307–20.

Lynch, G. (2014) 'Saving the child for the sake of the nation: Moral framing and the civic, moral and religious redemption of children'. *American Journal of Cultural Sociology,* 2 (2), 165–96.

Mayhew, F. (2014) 'New council leader speaks about vision for Barking and Dagenham'. *Barking and Dagenham Post,* 2 June. Online. www. barkinganddagenhampost.co.uk/news/new_council_leader_darren_rodwell_ speaks_about_vision_for_barking_and_dagenham_1_3624141 (accessed 1 August 2016).

Noyes, J. and Blond, P. (2013) *Holistic Mission: Social action and the Church of England.* London: ResPublica. Online www.respublica.org.uk/wp-content/ uploads/2013/07/mfp_ResPublica-Holistic-Mission-FULL-REPORT-10July2013.pdf (accessed December 2016).

O'Connor, A. (2007) 'Swimming against the tide: A brief history of federal policy in poorer communities'. In J. DeFilippis and S. Saegert (eds), *The Community Development Reader.* New York: Routledge.

ONS (2011) *2011 Census: Quick statistics for England and Wales on national identity, passport held, and country of birth.* Office of National Statistics. Online. http://tinyurl.com/grrhzxu (accessed December 2016).

Powell, F.W. (2007) *The Politics of Civil Society: Neo-liberalism or social left.* Bristol: Policy Press.

Prochaska, F. (1988) *The Voluntary Impulse: Philanthropy in modern Britain.* London: Faber and Faber.

Rochester, C. and Torry, M. (2010) 'Faith-based organizations and hybridity: A special case?' In D. Billis (ed.), *Hybrid Organizations and the Third Sector: Challenges for practice, theory and policy.* Basingstoke: Palgrave Macmillan, 114–33.

Ryan, B. (2016) *Catholic Social Thought on Catholic Charities in Britain Today.* London: Theos.

Sandel, M.J. (2010) *Justice: What's the right thing to do?* Basingstoke: Macmillan.

Sider, R.J. and Unruh, H.R. (2004) 'Typology of religious characteristics of social service and educational organizations and programs'. *Non-profit and Voluntary Sector Quarterly,* 33 (1), 109–34.

Taylor, C. (2007) *A Secular Age.* Cambridge, MA: Harvard University Press.

Trussell Trust (2016) *Foodbank Use Remains at a Record High.* Online. www. trusselltrust.org/2016/04/15/foodbank-use-remains-record-high/ (accessed December 2016).

Trust for London (2014) *London's Poverty Profile: Barking and Dagenham.* Online. www.londonspovertyprofile.org.uk/indicators/boroughs/barking-and-dagenham/ (accessed December 2016).

Wilkinson, D. and Appelbee, E. (1999) *Implementing Holistic Government: Joined-up action on the ground.* Bristol: Policy Press.

Chapter 8

Voluntary action: Micro-organizations and infrastructure support

Truly Johnston

The Coalition government (2010–15) signalled 'a new relationship between the third sector and the state' (Macmillan, 2013: 187). However, this changed relationship recast the third sector's role in service provision from 2010 onwards, and a further deterioration in relationships followed under the subsequent 2015 Conservative government. The Office for Civil Society's (OCS) proposals for Supporting a Stronger Civil Society provide insights into the nature of changes expected, recommending that civil society organizations 'improve their business skills [and] become more entrepreneurial' (OCS, 2010: 6). Government approaches to funding have subsequently reflected this shift in approach, with reduced central and local government grants to the voluntary sector, an intensely competitive culture generating increasingly large-scale public service contracts, and a drive towards civil society organizations seeking greater reliance on social investment. For formal voluntary organizations, these changes have posed critical dilemmas as to whether to continue on a path of service delivery, growth, and further professionalization and potentially engage in delivery for corporate contractors, all changes that would significantly transform their cultures of operation. For micro-organizations – often under the radar – meeting the new challenges arising from reduced public services, a smaller state, and a politically contentious focus on local, volunteer-led services, also poses acute questions. For example, can small voluntary organizations adapt to this new policy agenda and still maintain their own distinctive qualities without being overly remodelled by these external pressures?

This chapter will explore the relationship between Councils for Voluntary Services (CVS) and micro-organizations for whom they provide local infrastructure support. A primary study illustrates how the territory of both CVS and micro-organizations is changing rapidly, driving them both to adapt their working practices.

Councils for Voluntary Services (CVS): Facing the pressures to change

CVS have been integral to the voluntary sector landscape since the early twentieth century, and have been regarded as vital building blocks for local voluntary and community organizations (Rochester, 2012). Their role and purposes are long-standing, and recent definitions of their core functions as providing 'development, support, liaison, representation and strategic partnership work' (NAVCA, 2013) echo those outlined in influential policy of some 35 years earlier (Wolfenden Report, 1978). While this 1978 report also highlighted 'direct services to individuals', most CVS regarded service delivery as outside their remit until relatively recently. However, with competing demands and insufficient resources, some CVS are now directly engaged in service contracts and selling consultancy and advice (Walton and Macmillan, 2014).

Voluntary sector growth over the previous 20 years saw CVS organizations develop to address the training and support needed by many small and medium-sized organizations and to broker links with local authorities. The scale of support and reasons for providing it vary by area and reflect the different political stances of mainly local authority funders. As Macmillan describes, even when policymakers have applauded what voluntary organizations do, they invariably seek to change them. '"Support" is potentially a powerful set of policy interventions, in discourse and practice, to achieve this' (Macmillan, 2011: 122). Capacity building, widely promoted as a supportive strategy to extend service provision and raise professional standards, offers a germane example. Alongside pressure to expand their own capabilities and funds, CVS have been tasked with exerting pressure on small organizations to build service capacity. However, capacity building is conceptually 'nebulous and ill-defined' (Cornforth and Mordaunt, 2011: 430) and the tendency is to assume a simple path to its achievement when organizational development is both complex and time consuming. Additionally, expectations on CVS are disproportionate to their abilities to provide the kind of support needed (Rochester, 2012).

More importantly, capacity building, as in NAVCA's (2013) definition, often implies a deficit model, rather than an empowerment (Cairns *et al.*, 2005: 873) or an 'asset-based' model (Foot, 2012: 5), which involve approaches to working with groups that recognize their existing strengths. The first, deficit model assumes that CVS experts impart recommended knowledge and skills to small uninformed organizations; but this is problematic if organizations do not wish to develop, professionalize, or engage formally in service delivery in the ways prescribed. Capacity building, then, could provide a means through which government policymakers can remodel small voluntary organizations in ways that match policy agendas, potentially increasing their abilities to deliver services (Cairns *et al.*, 2005). This places additional external pressures on volunteer-run groups already trying to fill the growing gaps left by cuts in welfare and public services.

Growing contradictions and tensions exist in this evolving policy context. In order to carry greater responsibility, small organizations need support, yet resources for support systems are diminishing rapidly. The stance of local authorities to funding local CVS is key; it varies markedly by area and can be highly politicized. Some councils have a well-developed collaborative approach and there is mutual understanding of the different roles involved; others have cut funding entirely, leading to CVS closure. Some have combined local district-level CVS into new county-wide structures; others have tendered and outsourced the CVS role, awarding contracts to large national charities, resulting in loss of services and new charges levied. Offering a sharply contrasting example, Camden Council has committed to stable seven-year funding of key voluntary infrastructure organizations (London Borough of Camden, 2015) despite major overall budget reductions.

The general context for CVS, however, is now one of continual pressure to justify their existence. The widespread cuts to voluntary sector funding and changing political agendas have affected the capacity of local infrastructure organizations to deliver intensive support to community organizations. The challenge for many CVS is now to find cost-effective alternatives to previous one-to-one support. At the same time, volunteer-run micro-organizations have gained a higher profile in response to growing social need and politically contested government pressures on civil society to plug welfare gaps.

Micro-organizations and Councils for Voluntary Services (CVS)

Policymakers have a particular view of how micro-organizations fit their programmes, but alternative definitions persist (Phillimore and McCabe, 2015). The term 'micro-charity' has been used to define organizations with annual incomes of below £10,000, registered with the Charity Commission, estimated as some 49 per cent of registered charities but accounting for only 0.6 per cent of the total income (NCVO, 2015). However, these figures exclude a far greater number of organizations not registered with regulatory bodies, often identified as 'below-the-radar' (McCabe *et al.*,

2010) and estimated as perhaps 900,000 groups, compared with a total of some 163,000 registered charities. This chapter uses the term 'micro-organization' (Donahue, 2011), which seems to best describe the small-scale voluntary activity of unregistered groups that nevertheless have a clear vision and purpose.

The key distinctive features of micro-organizations have been identified as informality, a focus on networking, and reliance on volunteers (Phillimore *et al.*, 2010; Donahue, 2011), and their informality and flexibility are rightly seen to offer particular advantages in accessing hard-to-reach groups in the population. Micro-organizations have limited financial or physical resources, but compensate through enthusiasm and the 'knowledge and skills brought by activists' (Phillimore *et al.*, 2010: 2). While groups vary greatly, most operate on an associational basis, led by active members, often with a committee structure and wider membership of volunteers (Ockenden and Hutin, 2008). This contrasts with the more formalized, hierarchical structures of larger voluntary organizations.

Micro-organizations often feel unsupported by CVS (McCabe, 2010; Harker and Burkeman, 2007). Ockenden and Hutin (2008: 40) similarly argue that 'volunteer-led groups' need wider recognition, as they are 'equally valuable, and possibly more prevalent than' volunteers in larger organizations. However, the diversity of groups and their differences from more formalized voluntary organizations highlight difficulties for CVS. With limited resources to engage with multiple groups, a CVS working within an empowerment model needs to offer support tailored to the specific strengths defined by micro-organizations.

Researching changing roles

An interview-based study involving three CVS and two micro-organizations investigated how the role of CVS working with micro-organizations was being recast and considered emerging adaptations to their working practices. The organizations were located in culturally diverse, inner-city areas, and all had experienced budget cuts.

Each CVS was, to some extent, reconsidering its stance on organizational development work, and the development workers interviewed were keen to explore and reflect on their positions. Their funding came mainly from their local authority, although two were also delivering projects under a programme to transform local infrastructure, and all three were exploring ways to generate income by charging for services. One CVS had a good working relationship with its local authority funder but fear of redundancy and fraught relationships were dominant in the other two. The four CVS development workers interviewed were: Sarah (Springdale CVS), Cathy (Brook CVS), and Andy and Jo (Oakville CVS).

Interviewees from two micro-organizations located in these CVS areas are also discussed below. Both micro-organizations were members of their local CVS and both primarily offered services rather than being activist campaign groups.

Rootreach Centre, in the Brook CVS area, is a recently established volunteer-run group that focuses on local social and community action, providing facilities and services for local residents. The organization stems from a faith-based group, and the parent faith organization provides some infrastructure and funding support, together with premises. Jonathan, the programme director, and Vera, the programme co-ordinator, were interviewed.

The Women's Empowerment Network (WEN), in the Oakville CVS area, was established in 2004 and supports women with HIV and victims of domestic violence. For most of its life, it has been volunteer-run and the group survives with funding from local government and the health sector, supplemented by income from trusts and foundations. Nina, the founder and director of WEN, was interviewed.

Four themes emerged from the research findings as key to the inter-relationship of CVS with micro-organizations.

Formality and informality: Different ways of operating

Formality and informality represent different ideas about what an organization is, its ways of working, and by implication its different development needs. Interviewees regarded formality and informality as defining organizational identity to a certain extent, and this applied to both CVS and micro-organizations. The formality of the CVS was contrasted with the informality of micro-organizations, and this emerged repeatedly from interviews, highlighting the different approaches of the two types of organizations. Various studies have highlighted this distinction between formal and informal practices as presenting barriers to micro-organizations engaging with CVS services (Harker and Burkeman, 2007; McCabe *et al.,* 2010). However, the examples here illustrate that this is not necessarily the case.

Sarah (Springdale CVS) mused on why micro-organizations might not approach the CVS for support, and highlighted the formality of CVS as a potential barrier: 'they've got lots of preconceptions about it, and expect it [support from the CVS] to be quite formal'. Cathy (Brook CVS) and Andy (Oakville CVS) expressed similar views: 'initially without coming here, they would possibly ... just have this idea that no, no I can't go there, or it's not sort of informal enough' (Andy).

However, the micro-organizations Rootreach and WEN took a different view and did not recognize CVS formality as a barrier to accessing support. Both organizations had used the CVS as an information source and had also sought support tailored to their specific needs to help them develop and engage with more formal requirements in ways that they had chosen. WEN had grown from a volunteer group operating from the founder's home and approached the CVS when they decided to form a formal organization to attract more funding. As Nina explained, 'then I went to see [CVS worker] and ... started looking at how to get an office and be properly based, getting first of all a bank account'. Rootreach similarly had approached the local CVS in order to expand its local networks. Jonathan described looking for support, 'kind of anything and everything. We picked up brochures, we scouted the papers', eventually locating the CVS through another link.

Changing approaches to development

The three CVS all aimed to provide a bridge to more formal parts of the voluntary sector for micro-organizations wanting to grow, and this was reflected in the development approaches that the CVS workers adopted. Echoing criticisms discussed earlier, Jo (Oakville CVS) said, 'Capacity building is a word that you shouldn't even use!' and was keen to describe their approach as an 'asset-based community development model', which acknowledged the strengths that the groups brought, while also trying to link them with the wider community sector. Andy (Oakville CVS) described translation between different sectors and agencies as an important part of their work with micro-organizations: 'the responsibility of people like Jo and myself is that we are translators'.

However, because the CVS workers were embedded in the formalities and regulations of the sector in gaining funding, and in planning and managing risk, they were sometimes unable to see how micro-organizations could operate without changing and compliance with formal structures. At the same time, they also expressed ambivalence:

> And I felt like I was just kind of smashing his dreams, because I was coming down on him with all of this regulatory stuff which I've learnt is important in the course of being a development worker, and we sort of worked it through that there were ways that he could probably do it.
>
> Cathy, Brook CVS

Identifying alternatives to normative expectations amid these externally driven changes was hard. These cases show CVS workers and micro-organizations struggling to find an acceptable balance between informal volunteer-run activities and formal processes and structures. Safeguarding, insurance, risk management, governance, and access to funds are inevitably onerous, and the CVS workers saw no ready-made or 'light' version for small organizations, raising the fundamental question of whether volunteer-run groups that remain small can or should expand the service provision they take on.

The CVS workers adopted diverse approaches in working with micro-organizations with limited capacity to take on formal practices. Micro-organizations are encouraged to develop and adopt formal arrangements so that they can operate safely and legally, a view shared by both the CVS and funders. CVS development workers all highlighted the problem of communicating the necessary information and arrangements in ways more accessible to small groups, reiterating their translation and demystification roles. The orthodoxy reinforcing formal arrangements was strong, and CVS workers found it hard to find creative and relevant alternatives for micro-organizations that would also satisfy funders.

CVS workers also underlined the importance of intensive work, over time. Micro-organizations similarly agreed that a one-to-one approach best suited their needs, and the value of this approach is well documented elsewhere. For example, research on infrastructure support services needed by community organizations confirms that they, 'need some handholding through difficult situations, and certainly need someone to "translate" mystifying language and to share information' (Newton, 2010: 21). Cathy (Brook CVS) and Jo (Oakville CVS) also stressed the importance of networks, which they viewed as well-suited to the informality of grassroots groups and valuable in enabling the development of peer-learning relationships. Corroborating other research, the findings here suggest that micro-organizations will reap few benefits from the 'supply-led programmes of capacity building which have come to dominate the capacity building landscape' and which are poorly 'attuned to the practical realities of small organizations' (IVAR, 2010: 6). However, in this study, the CVS development workers were often more attuned to the realities and limitations for micro-organizations than some other studies suggest, seeking a means of support more in line with an asset-based approach.

Emerging tensions

Despite their aspirations, interviewees recounted significant changes affecting the ways in which they worked. These included: increased demands on services provided by micro-organizations, growing numbers of organizations choosing social enterprise over charitable models, and the need to find different methods to generate income. Both Oakville and Brook CVS discussed the priorities of developing consortia among larger organizations, for which Brook had appointed a new dedicated worker. However, this meant that this consortium development work was separated from the support for small and micro-organizations. Cathy (Brook CVS) described misgivings because it would look from the outside as if CVS work with small organizations took second place to consortium development and as if priorities were moving away from micro-organizations.

Yet all the CVS workers reported growing numbers of small and micro-organizations seeking their support in the past few years. Sarah (Springdale CVS) said, 'a lot of the established organizations are sort of imploding, whereas the energy is more at the grassroots sort of level'. This increased demand on CVS support seemed to be a direct response to micro-organizations trying to tackle growing social needs:

> They're not doing it because they want to get to know their neighbours and provide social capital in the community and all that. They're doing it because they're like, things are really difficult, and no one else is doing this.
>
> Cathy, Brook CVS

Micro-organizations similarly identified increased demands on their services. However, CVS workers indicated that it was extremely challenging to adequately support the development of more micro-groups seeking to respond to growing social needs, while they were also being pressured to shift their focus away from frontline face-to-face work in order to concentrate on generating income through work with larger organizations.

Lack of funding and time emerged repeatedly as serious challenges, both for CVS workers and micro-organizations. Reduced funding was leading to a scaling back of CVS services, while workers were experiencing growing pressure to demonstrate the value and impact of activities. Two of the three CVS had decreased the level of support offered to micro-organizations. Springdale CVS was reviewing whether it could continue to fund the worker liaising with small groups. Oakville CVS had reduced the number of one-to-one support surgeries provided and the hours of one of the development workers. CVS workers also expressed frustration with their limited time to carry out the kind of outreach with micro-organizations that was needed. Previously, Oakville CVS had funds to support community groups, and both Andy and Jo recognized that, with fewer resources they would not meet the needs of the many small organizations.

There was a shared perception among both CVS and micro-organization workers of being undervalued by policymakers, the local authority, and, occasionally, within their own organizations. Sarah (Springdale CVS) described the view of infrastructure organizations as, 'politically, it's like "why would you need that? Just do it – just go out there and get your volunteers to do it"'. Her opinion was that policymakers simply failed to understand the relevance of CVS support work. This view was echoed by other CVS development workers who similarly considered that policymakers failed to understand the wider value of their roles:

> I think some … people would see us as almost middle management of the voluntary sector. Like I think this government is like, 'well what is the point?' And also what evidence is there that we do any good?
>
> Cathy, Brook CVS

There was resentment at this lack of recognition, which they also felt devalued their local expertise:

> We are not acknowledged, ok, in terms of community intelligence, in terms of community experts, having, being in this locality … for so long we have educated ourselves and been educated by the community on their needs and their issues, you know, and it's not really used.
>
> Andy, Oakville CVS

Micro-organizations expressed similar resentment that despite growing challenges and increased difficulty in finding funding, their work was not adequately recognized by their local authority. Nina from WEN explained: 'I always insist that grassroots organizations do deliver lots, and they change people's lives, but they are not acknowledged.' Overall, scaling back public services, increased policy pressures to do more for less, and reduced funds were creating tensions, undermining the support needed by micro-organizations, and exacerbating feelings of resentment around their grassroots activities being undervalued.

Adapting for the future

A decade ago, Harker and Burkeman (2007: 1) argued that CVS were operating 'in a very difficult environment, with pressures on them from all sides, while attempting to manage high expectations and heavy demands'. Since then, declining resources and changing political priorities have intensified the problems and the limitations on one-to-one support:

> What our groups ... want is that time with the 'doctor'. We know that ... just like public health, there's a squeeze on the doctor's time and the money attached to the doctor's time, but we know that's what groups want.
>
> Jo, Oakville CVS

Despite this squeeze on the development worker's time, the CVS workers maintained a strong commitment to this type of service for micro-organizations and to it being free of charge. Brook CVS was still considering targeted work with a small number of micro-organizations over the next year, intending to track the changes resulting from intensive support. However, because they identified one-to-one support as becoming ever harder to sustain, CVS workers had started to explore new approaches for supporting micro-organizations, and discussed ways in which they were helping to fill the current gaps in services identified by micro-organizations. At Oakville CVS, bi-monthly, 'one-stop advice surgeries' allowed groups to meet and consult multiple advisers. Springdale CVS had recently held a forum for micro-organizations with an 'open space' approach where groups set the agenda. Some of these developments facilitated valuable 'opportunities to share experiences and exchange knowledge, as well as to coordinate their actions' (Rochester, 2012: 109).

The CVS development workers all acknowledged that frontline work with micro-organizations was inevitably changing but were committed to sustaining it in some form free of charge. They also discussed ideas for future approaches, including undertaking more paid consultancy work for larger organizations, contracts for tailored training or development work, and seeking alternative streams of funding despite diverse funding sources also declining. Jo (Oakville CVS) referred to 'social prescriptions', using public health database listings as a means for local doctors to signpost their patients to community activities, when otherwise micro-organizations might be less visible. Cathy (Brook CVS) highlighted a significant future role for CVS in influencing the policy and changes affecting the voluntary sector: ''cause I think that's the thing you've got to kind of look at, the structural things, longer-term things, which I worry that we don't tell people that we're doing that enough'. However, recent legislation in the form of the Charities Act (UK Parliament, 2016) is likely to restrict the scope for this.

Micro-organizations had different views on the support a CVS should offer. WEN had received a lot of support from the local CVS in its formative years, and also some funding. It had witnessed the recent decline in CVS support services, and Nina (WEN) expressed her pessimism about the future: 'I feel that the CVS is dying.' She maintained that the CVS should provide funding for small groups, while Rootreach, which had never received funding from the CVS, had no expectation of it. Jonathan was positive about the CVS support received and his organization's experience of it: 'they come for free, maybe people take it for granted here, but I'm quite impressed that such a thing exists'.

These different assumptions highlight the diversity of experiences among micro-organizations and how established and relatively new groups may carry different, historically shaped expectations of CVS into the future. CVS are able to manage the expectations of support for new groups more readily, but communicating changing conditions to existing groups requires more work. CVS can hardly return to the intensive and involved support that they once offered to all micro-organizations, despite recognizing that this generates positive outcomes. The challenge for CVS is in reframing the value of what they can now offer and communicating that to groups effectively.

Adapting or threatening independence?

This chapter began by considering the extent to which the formal approaches of a CVS pressure micro-organizations into change. Other research suggests that 'local CVS have a tendency to push organizations into growth and professionalization rather than finding ways of helping those organizations to remain volunteer led and run' (Donahue, 2011: 395). While the CVS workers in this study also voiced this concern, it was not generally shared by the micro-organizations.

Micro-organizations viewed their current survival as particularly difficult because of increased social need, loss of public welfare provision, and limited support to access funding. They experienced external pressures to change in specific ways and had limited resources to explore alternatives that would allow them to retain their independent ethos while delivering badly needed local services. Despite reservations about externally imposed priorities, WEN was planning to engage in service delivery contracts. It had previously delivered local authority contracts and had applied to be on the local authority's preferred providers' list in health and social care, offering its particular expertise in reaching marginalized groups. By contrast, Rootreach identified its primary motivation as 'voluntary altruism', aiming to provide services for local people but not necessarily through outsourced public services.

All of the CVS interviews exposed significant pressures to change, including generating income and new approaches for delivering (less costly) infrastructure support. The growth of micro-organizations and the spread of regulatory frameworks also added considerably to demands on the resources needed for support. Two of the three CVS were developing consortia to enable combined bids for large contracts. These multiple pressures to change emphasis were largely externally driven and reflected wider political and policy shifts affecting arrangements between the state and civil society. Study participants revealed a level of compliance with changes but were also ambivalent in other respects. Most highlighted the importance of taking a reflective stance on their roles, including the potential exploitation of voluntary activities:

> ... because it's like 'you guys are the great society' or whatever, but on the other hand, I don't always agree with that perspective ... and you can get into that, oh god we're in this kind of bad Victorian charity mode where we're just kind of fixing problems without looking at the larger solutions.

> Jonathan, Rootreach

A complementary or co-opted role?

Understanding the context of growth for grassroots groups is crucial, as McCabe and others highlight; in particular:

> ... the extent to which 'under the radar activities' or small community groups offer organic solutions to many of the social ills associated with recession and projected cuts in public spending or become co-opted by the state, and are pushed towards, or actively collaborate with, formalisation in ways which prevent or inhibit grass roots community action.

> Attributed to Dominelli, 2006, in McCabe *et al.*, 2010: 21

The changing emphasis of grassroots organizations reopens the question of the voluntary sector's role in public service delivery and the extent to which grassroots organizations should remain distinct from outsourced state provision. The micro-organizations in this study illustrate small-scale voluntary provision, which, up until recently, has supplemented and added value to public services at local levels. However, as welfare cuts deepen, other recent studies (Phillimore and McCabe, 2015) indicate that such organizations are being tasked with shoring up provision with inadequate, largely voluntary, resources. Both WEN and Rootreach are facing growing social needs and their aims to support these adequately may, over time, affect their distinctive ethos and independent activities as grassroots groups with specific local ties. If WEN succeeds in becoming a preferred local authority provider, the pressures to change may be greater, while Rootreach, with its strong faith-based focus, may succeed in retaining greater independence.

Voluntary organizations are recognized for offering important alternative and innovative approaches in reaching marginalized groups not otherwise accessing provision (Boateng, 2002), but greater service involvement has increasingly compromised independent activities (Baring Foundation, 2015). Many micro-organizations, like Rootreach, are driven more by ideas of solidarity, mutuality, and voluntary altruism than by providing professionalized services (Barnes *et al.*, 2006). However, sustaining a critical, reflective, and altruistic stance amid competitive, contractual arrangements is hard, and immersion in associated professionalized and regulatory frameworks can readily divert micro-organizations from their core purposes.

Transformation or demise of infrastructure support?

This study highlights how both CVS and micro-organizations viewed their work as widely discounted by policymakers, raising questions about the spaces now available for the independent and alternative contribution of voluntary action. The research also illustrates the important role that CVS still play in mediating and decoding regulatory frameworks and technical language, and making links between grassroots organizations and outside bodies. However, with severe constraints on time and funding, the CVS studied here were struggling to address growing support needs and turning to other methods of providing support. Open fora and networks offered benefits for micro-organizations in sharing concerns, expertise, and co-ordinating action, still allowing some degree of in-depth support tailored to the needs of individual micro-organizations.

The study emphasizes the rapid pace of development among micro-organizations facing growing demands resulting from the reduced scope of public services. Micro-organizations anticipated extending services to tackle these unmet social needs, but faced increasing pressures to grow and professionalize to attract more service funding. In parallel, they recognized that this potentially jeopardized their independent goals and activities as small, volunteer-led groups. The CVS workers lacked the capacity to fully support them in the flexible ways that they wanted, with time for support work and workers' hours declining. They recognized that new ways of working and generating income other than from local authority sources had become essential, but their shift towards developing networks and away from resource-intensive one-to-one work and development funding still needed acceptance by some groups. However, workers hoped it might generate new spaces for collective action.

CVS workers clearly feel challenged in a climate where they face growing pressures to prove their worth and relevance, yet can offer far less support to small organizations. Both CVS and micro-organizations are grappling with developing different approaches to address a future with inadequate resources. This research illustrates areas where local authorities were still investing in infrastructure organizations, whereas discussion earlier maps a harsher overall picture, with support services outsourced to cost-cutting contractors and some decimated. The territory that CVS have operated in has changed, together with their former roles and purposes. They face new challenges in negotiating competing strands of work and adjusting to reduced income and the changing demands of grassroots groups. Articulating the value of their work and asserting their specific place within a politically contested understanding of the purposes of voluntary organizations are crucial as the welfare state is progressively dismantled.

References

Baring Foundation (2015) *An Independent Mission: The voluntary sector in 2015*. London: Baring Foundation.

Barnes, M., Newman, J., and Sullivan, H. (2006) 'Discursive Arenas: Deliberation and the constitution of identity in public participation at local level'. *Social Movement Studies*, 5 (3), 193–207.

Boateng, P. (2002) *The Role of the Voluntary and Community Sector in Service Delivery. A cross cutting review*. London: HM Treasury.

Cairns, B., Harris, M., and Young, P. (2005) 'Building the capacity of the voluntary non-profit sector: Challenges of theory and practice'. *International Journal of Public Administration*, 28, 869–85.

Cornforth, C. and Mordaunt, J. (2011) 'Organisational capacity building: Understanding the dilemmas for foundations of intervening in small and medium-size charities'. *Voluntas: International Journal of Voluntary Nonprofit Organizations*, 22 (3), 428–49.

Donahue, K. (2011) 'Have voluntary sector infrastructure support providers failed micro-organisations?'. *Voluntary Sector Review*, 2 (3), 391–8.

Foot, J. (2012) *What Makes Us Healthy? The asset approach in practice: Evidence, action, evaluation*. Online. www.janefoot.co.uk/page3/index.html (accessed November 2015).

Harker, A. and Burkeman, S. (2007) *Building Blocks: Developing second-tier support for frontline groups*. London: City Parochial Foundation.

IVAR (2010) *BIG and Small: Capacity building, small organisations and the Big Lottery Fund. Final report for the BIG Lottery Fund*. London: Institute of Voluntary Action Research.

London Borough of Camden (2015) *Camden Council and Camden's Voluntary and Community Sector: Investing in a sustainable strategic relationship*. London: Camden Council. Online. https://consultations.wearecamden.org/culture-environment/camden-council-and-camden-s-voluntary-and-communit-1/supporting_documents/Camden Council and Camdens Voluntary and Community Sector Consultation.pdf (accessed December 2016).

McCabe, A. (2010) *Below the Radar in a Big Society? Reflections on community engagement, empowerment and social action in a changing policy context* (Third Sector Research Centre Working Paper 51). Online. www.birmingham.ac.uk/generic/tsrc/documents/tsrc/working-papers/working-paper-51.pdf (accessed December 2016).

—, Phillimore, J., and Mayblin, L. (2010) *'Below the Radar' Activities and Organisations in the Third Sector* (Third Sector Research Centre Working Paper 29). Online. www.birmingham.ac.uk/generic/tsrc/documents/tsrc/working-papers/working-paper-29.pdf (accessed December 2016).

Macmillan, R. (2011) '"Supporting" the voluntary sector in an age of austerity: The U.K. coalition government's consultation on improving support for frontline civil society organisations in England'. *Voluntary Sector Review*, 2 (1), 115–24.

— (2013) 'De-coupling the state and the third sector? The "Big Society" as a spontaneous order'. *Voluntary Sector Review*, 4 (2), 185–203.

NAVCA (2013) *NAVCA Quality Award. 2013 Performance standards and introductory notes*. National Association for Voluntary and Community Action. Online. www.rva.uk.com/wp-content/uploads/NAVCA-Standards-Web-version-2013-Edition-2.pdf (accessed December 2016).

NCVO (2015) 'Workforce'. In *UK Civil Society Almanac 2015*. London: National Council for Voluntary Organisations. Online. https://data.ncvo.org.uk/a/almanac15/workforce/ (accessed December 2016).

Newton, D. (2010) 'The infrastructure support services needed by community organisations in London, 2009 onwards'. London: LVSC. Online. www.lvsc.org/yourvoiceyourcity/wp-content/uploads/downloads/2012/09/NSG-report-April-2010.pdf (accessed March 2017).

Ockenden, N. and Hutin, M. (2008) *Volunteering to Lead: A study of leadership within small, volunteer-led groups*. London: Institute of Volunteering Research.

OCS (2010) *Supporting a Stronger Civil Society: An Office for Civil Society consultation on improving support for frontline civil society organisations*. London: Cabinet Office, Office for Civil Society. Online. www.gov.uk/government/uploads/system/uploads/attachment_data/file/78926/support-stronger-civil-society_0.pdf (accessed December 2016).

Phillimore, J., and McCabe, A. (2015) 'Small-scale civil society and social policy: The importance of experiential learning, insider knowledge and diverse motivations in shaping community action'. *Voluntary Sector Review,* 6 (2), 135–51.

—, Soteri-Proctor, A., Taylor, R. (2010) *Understanding the Distinctiveness of Small Scale, Third Sector Activity: The role of local knowledge and networks in shaping below the radar actions* (Third Sector Research Centre Working Paper 33). Online. www.birmingham.ac.uk/generic/tsrc/documents/tsrc/working-papers/working-paper-33.pdf (accessed December 2016).

Rochester, C. (2012) 'Councils for voluntary service: The end of a long road?'. *Voluntary Sector Review,* 3 (1), 103–10.

UK Parliament (2016) *Charities (Protection and Social Investment) Act 2016.* London: Cabinet Office. Online. http://services.parliament.uk/bills/2015-16/charitiesprotectionandsocialinvestment.html (accessed 20 August, 2016).

Walton, C. and Macmillan, R. (2014) *A Brave New World for Voluntary Sector Infrastructure? Vouchers, markets and demand led capacity building* (Third Sector Research Centre Working Paper 118). Online. www.birmingham.ac.uk/generic/tsrc/documents/tsrc/working-papers/working-paper-118.pdf (accessed December 2016).

Wolfenden Report (1978) *The Future of Voluntary Organizations: Report of the Wolfenden Committee.* London: Croom Helm.

Part Three

Shadow conversations
of workers

Chapter 9

Workers in voluntary organizations: Space for political awareness?

Alexandra Molano-Avilan

This chapter examines the perspectives of voluntary sector workers against a backdrop of austerity measures and political and policy changes that have had a detrimental effect on working conditions. Recent research indicates that many workers in voluntary organizations are poorly paid, over-burdened, and embedded in a culture of working excessive hours, which leaves them stressed and demoralized. However, the extent to which their everyday professional discussions involve reflection on their organizational roles within a wider political context is unclear. This chapter considers the presence or absence of critical discourse in workplace discussions, drawing on a study of the views of ordinary voluntary sector workers, who rarely feature in research. It also explores workers' perspectives on recent changes, questioning their sense of agency or influence in their working environments and their access to external debates.

The research was inspired by personal experience. During my post-graduate studies, I experienced a critical moment as I realized that analysis of my professional setting had come entirely through interaction with my academic course, rather than from workplace discussions. This prompted me to explore how my contemporaries in voluntary organizations were able to contextualize their roles amid rapidly changing conditions. The chapter asks how far voluntary organization workers regard their roles as apolitical and what this may mean for longstanding practices related to advocacy and campaigning. It first considers recent political and policy changes and their effects on voluntary sector workers' roles and then examines the research findings, which illustrate how few workers receive support to make sense of their changing conditions or place them within any wider political frame.

Politics, policy, and practice

A raft of political and policy changes since 2010, outlined in chapter 1, have significantly changed the landscape of voluntary organizations, placing smaller organizations in sharp competition for service contracts with private sector companies and major charities. Additionally, budget reductions have significantly undermined welfare services affecting the most vulnerable in society, for whom voluntary organizations have traditionally provided support. This has resulted in organizations struggling with inadequate resources to meet growing welfare demands, often dependent on extensive voluntary efforts.

Voluntary sector research has been slow to address the impacts of recent changes, but growing disquiet and critical dialogue is emerging (NCIA, 2015), alongside arguments for greater independence from external influences (Civil Exchange, 2016). Rochester (2013) contends that many voluntary organizations have been sleepwalking into compliance with state and now corporate arrangements, conceding their own values and practices. Consequently, many voluntary organizations now find themselves embedded in a rapidly privatizing, contract culture, where workers feel unable to operate freely, voice major concerns, or advocate for those with whom they work (Milbourne, 2013).

From 2010, the Coalition government further outsourced state welfare responsibilities, but experiences among voluntary organizations changed markedly, as their preferred provider status collapsed. Free-market ideology intensified and private companies accessed more local service contracts. When the 2015 Conservative government took up power, a fiercely competitive landscape was evolving, with massively scaled-up service contracts, often excluding smaller voluntary organizations. Funding has shifted rapidly towards corporations and into transaction costs, and away from existing frontline providers (NCIA, 2015). For voluntary organizations to remain in the frame, capacity building and sub-contracting have become widespread.

This discussion describes politically driven changes, with many voluntary organizations subscribing to the dominant ideology of markets as 'a superior model for improving efficiency and effectiveness' (Milbourne, 2013: 69). Yet underlying this rationale are the apparently apolitical identities that many voluntary organizations and charity leaders have assumed (Whitfield, 2014), as their priorities have shifted to competing for service contracts and adopting business models of operation.

Distinctiveness has long provided a justificatory narrative for voluntary organizations, both sustaining voluntary sector identity and implying superior value and better service models. Together with arguments around the need to change to meet current challenges, this narrative is upheld among sector leaders, but not necessarily shared by diverse organizations or the wider workforce. Amid current competitiveness, distinctiveness claims partly reflect a jostling for recognition, power, and resources (Macmillan, 2013), but they also deter less powerful players from promoting alternative approaches or fulfilling wider social aims. Additionally, with competition for resources undermining previous inter-organizational co-operation, the sector is becoming increasingly fragmented (Milbourne, 2013). Growing professionalization and inflexible management arrangements are also generating poor relationships with staff and volunteers and hindering improved cultural awareness, while the proliferation of self-censorship and gagging clauses in service contracts (Baring Foundation, 2015) are compounding other constraints on speaking out.

Even before many of these changes became evident in voluntary services, researchers argued that private sector involvement in welfare was suppressing the ethical foundations of public service (Mayo *et al.*, 2007). As managerialism and then market values became entrenched in voluntary services (Murray, 2013), an apolitical stance chimed pragmatically with external expectations and became the dominant voice. Thus, overt purposes lost their political edge, alongside aspirations for reform, social change, and former campaigns. New Labour drew many voluntary organizations into governability, better aligning them to assist in the subsequent neo-liberal trajectory of dismantling the welfare state (Milbourne, 2013), but few anticipated how vulnerable they would become in the increasingly ruthless service markets of later governments.

This describes broad trends, but local-level studies also illustrate many voluntary organizations as conflicted between their goals and the pressures of a competitive environment (Milbourne and Murray, 2014a). Additionally, some organizations, including several well-known international agencies, have allied in campaigns opposing government policies (Perry *et al.*, 2014). In particular, the Transparency of Lobbying, Non-party Campaigning and Trade Union Administration Act (Cabinet Office, 2014) and the mandatory Workfare schemes have stimulated new alliances and activism.

Conditions for paid workers

Income to voluntary organizations has reduced steadily since 2010, largely reflecting reallocated public service contracts. With local authorities facing draconian budget cuts, small grants have largely disappeared (Watt, 2014), and the hardest-hit areas are invariably the least affluent, with few community resources and facilities (Mohan, 2014). Conditions are well documented in regional studies, including in Greater Manchester (Dayson *et al.*, 2013) and Birmingham (Birmingham City Council, 2013), and by the trade unions UNISON (2013) and Unite (2015).

These reports show that underfunding from contracts is a widespread experience, with organizations mining reserves and voluntary resources to cover the gaps. There is also evidence that specialist local services are increasingly being displaced by large contractors (both corporations and charities), distanced from local knowledge about service needs, with services in some areas changing hands rapidly, producing elements of experiment and chaos. Many smaller voluntary organizations report sinking under growing demands and at risk of closure, a situation worsening with time (Unite, 2015). This evidence highlights the frailty of parts of the voluntary sector and the precarious nature of work for many staff, especially those in small organizations. Smaller organizations experiencing excessive pressures may simply fold or opt out (Milbourne and Murray, 2014b).

Steady growth in income from 2001 until 2010 led to an overall increase of employed workers and career expectations in voluntary organizations (NCVO, 2015). However, since 2010, this has reversed rapidly, although workers in large charities have been less affected. Trade union surveys of the voluntary sector workforce from 2012 to 2015 (TUC, 2012a; UNISON, 2013; Unite 2015) report a significant deterioration in working conditions, including pay cuts of 30 per cent or more, excessive workloads, widespread redundancies, extensive use of zero-hours contracts, volunteers replacing paid workers, rising unfair dismissal claims, and negative impacts on service quality. The increase in insecure and part-time jobs in voluntary organizations is echoed in Personnel Today (2013). Unite (2015: 23–4) identifies 'years of pay freezes and deteriorating conditions', resulting from 'government cuts and the race to the bottom caused by competitive contracts'. With a membership of some 17 per cent, trade unions identify a need to support members better, but highlight the lack of union recognition among many larger charities (TUC, 2012a; 2012b).

There is also a disparity in gender roles in voluntary organizations, with males over-represented in management and chief executive positions, whereas females predominate in lower-paid positions, where they form a significant majority (NCVO, 2015). Such disparities are even more marked when examining class and ethnic diversity, with the paid workforce being mainly white, middle class, and university graduates.

Workers face tensions within their daily work resulting from the competing cultures of state, private sector, and voluntary organizations (Hoggett *et al.*, 2008), producing conflicting demands on their time, from increased performance monitoring to growing pressures in service activities. These combine to undermine reflective practice, robbing workers of the mental space to think creatively and make judgements about problems (Cooper, 2001) or to develop the kinds of innovative approaches for which voluntary organizations have been valued. In 2014, such tensions erupted, leading to a week of industrial action to protect service quality by staff at St Mungo's, a housing charity (Unite, 2014). Cotton (forthcoming) has also highlighted the deepening crisis in mental health, including among charity providers, with low pay, high levels of unpaid staff (both trainees and retired volunteer professionals), and the growth of contract and agency working. She observes a general drift towards low-intensity well-being programmes as a substitute for proper therapeutic interventions.

Overwork and loss of reflective space also have emotional impacts, creating feelings of anxiety and guilt, as workers recognize that prioritizing organizational survival – chasing funds and new contracts – is displacing mission and values and narrowing their roles. Survival for some workers may also require unquestioning attitudes and adopting the professional roles expected, since, as Rahah and Dawood (2013) demonstrate, there are also high levels of workplace bullying. The authors suggest that this stems from a 'concentration of highly educated workers' in a rapidly contracting environment, where they lack 'control and participation' (2013: 68). In overly hierarchical organizations the lack of spaces for employees to shape strategies generates covert conversations (Stacey, 2003), but leaves the management view to dominate.

Reflecting on workers' voices

The qualitative study discussed below was based in one metropolitan area, and draws on interviews with six participants located in different types of voluntary organizations and across a range of service fields. Online platforms and networks were used initially to distribute a questionnaire seeking voluntary participants, which ensured access to independent viewpoints. Suitable participants were selected for subsequent in-depth interviews.

The workers interviewed were from different voluntary organizations and are identified with pseudonyms. They came from the following diverse fields: international non-governmental organizations (INGOs) (Karen, Mike, and Susan); disability rights and advice organizations (Charlotte and Julia); and sexual health and advice services for young people (Carroll). All occupied non-managerial roles, which ranged from campaigning to telephone advice, marketing, policy development, and fund-raising. The findings from these interviews are organized thematically, using six key conceptual themes that emerged from the experiences and viewpoints conveyed.

Attitudes to working in voluntary organizations

The participants all chose to work in voluntary organizations, and the sector's growth up to 2010 meant that employment opportunities and a credible career had been feasible until recently. Participants' views on work in other sectors varied but most were critical of both corporate and state practices, with one stating: 'I tried to find a job that I thought wasn't evil.' Most participants identified state and corporate interests as too close, criticizing government agencies for being increasingly embedded in market values.

However, some stories recounted about their workplaces belied implications that voluntary sector work was necessarily better. Most participants were extremely anxious for assurances of anonymity, and one participant, worried about identification, described an experience that she subsequently asked the researcher not to use in the study. Most came to the interviews with something they seemed to want to unburden and described their workplace environments as lacking any space to share, reflect, or act on the concerns and experiences they recounted. Another participant shared an emotive account of an unfair experience, confirming research findings on bullying within voluntary organization workplaces.

Alienation and problematic workplace practices

Negative views on collaboration, decision-making processes, and influence within their organizations were remarkably uniform. Many also struggled to identify themselves as a part of a wider voluntary sector, highlighting the disconnected nature of organizations with different specialisms. Unsurprisingly, austerity, with increasing demands and reduced resources, had strained relationships within the office environment. Growing job insecurity and more hierarchical roles were causing tensions, which Karen felt were widespread, and Julia similarly emphasized that negative behaviours and tensions were frequent but rarely 'acknowledged, as a lot's happening from the top layers of management'. She highlighted power imbalances and exclusions as exacerbating workers' feelings of isolation in their roles.

Participants complained about changes in their roles and the limited value they were accorded as staff, with Mike highlighting trends towards professionalizing management as partly responsible since they encouraged distance and disconnection from ordinary workers. Julia pointed to the excessive voluntary work expected of them, stressing the extent to which, 'staff are volunteers, we all work well beyond our paid hours'. Karen also emphasized the problems of low pay and depending on volunteers, which additionally undermined cultural diversity:

It's really important people are paid ... people need to afford to live. If you don't pay workers then you're attracting elites [who can] work for free, you're only getting people with a specific perspective ... that's already problem enough with paid staff because so many ... entry level jobs are unpaid, so diversity is a huge problem.

Human resources departments, which Julia considered should support workers and improve job profiles, were experienced as acting narrowly for the organization and provided little independent advice, as she explained: 'HR are now more about the organization than the individual.' The organizational cultures that participants described, with distant managers and decision making, strongly hierarchical attitudes, and unsupportive human resources departments, reflect elements of institutional isomorphism (DiMaggio and Powell, 1983), with voluntary organizations emulating the management styles and arrangements of other sectors. Participants found many recent shifts deeply frustrating, with organizational strategy and decision making experienced through 'lifeless' consultations (Hoggett, 2004: 123), largely excluding their views.

Support for workers' rights

If support within organizational structures was absent, support was similarly lacking through external connections with trade unions, despite worsening pay and conditions. As Unite reports (2015), many recent service changes have contributed to an ethos where voluntary sector workers are pressured to take on more while their pay and conditions are eroded. Yet often, as Julia observed, 'my organization doesn't actually recognize unions' and they relied on what office discussions they could manage. This left workers feeling vulnerable, as Charlotte explained, because, 'it's ... about power all the time ... structures are really hierarchical and just don't permit the right voices at the right time'. The effect, however, was to create hostile workplaces and isolated, demotivated workers.

Also echoing Unite's (2015) report, this study found that collective bargaining and external representation for workers were largely absent or discouraged. Julia felt that union support 'would be an amazing thing ... the third sector are getting screwed all the time on things like pay freezes, pensions, leave, job security'. She added that 'in an ideal world, I'd certainly be a member of a recognised union', identifying a recent restructuring process where union representation 'would have been massively beneficial'.

The embedded workplace cultures and practices together with non-recognition of unions undermined workers' rights and conditions but also affected their wider political awareness. Shielded by a supposedly apolitical workspace where unionization is regarded as extraneous, workers' identities as political beings become correspondingly marginalized. Attempts to reassert those identities are therefore treated as irrelevant to the main purposes of the organization, negating the need for critical debate.

Only the INGO workers were unionized and had used that support to negotiate workplace rights. Despite welcoming the idea, other participants lacked knowledge even of which union might represent them. More worrying were the workplaces where interviewees indicated that trade unions were expressly not recognized. While the traditional ethos of voluntary organizations encourages workers to regard unions as unnecessary and a diversion from commitment to the main endeavour, a refusal to recognize unions signals a recent tendency to assert managerial control. Surprisingly, most workers had not considered approaching a union; but outreach by relevant unions also seemed to be missing. However, workers' lack of trade union involvement also meant that they lacked knowledge about trade union roles in collective campaigns, such as against casualization, and signals participants' narrow focus and limited engagement in wider movements.

Curbing reflection and critical voices

The participants regarded the problematic workplace cultures and practices as symptoms of the growing inflexibility and risk aversion in organizational strategies. Karen described her INGO as 'too afraid of failure, meaning we're not learning and developing, and will eventually cease as we're not changing our narrative'. This culture of fear, often about not meeting external targets, added to growing service demands and resource pressures to constrain critical reflection and organizational learning. Equally, fears around losing funding suppressed criticisms, as Karen illustrated, describing her organization's self-censorship: 'We still haven't published a report because it was considered too critical of government and interfering with funding we're getting … which is a … nightmare.'

Other participants also recounted suppressing critical evidence and organizations instead complying with 'conveyor belt practices' that failed to challenge the status quo or generate positive changes. Mike cited 'Make Poverty History' as a classic example of a crucial campaign launched before adequate time was spent debating or reflecting on how to achieve poverty reduction:

> Make Poverty History came about, a very deep question … but you can't have a [philosophical] conversation while formulating a major campaign … but the fact that that conversation hadn't happened was very problematic and … needs to happen now.

Operational targets reliant on rapid results frequently displaced the diminishing spaces for critical discussion, but also generated dilemmas for workers, since this lack of reflection left ambiguity around purposes and actions. These dilemmas exposed the absence of a culture promoting organizational development and were paralleled by inadequate individual development opportunities. Mike stressed that even if training was available, there were barriers to implementing different approaches:

> It's about being given the space and support to implement [learning]... back in your work environment ... because you're constantly swamped, you never have a chance to change mode, change thinking, change your approach. You're just either fire-fighting or, you know, trying to cope! (laugh).

When asked about access to strategic information, most participants echoed Mike that it was limited to 'informal conversations with peers and colleagues'. Some participants identified conferences as useful for sharing information, but these often prioritized organizational agendas and rarely offered opportunities for wider reflection. Since informal, internal, organizational spaces provided the key sources of information, few participants were stimulated to reflect on their experiences within a wider political frame.

Welfare and wider reflections

Despite limited access to debates on wider issues, participants expressed critical views on trends in welfare provision. Carroll, reflecting other participants, commented on the unfair award of public services contracts and the consequences of corporate takeovers:

> The corporate giants are closer to government than they say ... So it's not on merit, if it was, G4S and Serco wouldn't exist ... they don't have the expertise ... there are people who are very good at it, and they don't get the contract. That makes no sense ... and the corporate sector, they're not people that care.

Collaboration was one policy solution proposed to encourage charities to compete more effectively for new scaled-up contracts, but participants regarded the increasingly competitive environment, alongside excessive workloads, as having undermined any genuine collaborative spirit, with collaboration often used instrumentally to win funding, as Milbourne (2013) describes. Alternatively, as Julia explained, organizations were too busy defending their specific identities to reflect constructively on collaborative priorities, whereas more focus was needed on 'what's best for beneficiaries'.

Most participants believed in state-funded welfare services, yet seemed to have accepted that voluntary organizations should 'step up their game' to address growing needs arising from austerity measures and shrinking public services. They had also assumed the need to compete more effectively for contracts, which Julia and Charlotte identified as imitating corporate arrangements. While participants seemed critical of general welfare trends, they offered little comment on the morality of declining public services, nor whether voluntary organizations should be challenging this. Only Carroll expressed a clear political view that the 'voluntary sector should not exist' to salvage flawed public services.

However, recent changes clearly troubled workers, and Karen discussed pressures to curtail statements that highlighted underlying social or policy problems and might jeopardize charitable or public income:

> A lot of charities doing service provision, actually the problems they're trying to tackle are structural … there's a tension because organizations are still offering services as well as campaigning, and the two … rub up against each other and … charity law puts a lot of pressure on to be less political … they want to get gift aid … and money from government which means they're less political.

Karen's awareness of recent political dilemmas suggested wider critical reflection, but alongside other participants, she seemed to accept the idea of a shrinking state as given, rather than open to challenge. This illustrates workers and organizations embedded in everyday social welfare activities largely neglecting wider ideological reflection. Thus, while participants were critical of current policy and operational arrangements and ways in which they constrained their organizational activities and autonomy, criticisms were often general and sometimes self-directed, but rarely analytical or concerned with seeking spaces for challenge or wider social changes. In this sense they had apparently internalized elements of external conditions as given and failed to locate themselves conceptually within any wider ideological movements.

A site for change?

When asked to reflect on what voluntary organizations could or should do, participants shared a vision of voluntary organizations as potential sites for innovation. This was noticeably at odds with the organizational cultures that they had described – that is, as lacking the space or energy for creative developments. Equally, participants stopped short of extending their wider critical reflections into ideas of activities that could achieve changes. However, they viewed many voluntary organizations as concentrating on policy change at the expense of challenging public assumptions. For example, within the disability field, Charlotte criticized failures to prioritize changing attitudes to disability or to mobilize public opinion. Carroll and Karen both condemned the focus on seeking 'policy wins' as flawed, with Karen highlighting the ongoing compromises involved and 'shifting … further to the right', instead of engaging in 'a movement of structural change'. Yet Karen seemed not to entertain this as a real possibility. Mike similarly deplored the failure of recent poverty campaigns to sustain public support and recognized that failing to take action to counter the way things were was paramount to acceptance, with too many workers focused simply on 'getting by' or 'fire-fighting'. However, while critical of charities (and implicitly self-critical), he failed to locate the problems within a wider ideological frame, distancing himself conceptually from a politics of change:

> Rather than seeing it as a moment of retrenching … holding the fort, trying to ride out the storm, why not see a time like this as an opportunity to get a different message out there, an alternative … and that's what I don't think any of them [charities] are doing, unfortunately.

Contradictions and myopia

The study found reflective, well-qualified staff, mostly underpaid and overworked, demoralized through exclusion from decision making and influence over their working environments, with management often regarding trade union roles as extraneous. Implied, although not always acknowledged, was that the participants' organizations had assumed the market values and managerial practices that they criticized in wider discussion of service provision. Voluntary organizations in general came under significant criticism for undervaluing and failing to support staff. As Caulkin (2007) underlines, while business models are often assumed to be superior, they are unlikely to produce creative organizational developments and have mostly produced more hierarchical systems in voluntary organizations, redirecting purposes and neglecting workers' welfare. Much advice on managing voluntary organizations is characteristic of wider UK managerialism (Rochester, 2013), while successful innovation, to which participants aspired, rarely emerges from these controlling models, but more often involves trust relationships, risk-taking, and outward-looking strategies (Milbourne and Cushman, 2013).

The study revealed contradictory perspectives on how workers understood their roles both within their organizations and in a wider political frame. It illustrated many workers as inward-looking organizationally, isolated from the debates and preoccupations of the wider voluntary sector, which they viewed as extraneous to their everyday concerns. Limited collaboration across different service fields also contributed to a sense that only the voice of remote national bodies was heard publicly. Workers were clearly overburdened by everyday tasks and demoralized because of lack of workplace influence, but had internalized many of the negative internal and external factors as unchangeable, despite making broader criticisms about trends in welfare and organizational cultures. They felt compelled to 'compete better' against corporate contractors and 'up their game', as if the skills of the voluntary services were inadequate. However, they also criticized the incursion of corporate businesses into service provision, with their poor expertise and lack of transparency, and voiced self-criticism about succumbing to these pressures.

Despite insightful comments on trends within their organizations and sometimes wider issues, participants distanced themselves from a role as actors who could challenge or change current conditions and neither sought, nor seemed aware of, research that could have connected their thinking and activities. This, surprisingly, included widely available reports (for example, Baring Foundation, 2014) identifying growing threats to voluntary sector independence and freedom of expression.

Participants' lack of awareness of relevant research illustrates the poor information flows to ordinary workers who lack organizational support and the capacity to engage in the kinds of discussions that such research could provoke. Pressures of work and organizational requirements thus posed barriers to workers extending their knowledge and engaging in wider reflection and development. Their nebulous information about research, alternative models, and wider campaigns demonstrate that many voluntary organizations and workers are not benefiting from existing analysis of problems. Surprisingly, they had not pursued a better critical understanding when reflecting on changes in public services and the inward-looking cultures of many charities.

With a lack of 'mind space' and opinions and reflections based largely on ad hoc experience and informal or covert discussion, participants found it hard to contextualize their situations or to analyse wider changes more coherently (Cooper, 2001). Thus they retained a myopic focus on issues within their organizations or specific service fields, but lacked the analytical tools or motivation to act differently or to imagine how their workplace cultures and arrangements could be constructed differently. They consequently described settings with few outlets for expression, resulting in frustrations, demoralization and intellectual inertia. While inadequate critical analysis is detrimental to workers and hinders organizational learning, the consequences ultimately result in poorer services.

The innovative vision that these workers asserted about voluntary organizations, while failing to interrogate the wider ideologies perpetuating their negative conditions, highlights a further contradiction. There is a considerable mismatch between workers' aspirations and actions, and the realities they experienced but did not expect to change. This may reflect a way of coping with diminishing control over their working environments.

What happened to democratic organizations?

Two decades of neo-liberal ideology have generated deep and sustained changes in the character of many voluntary organizations, and workers have suffered the effects. The study reveals caring but disempowered workers, often uneasy with their roles in diverse voluntary organizations. The varied workers' roles and different organizational types illustrate that this is broader than one service field. Critical reflection and debates among workers around changing trajectories in the voluntary sector were rare or non-existent occurrences in their workplace settings. Sense-making discussions (Weick, 1995) had been marginalized. While workers expressed critical views about different arrangements, few were 'joining up the dots', leading to the conclusion that they are failing to analyse their roles within a wider political context. The tendency to 'sit out the storm' may be a comforting practice for organizations and workers, but it fails to address the increasingly negative outcomes, including in service provision.

The pressures on workers and the lack of wider reflection are exacerbated by little support for securing workplace rights. Alongside other studies (UNISON, 2013; Unite, 2015), this research demonstrates the crucial role of trade union support in contexts where employees have experienced widespread job and salary cuts, growing casualization and excessive workloads. Research on the involvement of large corporations in public service contracts and their exploitation of voluntary organizations has raised significant concerns (Milbourne and Murray, 2014a), but these appeared absent from workplace discussions. This absence reinforces the perception of an apolitical attitude underlying mainstream voluntary sector discourse, which blocks critical response and opposition. As massively reduced public spending exacerbates conditions for voluntary sector workers and the most disadvantaged service users, it is vital that workers engage more widely with recent critical research and the growing academic and activist voices arguing for separation from market-driven arrangements.

This chapter draws the overall negative conclusion that the ideologies and organizational systems associated with managerial cultures, exacerbated by corporate involvement in public welfare, now pervade many voluntary organizations. This has marginalized the spaces for the kind of critical thinking and debate about alternative models apparent in earlier eras of voluntary sector history. Given this history, it provokes questions about how such passivity has now been manufactured among so many voluntary organizations, and what has happened to democratic leadership (Rustin and Armstrong, 2012) both in terms of management style and overall models of governance.

Rochester (2013) maintains that many voluntary organizations have been sleepwalking into this complicity for too long, but the growing evidence around the resulting damage argues that it is now time for workers to rediscover voluntary action and reposition themselves as dissenting actors rather than 'riding out the storm'. There is a need to challenge this pervasive culture and place importance on creating discursive spaces, whether in academic, organizational, or informal worlds or ideally across all three. Overt critical debate is needed, framing understanding within wider ideology and confronting the nonsensical dominant discourse that voluntary organizations can somehow be non-political. This is essential for the ongoing morale of workers and organizations and to achieve the goal of better services.

References

Baring Foundation (2014) *Independence Undervalued: The voluntary sector in 2014*. London: Baring Foundation.

— (2015) *An Independent Mission: The voluntary sector in 2015*. London: Baring Foundation.

Birmingham City Council (2013) *Health of Birmingham's Third Sector*. A report from Overview & Scrutiny. Birmingham: Birmingham City Council.

Cabinet Office (2014) *Transparency of Lobbying, Non-Party Campaigning and Trade Union Administration Act 2014*. Online. www.legislation.gov.uk/ukpga/2014/4/pdfs/ukpga_20140004_en.pdf (accessed December 2016).

Caulkin, S. (2007) 'Command, control ... and you ultimately fail'. *The Guardian*, 16 December. Online. www.theguardian.com/business/2007/dec/16/2 (accessed December 2016).

Civil Exchange (2016) *Independence in Question: The voluntary sector in 2016*. London: Civil Exchange.

Cooper, A. (2001) 'The state of mind we're in: Social anxiety, governance and the audit society'. *Psychoanalytic Studies*, 3 (3/4), 349–62.

Cotton, L. (forthcoming) *Surviving Work: How to manage working in health and social care*. Gower Books.

Dayson, C., Eadson, W., Sanderson, E., and Wilson, I. (2013) *Greater Manchester: State of the voluntary sector 2013*. Sheffield: Centre for Regional Economic and Social Research.

DiMaggio, P. and Powell, W. (1983) 'The iron cage revisited: Institutional isomorphism and collective rationality in organizational fields'. *American Sociological Review,* 48, 147–60.

Hoggett, P. (2004) 'Overcoming the desire for misunderstanding through dialogue'. In S. Snape and P. Taylor (eds), *Partnerships between Health and Local Government*. London: Frank Cass, 118–26.

—, Mayo, M., and Miller, C. (2008) *The Dilemmas of Development Work: Ethical challenges in regeneration*. Bristol: Policy Press.

Macmillan, R. (2013) '"Distinction" in the third sector'. *Voluntary Sector Review,* 4 (1), 39–54.

Mayo, M., Hoggett, P., and Miller, C. (2007) 'Ethical dilemmas of front-line regeneration workers'. In S. Balloch and M. Hill (eds), *Care, Community and Citizenship: Research and practice in policy context*. Bristol: Policy Press, 75–88.

Milbourne, L. (2013) *Voluntary Sector in Transition: Hard times or new opportunities?* Bristol: Policy Press.

— and Cushman, M. (2013) 'From the third sector to the Big Society: How changing UK government policies have eroded third sector trust'. *Voluntas,* 24 (2), 485–508.

— and Murray, U. (2014a) '*The State of the Voluntary Sector: Does size matter? Paper 1* (NCIA Inquiry into the Future of Voluntary Services Working Paper 9). Online. www.independentaction.net/wp-content/uploads/sites/8/2014/07/Does-Size-Matter-paper-1-final.pdf (accessed December 2016).

— (2014b) *The State of the Voluntary Sector: Does size matter? Paper 2* (NCIA Inquiry into the Future of Voluntary Services Working Paper 10). Online. www.independentaction.net/wp-content/uploads/2014/07/Does-size-matter-paper-2-final.pdf (accessed December 2016).

Mohan, J. (2014) 'Why are charitable resources not targeted where they are most needed?' *The Guardian,* January 15. Online. www.theguardian.com/society/2014/jan/15/charitable-resources-not-targeted-where-needed?dm_i=A1N,26SYV,9AI2BR,7XM9U,1 (accessed December 2016).

Murray, U. (2013) 'To what extent is the voluntary sector colonised by neo-liberal thinking?' Paper presented at the 8th International Critical Management Conference *Extending the Limits of Neo-liberal Capitalism*, Manchester, 1–12 July. Online. www.independentaction.net/wp-content/uploads/2013/09/Voluntary-Sector-Neo-Liberal-thinking-Ursula-Murray.pdf (accessed December 2016).

NCIA (2015) *Fight or Fright: Voluntary services in 2015* (NCIA Inquiry into the Future of Voluntary Services Summary and Discussion of the Inquiry Findings). London: National Coalition for Independent Action. Online. www.independentaction.net/wp-content/uploads/2015/02/NCIA-Inquiry-summary-report-final.pdf (accessed December 2016).

NCVO (2015) 'Workforce'. In *UK Civil Society Almanac 2015*. London: National Council for Voluntary Organisations. Online. https://data.ncvo.org.uk/a/almanac15/workforce/ (accessed December 2016).

Perry, J., Williams, M., Sefton, T., and Haddad, M. (2014) *Emergency Use Only: Understanding and reducing the use of food banks in the UK*. Oxfam GB. Online. www.cpag.org.uk/sites/default/files/Foodbank%20Report_web.pdf (accessed December 2016).

Personnel Today (2013) *Latest Voluntary Sector Employment Statistics: Increased instability + impact on training/career planning investment*. Online. www.personneltoday.com/pr/2013/02/latest-voluntary-sector-employment-statistics-increased-instability-impact-on-trainingcareer-planning-investment/ (accessed December 2016).

Rahah, S. and Dawood, S. (2013) 'Prevalence and forms of workplace bullying in the voluntary sector: Is there a need for concern. *Voluntary Sector Review*, 4 (1), 55–77.

Rochester, C. (2013) *Rediscovering Voluntary Action: The beat of a different drum*. Basingstoke: Palgrave Macmillan.

Rustin, M. and Armstrong, D. (2012) 'What happened to democratic leadership?' *Soundings*, 50, 59–71.

Stacey, R.D. (2003) 'Legitimate and shadow themes'. In R.D. Stacey, *Strategic Management and Organisational Dynamics: The challenge of complexity to ways of thinking about organisation*. Harlow: Prentice Hall, 363–74.

TUC (2012a) *Outsourcing and Austerity: Civil society and the Coalition government., Conference report*. London: Trades Union Congress.

— (2012b) *Localism: Threat or opportunity?* London: Trades Union Congress. Online. www.tuc.org.uk/sites/default/files/tucfiles/localism_guide_2012.pdf (accessed December 2016).

UNISON (2013) *Community and Voluntary Services in the Age of Austerity: UNISON voices from the frontline*. London: UNISON. Online. www.unison.org.uk/content/uploads/2013/11/On-line-Catalogue219293.pdf (accessed March 2017).

Unite (2014) 'St Mungo's Broadway staff to strike for 10 days in battle to maintain quality services at housing charity'. London: Unite. Online. www.unitetheunion.org/news/st-mungos-broadway-staff-to-strike-for-10-days-in-battle-to-maintain-quality-services-at-housing-charity (accessed December 2016).

— (2015) *A Strong Voluntary and Community Sector. The foundation for a thriving society*. London: Unite. Online. www.unitetheunion.org/uploaded/documents/0000042-Unite%20Manifesto_Our%20Society_A4_Finalv411-22933.pdf (accessed December 2016).

Watt, N. (2014) 'Local government cuts hitting poorest areas hardest, figures show'. *The Guardian*, 30 January. Online. www.theguardian.com/society/2014/jan/30/local-government-cuts-poorest-areas (accessed 3 August 2016).

Weick, K.E. (1995) *Sensemaking in Organizations*. Thousand Oaks: Sage.

Whitfield, D. (2014) *The Ideological Content* (NCIA Inquiry into the Future of Voluntary Services Working Paper 4). Online. www.independentaction.net/wp-content/uploads/sites/8/2011/03/Ideological-Context-final.pdf (accessed December 2016).

Chapter 10

Personalization in adult social care: A shadow conversation ignored

Dawn Thorpe

The personalization agenda, initiated by the 'New' Labour government and carried forward by subsequent governments, has been at the heart of the modernization of social care services (Ferguson, 2007). Ideologically, personalization was promoted as giving people more control over services by tailoring or personalizing support to meet their needs (Dayson, 2011). However, it has moved provision away from service-led commissioning towards market-driven services. Against a backdrop of austerity measures and efficiency savings, it was hoped that tailoring services to individual needs would also be more cost-effective. Conceptually, personalization was widely accepted as good since it is hard to argue against giving individuals more control over the support that they receive. However, there were voices calling for caution (Beresford, 2009), and the concept and its practical implementation have subsequently proved problematic. The mechanisms underlying personalization, including direct payments and personal budgets, have imposed dramatic funding changes, threatening existing service providers and demanding a complete overhaul of their organizational cultures (Cunningham and Nickson, 2010).

The chapter first considers the policy background to personalization and associated theoretical debates and then turns to explore experiences of practice, drawing on a case study of a medium-sized voluntary organization.

Researching lived experience

Significantly, the disability rights movement was the driving force behind personalization, and many organizations have campaigned for more control for service users for many years (Dickinson and Glasby, 2010). My own awareness first came from a 2007 conference, In Control, where the concept of personalization had widespread support. However, from observing the different ways in which local authorities were introducing personalization, I started to seriously question the effects on service providers and staff. As time passed, I noticed that many staff, in both public and voluntary services, had reservations about the future under personalization. Such doubts and fears were rarely voiced publicly or in professional forums but they permeated peer conversations. These discussions, always firmly in the shadow, struck a chord with literature, in particular Stacey's (2003) discussion of 'legitimate' and 'shadow' themes in organizational discourse. I reflected that these shadow conversations expressing critical concerns stood in opposition to the positively framed and widely disseminated, and supposedly legitimate, public discussion on personalization. The hidden conversations highlighted professionals' fears and concerns for their own livelihoods, the safety of those they supported, and the future of their services.

Despite many concerns expressed, implementation of personalization moved forward swiftly, with guidelines published in the *Putting People First* concordat (ADASS *et al.*, 2009), and local authorities were required to place 30 per cent of those eligible for services on personal budgets by April 2011.

The rationale for the research in this chapter stems from a perceived contradiction emerging in the field of adult social care between the potentially positive outcomes for service users from personalization and the potential threats to existing services and staff conditions. This suggests a conflict between ideological aims and practice, also highlighting the 'conflictual interdependence' of workers and service users (Hoggett, 2000b: 147).

Personalization: Theoretical debates

Personalization is defined as:

> Services ... tailored to the needs and preferences of citizens. The overall vision is that the state should empower citizens to shape their own lives and the services they receive.
>
> Cabinet Office, 2007: 7

Its origins date from the 1996 Community Care Act, which introduced direct payments (DoH, 1996). However, the recent conceptualization and terminology of personalization is usually attributed to Charles Leadbeater, policy adviser to Tony Blair (Ferguson, 2007). Personalization was launched with the publication *of Putting People First* (ADASS *et al.*, 2009: 2), which recommended the 'development of a new adult care system: a personalised system ... on the side of the people needing services and their carers'. This document also set personalization within a framework of funding changes and signalled an ideological shift away from state responsibilities to what subsequently became known as the 'Big Society', highlighting the need:

> ... to explore options for the long term funding of the care and
> support system, to ensure that it is ... unambiguous about the
> respective responsibilities of the state, family and individual.
>
> ADASS et al., 2009: 2

There were other influential forces behind personalization, including long-standing criticisms from within the disability rights movement concerning social care provision promoting dependency rather than independence (Morris, 2006). Simon Duffy, from In Control, originally a government social enterprise and later an independent charity, pioneered many early practical developments for implementing personalization, including the resource allocation system, direct payments, and individual budgets (In Control: 2011).

Implications for services and staff

Research on impacts for service users under personalization largely indicated improved outcomes and satisfaction (Samuel, 2011), but this dominant line of thinking was also contested. The stark contrast between the assumed positive outcomes for service users and the potentially negative outcomes for staff and service providers are visible from other research. Ferguson (2007) argues that the popularity of personalization derives from the promotion of choice, individualization, and responsibilization in New Labour rhetoric; however, in line with its neo-liberal agenda, risk was also transferred from the state to the individual. Ferguson therefore exhorts social workers to challenge uncritical acceptance of the philosophy of personalization, which, he argues, appears so irrefutably positive, especially linked to a choice agenda, that the word has taken on its own undeniable symbolic meaning (2007: 388).

Ferguson (2007) analyses the sub-text of policies with good reason, revealing the underlying motivation to cut costs and the transfer of responsibilities and risks with direct implications for service provision. The focus on responsibilization illustrates the beginning of the stigmatization of state dependency, legitimizing new policies and seeking to move people away from disability benefit. Ferguson (2007: 19) aptly demonstrates the underlying neo-liberal ideology and moves to reduce public responsibilities, quoting Leadbeater's analogy between privatization, 'putting public assets into private ownership' to incentivize efficiency and innovation, and personalization:

> Personalisation is just as simple: by putting users at the heart of
> services ... participants in design and delivery, services will be

more effective by mobilising millions of people as co-producers of the public goods they value.

Despite the conceptual simplicity and consensual good in ideas of personalization, little in the discourse acknowledged the scale of changes and the extent of the practical implications for the service field, which Beresford (2009: 9) describes as a 'fundamental shift in the care market', while Harlock (2010) predicts widespread restructuring and some organizations closing. Change on a massive scale can create anxiety, and Beresford (2009) reports staff feeling unsure about their futures, illustrating the mismatch between the philosophy of personalization and its practical implications.

Organizational dynamics of change

Priestly *et al.* (2010) indicates considerable anxiety and resistance among organizations and workers involved in transitions to personalized services, whereas Dayson (2011) offers a more detailed analysis, categorizing three organizational types. First, he identifies the 'fully developed': those aware of what is required of them, typically with a wide funding base and capacity to respond. Second, 'the underdeveloped and at risk': those aware of personalization but with little capacity and understanding to address the challenges, typically smaller and medium-sized organizations with limited funding; and third, the 'underdeveloped but not at risk', small organizations with low awareness of changes and limited resources. He also differentiates 'external' challenges over which an organization has little or no control, and 'internal', such as funding transitions, pricing, and managing monies (Dayson, 2011: 100). However, organizations consist of people and reflect their identities and experiences, and organizational change, especially where risks appear high, directly affects anxieties felt by staff.

Organizations are 'continually iterated' and negotiated processes of relating (Stacey, 2003: 358) and reflect their collective and individual constituents. Stacey also underlines that talking freely in organizations is not always possible and that the legitimate themes are those that can be discussed openly with anyone, reflecting the official position and acceptable opinions. Shadow conversations, in contrast, are the informal conversations exchanged with close and trusted colleagues that cannot be conducted freely. Stacey also suggests that these themes are underpinned by ideology, which may be official or unofficial, but serves to legitimize them: 'sustaining current power relations that make conversation feel natural, acceptable and safe' (Stacey, 2003: 364). Stacey's work, together with Ferguson's (2007), illustrates how personalization as a positive became a legitimate theme in social care discourse, while criticisms were suppressed or reduced to covert conversations.

Within dominant discourse, successive governments have demonized welfare dependency, privileging individualization and paid work while undermining notions of human interdependency, which underpin ideas of empowerment in developmental welfare work (Hoggett, 2006). Yet the interdependence of welfare relationships is notably missing from the language of personalization.

Control is central to personalization: who controls finance, who controls services provided or chosen, the loss of control experienced by service users, and fears around loss of control experienced by staff and service providers. As Hoggett (2000a: 147) argues, public sector workers can easily be seen as 'agents of disempowerment [rather than] actors also caught within the inherently contradictory logics of care and control, equity and rationing, and empowerment and exploitation'. Personalization has apparently reversed the axis of power, giving full power to service users. Yet, as Hoggett emphasizes, the relationship between service user and worker is one of 'conflictual interdependence', while the ideology of consumer sovereignty serves to undermine workers in providing care or managing resources effectively.

Researching the contradiction

As noted earlier, I had witnessed shadow conversations in private forums about people's fears and anxieties. The rationale for this case study in adult social care stemmed from acute awareness of the contradiction between the potentially positive outcomes for service users and the potential threats to services and staff terms and conditions. The research explores the apparent conflict between ideology and practice, reflecting the conflictual interdependence of workers and service users explained above.

Overall the study aimed to explore whether personalization has generated fragmentation and deprofessionalization of the workforce in adult social care. It investigated several questions, including: how staff felt about personalization, the ways in which work and working conditions had changed, and the nature of the shadow and legitimate conversations concerning personalization. It also considered whether changes were leading to a truly personalized service and the role of personal assistants in this. Given that personalization demands major changes in the organizational culture of adult social care providers (Cunningham and Nickson, 2010), the study questioned the importance of pre-existing culture for organizations faced with such massive changes.

The study adopted a qualitative approach using Stacey and Griffin's (2005) personal narrative methodology, using semi-structured, 'intensive interviews' as a method to draw out interviewees' interpretations of their experiences (Charmaz, 2006: 25). Seven interviewees were selected from the case study organization, Support Link, discussed below, all with prior knowledge of personalization and all frontline staff or volunteers. Two of the interviewees were also personal assistants (PAs) working outside Support Link but with continuing connections, having gained their PA jobs as a direct result of their Support Link work. The seven interviewees were all women, and ranged in ages from mid-20s to mid-40s. All names below are pseudonyms.

The research was conducted with a team and in a location unfamiliar to me, but my work for another part of the organization meant that I was able to collect data to which I would otherwise not have had access, including shadow conversations that might have remained hidden. It is often argued that research should be conducted in an unfamiliar setting, but, as Charmaz argues, 'we are a part of the world we study and the data we collect' (2006: 10). Thus, my stance of 'detached involvement' (Stacey and Griffin, 2005: 2) included reflexivity as a vital element of the research, and this forms a part of the discussion below. A number of key themes emerged from interpreting the data and were used to organize the material that follows.

Support Link: A case example

Support Link is a medium-sized national charity providing tenancy-related support to adults with learning difficulties living independently in their own homes. It has approximately 100 services across England and Wales. Support Link was founded some 20 years ago on the principle that people with learning difficulties have skills that should be valued to enable them to live independently in their homes with support from their local communities, volunteers, friends and family, aided by professional staff. The mission statement emphasizes a vision for vulnerable people at the heart of their communities, sharing skills and talents for everyone's benefit. Support Link identifies its role as improving the life chances of service users, and interviewees stressed these organizational values and associated culture as important throughout the study.

Until the onset of personalization, Support Link was completely reliant on local authority funding, largely based on block contracts. In this respect, it falls into Dayson's (2011) second organization type, underdeveloped and at risk, with limited capacity to deal with the challenges because it was neither large enough nor attracted sufficiently diverse funding. Closer examination, however, suggests a different perspective, and five of seven interviewees believed it was an organization that 'tries to stay ahead of the game'. They explained that the organization had volunteered to be involved in developing personalized services in one pilot area when the opportunity arose and now has a number of projects part-funded by service users' individual budgets. Projects included in the pilot scheme are therefore partly resourced by the Supporting People fund, with the remaining funding coming from individual budgets, which in turn are part-funded by the local authority.

There is evidence already that these funding changes in social care are affecting Support Link. The organization has lost approximately six contracts in the past year or so, which is a significant new experience as Support Link had previously experienced growth for some 20 years. The complexity of funding sources means that it is unclear whether contracts were lost due to the implementation of personalization specifically; but there is evidence that they resulted from the transformation of social care funding regimes.

Organizational culture

All interviewees showed high levels of regard for the organization, including its values, ethos, and ways of working:

> ... it's got a model that works which is quite different to anywhere else really, it's community-based, it relies on volunteers, it relies on paid staff and on the community to provide support ... that's quite unique to Support Link, that it appears at the moment that lots of other agencies are trying to mimic.
>
> Emma

> I think it's the culture as well isn't it? ... Support Link ... you know values. When people join and start working for Support Link I think there's a certain something you've been attracted to Support Link for and people have got certain values and work ethic and there's just a culture created [which is] very person centred.
>
> Ingrid

However, three interviewees also offered more critical assessments of the organization, highlighting a separation between management and frontline workers:

> I think some of the people making the decisions don't understand the frontline roles that we're all in ... they've never experienced it.
>
> Emily

Asked whether they had felt able to talk to anyone about their concerns around personalization, most echoed the comments below:

> No, it wouldn't be seen as constructive ... um I wouldn't be seen as constructive and it would be seen as obstructive and I ...
>
> Emily

> [we] are kept out of the loop, we're not invited to meetings ... god knows what's talked about in them, but you'll get snippets, they'll all tell you something different! ... we just talk to each other.
>
> Jeanette

As well as a split with management, these examples also provided evidence of shadow conversations among staff. While much emphasis was placed on positive organizational culture and values, there was also considerable strain visible in discussing management issues, indicating the organization's alignment with dominant ideology around personalization. Implementing personalization seemed to challenge the very culture of the organization, even though there was obvious synergy between the principles of personalization and the organizational values.

Problems with personalized services

Workers expressed real concerns around the problems they were experiencing with personalization. These have been separated between general day-to-day problems, problems concerned with the management of personalization, and workers' fears surrounding personalization. The comments below initially voice concerns about experiences of actual, everyday problems.

> I found in one and [a] half hours a week I wasn't getting very much done ... his last PA, all he ever did was take him out for coffee, or never turn up ...
>
> Shirley

> ... the lady [PA] she had last year ... from what I can gather, she was always on the phone ... on Facebook while Betty [client] was there ...
>
> Tina

> I just couldn't get in touch with him [the PA] and when I did he was really quite obstructive, I asked if we could meet, you know for a three-way with him and Peter [client] but he was like, blah, blah ...
>
> Emma

And:

> I contacted Meadows [the brokerage organization] and said this needs to be dealt with because there are real problems ... but they were being obstructive too, they were like 'it's really up to Peter, he's the employer' but Peter isn't able to advocate for himself.
>
> Emma

> ... and it's like you get choice but you get told how to choose ... this PA had been employed to work with a person I support but he [the client] wants to go out and do things but the PA is employed to do housework with him, so if the PA does what this person asks him to do he isn't really doing his job, but isn't it supposed to be up to the person what he wants? That's what I don't get.
>
> Sarah

All four staff members who had personal experience of working with PAs highlighted significant practical problems with the provision.

Management of personalized services

The four interviewees with direct experience of personalization indicated problems with how services were managed, including, for example, poor support, lack of monitoring, and inadequate funds. The three employed at a management level also questioned 'the real driving force' behind personalization, which they linked to cost-cutting, expressing this as a 'perceived concern'. In Emma's words:

> I know of service users who have been reassessed this year and they have had their individual budgets cut already, how is that about choice?

Shirley also discussed a PA not turning up for work, and when I asked whether this would have been discovered if the man had not also been receiving support from Support Link, she confirmed:

> it would never have been picked up because the way that adult social services work here, they don't review for years on end ...

Tina's response to 'Do you have a boss?' highlighted problems around who actually manages provision, together with the lack of staff supervision:

> No ... well I supposed Betty is my boss really.

> If I had a really bad shift with Betty, I'd go home and offload on my daughter, or I'd call Fiona, I've had to do that a few times when I have been worrying about things.

Absence of support was echoed by Shirley:

> ... because I got Fiona, it helps a bit, whereas if I didn't work for Support Link who would I go to?

Shirley and Tina had access to Fiona (Support Link manager) through their Support Link work. Fiona confirmed that she provided this unofficial supervision and support for them.

Additionally, these two PAs confirmed the lack of a support plan or assessment for their clients.

The research indicates that the PA system being implemented under personalization potentially has huge problems without either management or formal support for staff. Equally, there is no guidance or structure for roles or activities, which overall generates considerable scope for the abuse and neglect of vulnerable people.

Fears and perceived problems of personalization

All interviewees expressed uncertainty about the practicalities of personalization, with concerns focused more on anticipated problems rather than concrete experiences. The examples below reflect anxieties voiced around worsening services, despite the underlying client-led philosophy. As Emily explained:

> Well ... they won't get what they want; they won't even get what they need because they won't be able to afford it.

> I think the bad side is some services will fall by the wayside, and that will be some excellent services.

> I think personalization will lead to more isolation, for example, if a service user says 'I don't want to go to that meeting, or attend that social function', under individual budgets we won't be able to do anything, but ... our [Support Link] model is geared around people getting involved ... it's in the agreement we have with them.

Workers also feared extended commitments and threats to jobs and income:

> I am worried there will be an expectation for me to be available all hours, or what if someone's PA can't turn up, will I have to

spend time looking for another or … go instead? I worry I won't be able to keep the service full, then my job will be at risk, they could cut my hours, give me a zero-hour contract … where you are basically fighting for your salary … I don't want a job … not knowing what I am going to earn, I can't live life like that … I've got a mortgage.

Emily

The evidence of anxiety around the shift to personalization was considerable, often focused on experiences with service users, uncertainty around roles, absence of formal management or support, and especially fears for a worsening future.

Deprofessionalization and changing conditions of employment

The PAs, working directly under personalization, recounted examples that again illustrated ambiguity around roles and arrangements:

I wasn't interviewed; I got the job through Fiona … I had a chat over the phone and got the job.

Shirley

I'm not really sure who my employer is, I mean I get a wage slip from Meadows.

Tina

I was interviewed by the brother, they didn't do a CRB check though they did look at an old one.

I'm not really sure about days off and sick and stuff, I mean I did take a holiday … when they were away with their parents. I think if I was off sick then I'd just make it up.

[Laughs] no, there's no training but some of the training I've had at other jobs stands me in good stead.

I went on holiday with her that was working for 24 hours a day. I got paid for it though.

Ambiguous boundaries around professional roles and multiple ad hoc arrangements offered considerable evidence of frontline workers' roles becoming deprofessionalized by personalization. The usual structures associated with paid employment were lacking and numerous examples emerged of uncertainty around the PAs' knowledge of their terms of employment.

The interdependent relationship between workers and service users

All participants found it difficult to detach their feelings about their own experiences from the experiences of those they supported, and they often responded from service users' rather than their own perspectives. There were examples, however, of conflictual relationships arising between workers and service users.

When asked how accountable they felt, Tina offered an example of working with a client:

> Well at first I had a few difficulties with her behaviour, you know, and I was concerned and would contact her brother. He … said that he's really pleased because you know we go to a writing class and she's taken the work home with her, we're going to have a little book printed.

> There's been the odd occasion when I've had to send Betty home, she was very rude and very nasty. She went to swing for me, I can take that but I said 'you're going home', right, so she stomped off but she came back and said I'm sorry and gave me a big hug and I said 'I'm not having this behaviour Betty'. We were alright and went for a cup of tea.

Betty's behaviour is at odds with what is expected of her by the worker, and this exchange illustrates a clear power imbalance between client and worker. However, this is problematic if Betty, or her brother, is the employer. Betty's brother may be pleased with the activities organized, but Betty's individual budget pays the worker, and the usual power structure of employer and employee has been reversed. An already potentially conflictual relationship is exacerbated by this payment system and the ambiguity in employer.

What do these stories convey?

This research aimed to gain insights into the impact of personalization on staff and voluntary organizations working in adult social care. The findings were consistent with literature explored earlier, particularly Beresford (2009), who speaks of 'large scale anxiety'. Staff provided considerable evidence of perceived threats to organizational values, approaches, and their own security. It was also evident that these fears were being borne out in practice, with the organization losing contracts, having little management, supervision, or support for independent PAs, and experiencing failures in reviewing care plans and direct payments for service users. The frontline workers in the study felt unable to openly challenge the dominant positive discourse or legitimate themes surrounding personalization and discussed their fears and anxieties only in shadow conversations (Stacey, 2003).

There were also significant changes in relationships between service users and staff, generating a conflictual but dependent power balance, with staff through their professional positions holding power over service users, who perversely had become their employers. Lastly, there was ample evidence of workers' roles changing and becoming deprofessionalized. Responsibility for providing care, once a public sector responsibility, was being transferred to a privately employed, unregulated, and potentially untrained workforce, also shifting responsibilities from the state to individuals (Ferguson, 2007), including to vulnerable adults in their new employer roles.

The future of adult social care

Since the research was conducted, the 2014 Care Act (UK Parliament, 2014) has secured the future of personalization. The findings from this study, reflecting the anxieties of frontline staff voiced in shadow conversations, now appear prophetic. Personalization has increasingly become synonymous with cost-saving as the neo-liberal austerity agenda has advanced. The drive for efficiency savings, partly obscured within the early personalization agenda, is now overt in the public domain, and integral to dominant discourse. Personalization of adult social care has become a vehicle for local authority savings, and a recent council budget document (BHCC, 2016: 69–76), different from the study area, repeatedly refers to personalization as a 'model ... to reduce reliance on publicly funded services'. Its growing reputation for 'ideological efficiency' (West, 2013) therefore chimes well with aims for reduced state dependency and austerity measures. Its underlying philosophy promising choice for service users remains hard to refute, echoing the question that precipitated this study: 'How can one argue with personalization?'

Personalization is now being used overtly to cut costs, and it is therefore hard to assess the extent to which the changes integral to implementing personalization alone have led to the problems identified. Social care has been a significant victim of austerity, with some 30 per cent cut from net budgets between 2010 and 2015 (ADASS, 2015). Since this study, Support Link has suffered further contract losses and five separate organizational restructures, the combined effects of policy changes and wider-ranging austerity measures.

A key insight from this study concerned the changing relationship between service users and providers. Time has shown that devolving personal budgets has fulfilled the neo-liberal goal of repositioning the service user as a customer (technically with choice). However, it has changed the relationship between frontline staff and service users as well as their relationships with the state. With the implementation of personal budgets, local authorities can devolve responsibilities and transfer risks to individuals (Whitfield, 2012), which individualizes and fragments experiences. As Bolton (2014) suggests, 'personalised solutions could mark the end of collective services producing the expectation that self-provisioning must prevail in an era of chronic austerity'. This is confirmed in one council leader's statement:

> We will win devolved powers from government and devolve power down to local residents. Cuts to funding may mean we are no longer a provider or funder but we will be a proud enabler.
>
> BHCC, 2016

Whitfield (2102) argues that 'marketization creates the conditions whereby full privatization becomes inevitable', and many local authorities have sought to outsource most services. However, from experience over the past five years, clients with learning difficulties report that this market is non-existent. Two of the three local learning disability day centres have closed over the past two years with little to replace them. This lack of clarity around devolved responsibilities is well illustrated in this chapter, echoing other research, such as Needham (2015: 361), which concludes:

> the roll out of personalisation in a context of fiscal austerity ... ensures that as local authority services are withdrawn, it can be difficult for people to access or even know about what is replacing them.

Finally, a particularly enlightening development concerning personalization is the apology issued by Simon Duffy, who developed the resource allocation system and championed personalization, working directly with the government on its early implementation. His apology states that the criticisms made about personalization – namely that it would disempower social workers and service providers; that it would be used to disguise unfair cuts and cap budgets; that local authority calculations would be obscure; and the process would not empower disabled people and their families – have all, over time, been shown to be true. Duffy has devoted much of his career to campaigning for the rights of disabled people and sadly failed to envisage the potential for misusing his 'brainchild'. He argues that:

> These problems grew as local authorities started to adopt these approaches unthinkingly, without reference to the value of social

work or human rights ... [and] further accelerated in 2010, as the new government imposed 25% cuts on social care, and authorities began to use any tool possible to make these.

2012

The future of adult social care feels uncertain in many ways. What is certain, however, is that the present ideological programme of devolved responsibilities, alongside austerity and cuts, is set to continue year on year. By 2020, local authorities will be in receipt of little or no funding from central government. A future in which personalization can remain central to the delivery of social care is difficult to imagine.

References

ADASS (2015) *ADASS Budget Survey 2015. Report.* Association of Directors of Adult Social Services. Online. www.adass.org.uk/media/4340/adass-budget-survey-2015-report-final-v2.pdf (accessed July 2016).

ADASS, DH, and LGA (2009) *Putting People First, Transforming Adult Social Care: Progress measures for the delivery of transforming adult social care services.* London: The Association of Directors of Adult Social Services, Department of Health and Local Government Association.

Beresford, P. (2009) 'Whose personalisation?'. *Soundings: A Journal of Politics and Culture*, 40, 8–17.

BHCC (2016) Brighton & Hove City Budget Council Meeting. Online. http://present.brighton-hove.gov.uk/Published/C00000117/M00005638/$$ADocPackPublic.pdf (accessed June 2016).

Bolton, J. (2014) 'Finding savings in adult social care'. Report presented at ADASS Seminar. Online. www.adass.org.uk/media/4702/1-john-bolton-presentation-260914.pdf (accessed 8 March 2017).

Cabinet Office (2007) *Building on Progress: Public services.* London: Prime Minister's Strategy Unit.

Charmaz, K. (2006) *Constructing Grounded Theory: A practical guide through qualitative analysis.* London: Sage.

Cunningham, I. and Nickson, D. (2010) 'Personalisation and its implications for work and employment in the voluntary sector'. Workforce Unit Report, Coalition of Social Care Providers. Online. http://gcvs.org.uk/wp-content/uploads/2014/04/Personalisation_Report_Final_15th_November.pdf (accessed December 2016).

Dayson, C. (2011) 'The personalisation agenda: Implications for organisational development and capacity building in the voluntary sector'. *Voluntary Sector Review*, 2 (1), 97–105.

Dickinson, H. and Glasby, J. (2010) 'The personalisation agenda: Implications for the third sector' (Third Sector Research Centre Working Paper 30). Online. www.birmingham.ac.uk/generic/tsrc/documents/tsrc/working-papers/working-paper-30.pdf (accessed July 2013).

DoH (1996) *Community Care (Direct Payments) Act 1996*. Department of Health, Online. www.legislation.gov.uk/ukpga/1996/30/contents/enacted (accessed December 2016).

Duffy, S. (2012) 'An Apology'. *Centre for Welfare Reform*. Online. www. centreforwelfarereform.org/library/by-az/an-apology.html (accessed April 2013).

Ferguson, I. (2007) 'Increasing user choice or privatizing risk? The antinomies of personalisation'. *British Journal of Social Work*, 37 (3), 387–403.

Harlock, J. (2010) 'Personalisation: Emerging implications for the voluntary and community sector'. *Voluntary Sector Review*, 1 (3), 371–8.

Hoggett, P. (2000a) *Emotional Life and the Politics of Welfare*. Basingstoke: Palgrave Macmillan Press.

— (2000b) 'Social policy and the emotions'. In G. Lewis, S. Gewirtz, and J. Clarke (eds), *Rethinking Social Policy*. London: Sage, 141–55.

— (2006) 'Conflict, ambivalence and the contested purpose of public organizations'. *Human Relations*, 59 (2), London: Sage, 175–94.

In Control (2011) *Personalisation in Metal Health*. Online. www.in-control. org.uk/resources/health/personalisation-in-mental-health.aspx (accessed December 2016).

Morris, J. (2006) 'Independent living: The role of the disability movement in the development of government policy'. In C. Glendinning and P.A. Kemp (eds), *Cash and Care: Policy challenges in the welfare state*. Bristol: Policy Press, 235–48.

Needham, C. (2015) 'The spaces of personalisation: Place and distance in caring labour'. *Social Policy and Society*, 14 (3), 357–69.

Priestley, M., Riddell, S., Jolly, D., and Mercer, G. (2010) 'Cultures of welfare at the front line: Implementing direct payments for disabled people in the UK'. *Policy & Politics*, 38 (2), 307–24.

Samuel, M. (2011) 'Expert guide to direct payments, personal budgets and individual budgets'. *Community Care Online*, 19 August. Online (accessed April 2013). No longer accessible online. Archive may be accessed via www. communitycare.co.uk.

Stacey, R.D. (2003) 'Legitimate and shadow themes'. In R.D. Stacey, *Strategic Management and Organisational Dynamics: The challenge of complexity to ways of thinking about organisation*. Harlow: Prentice Hall, 363–74.

Stacey, R. and Griffin, D. (2005) 'Experience and method: A complex responsive processes perspective on research in organisations'. In R. Stacey and D. Griffin (eds), *A Complexity Perspective on Researching Organisations*. London: Routledge.

UK Parliament (2014) *Care Act. Chapter 23*. Online. www.legislation.gov.uk/ ukpga/2014/23 (accessed July 2016).

West, K. (2013) 'The grip of personalisation in adult social care: Between managerial domination and fantasy'. *Critical Social Policy*, 33 (4), 638–57.

Whitfield, D. (2012) 'UK social services: The mutation of privatisation'. Online. http://tinyurl.com/hsf5t45 (accessed December 2016).

Chapter 11

Less happy more often? Well-being in voluntary service organizations

Rachel Potts

The research in this chapter describes how the lived realities of many people currently working in voluntary organizations can often seem to have little to do with human flourishing. While problems are often located with material deficits such as lack of resources, this chapter argues that the central issue lies elsewhere, in the loss of the primacy of the relational link between practitioners and members or service recipients, and in the loss of spaces for meaning-making. Both have been suppressed and displaced by the language and demands of market thinking and, by extension, that of managerialism (Clarke *et al.*, 2000) and measured performance.

There is little research exploring either the roles of emotional labour (Hochschild, 1983) or that of well-being in voluntary organizations. The sense of alienation that exists behind the façade of a resilient sector, readily engaging with change and apparently sharing state and corporate imperatives, is unresearched. Cahalane (2015) highlighted the failure of charities to address well-being and proposed initiatives, such as introducing mindfulness sessions or Wellness Plans. Valuable though such initiatives may be in reducing an organization's stress and mental health issues, they avoid addressing the underlying source of a more systemic depression.

This stems from the changed environment of voluntary services provision. New Public Management (Hood, 1991) redefined public sector roles with a quality and audit system derived from a business model that dominates our modernized public services culture and now also pervades voluntary services. However, this change entails much more than the systems and arrangements that privilege managerial controls and judgements over those of welfare professionals. It fundamentally changes organizational cultures and values, reshaping priorities to comply with audit and funder requirements (Power, 1997). A gradual commodification of relationships between practitioners and service users thus ensues.

Does this sea change in the ways that service-providing voluntary organizations are now managed, monitored, and evaluated fundamentally thwart the traditional principles and values of those organizations? How has it impacted on the well-being of staff and members, and is it the case that all parties are now 'less happy more often' (Armatrading, 2003)?

The chapter first introduces the relevance of eudaimonic well-being in addressing such questions. This is a specific conceptualization of well-being rooted in Aristotelian ethics concerned with human flourishing and living a good, as in moral, life in accordance with classical virtues (Eagleton, 2003) that emphasize the central importance of human relatedness. Second, the chapter probes the implications of the changes occurring in language. Finally, it considers the role of narrative in researching the lived experience of well-being.

Contested meanings of well-being

The principles of eudaimonic well-being that frame the study discussed in the sections below identify individual well-being as inextricably linked to, and dependent on, the flourishing of others. They stress the 'primacy of the relational realm' (Ryff and Singer, 2006: 21). As noted above, this specific understanding of well-being derives from Aristotelian ethics, which is not aiming to be prescriptive, but rather to formulate ethical guidelines on how to live, which can be summarized as: self-acceptance, positive relations with others, personal growth, purpose in life, environmental mastery, and autonomy. While all of these conditions would ideally be present, positive relations with others, and purpose and autonomy appear of particular relevance to the discussion of well-being and voluntary action (Harris and Rochester, 2001). They are also especially reflected in the way Barnes (2007) describes a feminist ethic of care as living and deciding together and the positive experiences of acting collectively.

A lens of well-being carries a vocabulary of its own. It provides a frame for reflecting on individual and organizational actions and meanings, and also for discussing the wisdom of voluntary organizations partnering, for example, with large housing associations or becoming involved in the Work Programme and Workfare (Baring Foundation, 2012; Milbourne and Murray, 2014). Moreover, it has the potential to enable articulation of the potential rights and wrongs of adopting the discourse of vulnerability for service recipients.

While there has been an increased focus on the nature and importance of well-being and resilience within communities and for individuals, the main reason for growing attention from policymakers is that it can potentially reduce financial burdens on the state (Aked *et al.*, 2010). Local voluntary action groups have been promoted as positive ways to enhance well-being in communities and reduce welfare dependency and costs (Cabinet Office, 2010), but this strategy has increasingly been criticized for transferring responsibilities for gaps in welfare services to volunteer groups, who feel overburdened and undervalued (Ellison, 2011). The economic rationale for promoting well-being fundamentally avoids addressing eudaimonic well-being, a tenet of which, to paraphrase Bond (1996: 125), is that we find humans intrinsically valuable; we do not place a value on them. This chapter emphasizes that our own well-being is inextricably linked to, and dependent on, the well-being of others.

Well-being is often used interchangeably with happiness, which invariably focuses on individualized ideas of happiness and pleasure-seeking, frequently related to commercial and material satisfaction. A burgeoning and individually focused well-being or 'happiness industry' has been roundly critiqued by Davies (2015). Popular literature on resilience also fails to mention that there are limits to what an individual or an organization should be expected to endure, and that hardship and failures are not due to a deficit in the individual or organization (Sennett, 1998), but rather arise from environments and structural causes, such as those created by austerity politics (O'Hara, 2014).

Changing language

The continued trend towards a market-driven model and associated managerial practices among voluntary service providers has seen a parallel series of linguistic shifts that have ushered in and sustained a new business-oriented language of competition. These shifts in language may have seemed innocuous initially, and may have had limited impact on their own. But together and incrementally, over a sustained period, they have led to a situation whereby the traditional language of voluntary organizations has been all but stripped out. As language and vocabulary are the vessels within which individual and organizational narratives are contained, this 'language death' (Crystal, 2000: 1) has had various deleterious effects on well-being. Managerial language lacks the ability to convey the complexity and the richness of human experience. Its tendency is to neutralize, flatten, and, wherever possible, seek to achieve or give the appearance of consensus (Hoggett, 2004). Moreover, although there may appear to have been a desire to 'purge the sector of its language and its passions' (Miller *et al.*, 2006: 376), these changes were driven more by a series of conscious decisions to impose order and control over financial and administrative operations. But as a consequence, managerial language has seeped into previously relational spaces and has served to industrialize them together with the welfare support roles of many voluntary organizations.

Weick (1995) highlights the significance of exploring language use to understand how shifts in vocabularies affect workers' abilities to describe and make sense of their work and worlds, and to convey meanings in their work to a wider audience. At a societal level, we also see how a populist welfare discourse of 'makers and takers' in the US (Tirado, 2015) was translated into 'strivers' and welfare-dependent 'skivers' in the UK. A growing sense of shame now also attaches to frontline services for continuing to provide for the latter, and a rhetoric of poor-blaming (Lister, 2013) and fairness (Hoggett *et al.*, 2013) has replaced discourses about equality and social justice.

Alongside the gradual suppression of earlier vocabularies, there has been a process of 'semantic infiltration' (Ickle, 2010) in which an appropriation of apparently expert terms, previously well understood within specialist service fields, has given rise to ambiguity and changed meanings. For example, 'innovation', a term borrowed directly from the world of technology, can be particularly problematic within human and social services. A linear process or systemic tool kit used to increase efficiency is invariably incompatible with creative developments or the complex issues in human services (Darcy, 2002).

An example of shifting language is the now widespread adoption of 'service user', which is not an innocuous term. Voluntary organizations have traditionally been membership associations and involved stakeholders in decisions and shaping activities. But the term service user has gradually displaced 'members', changing the relationship and aiding commodification (McLaughlin, 2009). These relatively unexamined and unchallenged transitions in language signify voluntary organizations as indistinguishable from other service providers. A language of markets, competition, efficiency, targets, and performance outputs is now so embedded as to become normative. The effect has been to suppress alternative vocabularies, both expert practitioner language and earlier political discourse, which ironically represented the responsiveness and expertise in service delivery, the local experience, flexibility, and creativity for which voluntary organizations were previously applauded (HM Treasury, 2002).

Narrative forms of reflection

The disappearance of narrative forms of reflection in favour of 'numerical reductionism' (Thin, 2012: 313) is evident, not only in the way that services are monitored and evaluated, but also in the common experiences of workers, members and managers alike. The spaces in which narratives can be meaningfully expressed or find any expression appear to be shrinking in an organizational environment where numerical, standardized measurement and evaluation is privileged. The apparent distortion or loss of these narratives is significant because, as Schwabenland (2006: 8) states, narratives are particularly important within voluntary service organizations as the way in which 'we make sense of our experience ... We think in stories, we tell our lives to others in stories. As we tell our stories our experiences take shape and meaning.'

Narratives are the connective tissue or dark matter within and between organizations, trustees, managers, and staff, overarching socio-political movements, and individual members. Such stories are the vehicle through which effectiveness or value is conveyed. Narrative forms allow organizations to be contextualized historically and within their communities – they are highly condensed, dynamic, and necessarily conflictual (Hoggett, 2004). Emotional resilience also lies in the 'strength an organization derives from its history and values ... often grounded in organizational narratives' (Milbourne, 2013: 5).

Researching eudaimonic well-being using narrative

The wave of voluntary organizations and community development work that emerged during the 1960s and 1970s was linked to the revival of worldwide social movements and led to a growth of campaigning organizations and subsequently alternative service models, prompted by both state and voluntary sector practitioners challenging discriminatory practices (Challis *et al.*, 1988). In terms of eudaimonic well-being and the experience of human flourishing, it was a transformational moment for those involved; one in which collective endeavour was central and often linked to intense mourning for the subsequent loss of 'the movement' (Balbus, 2005: 80). In the 1990s, a comparable period of social activism arose specifically around mental health, linked to the closure of asylums and promotion of Care in the Community. Radical collective action around domestic violence and disabilities also arose in parallel. The availability of public funding to develop new and innovative services followed public pressure. Initially funded by Conservative governments, these projects encompassed experiences of transformational change that were then scaled up under New Labour.

This research set out to explore whether the present operational environment of voluntary service organizations is detrimental to eudaimonic well-being. Undertaken in 2014, the study involved six in-depth interviews with individuals who had experienced the innovative changes of the 1990s noted above and who continue to work in the same or similar organizations. The interviews were conducted with practitioners in voluntary service organizations or executive officers of infrastructure organizations. All were small organizations located in urban areas. The participants share longstanding connections to the voluntary sector and to particular specialisms: domestic violence, learning difficulties, LGBTQ, youth work, and supporting carers. The study adopted a narrative method to capture the lived experience of change over the intervening years. The interviews explored the reality of working in these services over several decades and were designed to uncover the participants' views, feelings, and experiences. However, it was a conscious decision not to ask questions about well-being directly so as to allow the participants' own narrative arc to develop freely. As a researcher, I was also conscious of the need to reflexively interrogate my own experiences of such change and separate these from the views of participants. 'RP' denotes my occasional interactions in the narratives below.

The 'affective turn' in research refers to a growing appreciation of the 'role that human feelings play in the life of communities, institutions, social movements and governments' (Hoggett *et al.*, 2013: 2). This finds expression through the layers of individual and organizational narratives. Worth (2004) considers that 'well constructed narrative … is a form of reasoning that can find morals, reasons, explanation … and all kinds of information'. It is the story element that carries the emotions (Chamberlayne *et al.*, 2000) and, as Stiles (1995: 125) suggests, 'when you have heard a story, you know more than you can say'. The stories that follow encompass an internal reasoning and resonance for participants, researcher, and reader through the process of making sense of the experiences recounted.

Findings from the study: Past and present experiences

Five key themes have been drawn from the interviews, which emphasize the motivations and experience of the participants in the narratives that emerged and organize the material that follows. The six participants below are: Ceri (learning difficulties), Lisa (domestic violence counsellor), Peter (domestic violence), Rhona (women's aid), Stephen (LGBTQ project), and Una (carers' association).

Radical non-compliance

Participants were asked about their motivations for working in their particular fields of expertise and why they chose the voluntary sector over state or private organizations. The motivations were radical, not only because of the personal socio-political principles and values that they associated with the voluntary sector, but also in the welfare fields to which participants were drawn and the attitudes that underpinned the relationships formed with clients and co-workers:

> Ceri: I initially came down to London to study at University, hated being the token working class kid [at a Russell Group University] so I left to work with people with learning difficulties, it was where my heart lay.

> Rhona: Then I got involved in Women's Aid [WA] but I did that because they were the happening political organization so it was political rather than personal ... those were my politics and it was great if you could work in your own political arena and that's what WA was ... a big, lively, organization.

> Lisa: Freedom. Particularly after nursing. ...concerned with looking for and having jobs that allow me to make a contribution in a way that I feel comfortable with.

> Peter: My own ego [as a police commander of an inner London borough] but also the credibility of the [domestic violence] organization made me sit up and listen.

> > RP: You could have just ignored it, given your position?

> Peter: I could have, but domestic violence is too important an issue – not much money in it! It was purely based on the motivation that CCR [Coordinated Community Response] (Pence and McMahon, 1997) is the solution.

> Stephen: I was particularly working with sex workers, male and female transgender, needle exchange, IV drug users and intramuscular drug users – so steroid abuse – that was, there was only one other service doing that, general drop in, doing work in schools – sexual health – it was so varied, every day was exciting – yes it could be challenging but that's the nature of it.

> Ceri: Learning difficulties as a user group is still far away from equality, rights – and it's a lifelong situation with learning difficulties, which it isn't with other social concerns, i.e. the elderly – I wanted to influence stuff ... stand next to people to support them with advocacy ... and what makes things work is

the quality of relationships ... Looking at the difference we can make to someone's lives – the way someone is spoken to, decision making, networking, being involved with self-determination, dignity ... is all very important.

Rhona: Unless you want to politicize and transform women's lives, you might as well leave it to the state [refuge provision] – because it's a tough job. ... Why are you getting all involved? It's the way in which we did it that mattered to us – it's about the content of it. So you ran the houses through house meetings with the women – you saw every person coming through the door as a potential member.

Past in the present: Developing a narrative arc

The interviewees were asked how they felt about their initial motivations and their current positions:

Stephen: Ah well this is something that I have been thinking about because I was made redundant recently. I was doing very targeted youth work and there are no jobs out there that do that at the moment, so I really had to re-think again – do I stay in this field? Is this something I still want to do? It's also the fact if I don't know what else would I do? I still want to create change. I am still passionate around doing that and having integrity with that as well, so looking at the client group I am no less passionate about the work I am doing.

Una: It just became meaningless and it became, just do as I say – essentially if the managers and the trustees could have said that explicitly, they would.

Ceri: Elements are still there ... I worked at various levels of senior management team. I never wanted to scale the greasy pole, no particular ambition to climb the ladder for my own ends ... it was driven by the ability to influence the further you get ... then you realize this is not necessarily true, you just dance harder ... at one point I had my post restructured when I was on leave. I had been there 8 years ... but everyone has to make those decisions to keep services afloat. So I know [making people redundant] what we were putting people through and their personal commitment to the organization was wasted.

RP: 8 years, just sitting with that ...

Ceri: I've never been a butterfly; I am in things for the long haul.

Taking up a 'true self' or 'false self' role

The core, transformative work of organizations appears increasingly hidden beneath the weight of output measurement and targets, and the examples below illustrate the extent to which practitioners now work by stealth:

> RP: If you could, what percentage of the organization would you say is driven by managerial systems and processes?

Ceri: It's high, loads higher than it should be. And again because of all the committees and layers of decision-making ... at every level people have loads of experience and knowledge – but we are so hierarchically organized we don't tap into that wisdom.

Lisa: The organization that I work for now works with domestic violence. We are counsellors so we are all experts ... we need regular meetings to 'check each other out' ... It's a matter of support but it's also about making sure that the organization functions. Because things have changed so much in the voluntary sector and everywhere, fewer people to do anything and more work to do, I've seen that side of processing become really nominal. So there are meetings, they are half an hour long. I mean that's just a waste of everybody's time. I find that offensive. It's just so we can say 'yes we are doing a meeting' – no you're not doing a meeting and the fact you are 'pretending' you are doing a meeting troubles me a lot.

> RP: Do you think your organization works by stealth then ... a false self – true self?

Lisa: My fear is they believe their false self is their true self. That's my fear.

Using marketized language

Asked about the extent to which they needed to use managerial language, the examples below show that despite deep scepticism towards managerial 'speak', interviewees regarded it as all-pervasive:

Ceri: We will take the mick out of each other and I can turn it on and off ... different settings require different ways of talking about things – we have KPRs and other acronyms ... again the managers as a group are quite witty.

Lisa: Our funders keep us open, they allow us to function. Therefore, anything they ask for, we will do it. I have been asked to write a case study for a funder. A fucking case study! So I just pushed that through my confidentiality filters and said to myself 'just shut up and do it' and lied and made up a client and did it in two paragraphs because it's not a case study.

RP: If I was to say to you 'case study' what would you say that that was?

Lisa: I would say that that's about 3,000-plus words, that it is carefully written, thinking about a client's anonymity and confidentiality, that it has a purpose, you are demonstrating that this, that, and the other occurred through this case study. That it's not a piece of work that I would do quickly, and so on.

RP: Speaking as a therapist …

Lisa: Yes. Of course that's not what they are looking for – what they want to see is the user received units of service from you that they went from broken dependant to hard-working tax payer.

A sense of loss

Different kinds of loss emerged in the interviews including material and financial losses, but the diminution of identities and purposes was foremost:

Stephen: Rapid change and turmoil – no time to settle own opinion, I think there is going to be a large deficit – loss of skills, smaller charities that have gone under, workers that are so disillusioned that they have moved on, particularly targeted and specialist work … a good example is social work.

Una: We are seeing another build-up … I also understand that some organizations have a natural life span, things change, client groups change … I think we are in a very interesting crossroads between quite large almost conglomerate charities defining areas of health or housing and have seen benefits of that, also the problems that can cause. … Influence is great, but the downside is that individual contribution is lost, the mission is lost and people feel disengaged with that organization.

Una: It's such a shame isn't it, there's that part of you, that journey you wanted to undertake and to feel that you failed because actually you've just been … 'I can't'… you get up and just get slapped down repeatedly, so of course, you're just going to move away. ... There is that part where you think it didn't seem that impossible – how could something possible become so impossible? So then you feel worse because it wasn't impossible, so have I been part of making it impossible? Did I collude in it in some way? And should I have been more ...?

Peter: Despite some successes, I feel that I have singularly failed to secure better outcomes for victims ... I want to remain in the sector, doing something useful to combat domestic violence but every time I think about it seriously my stomach begins to churn ... [working in the field] just became too damaging.

What do these stories tell us?

Most interviewees had first engaged in this work in the late1980s and early 1990s. They saw their work as responding to particular social needs in a political environment that had prompted the development of community-led voluntary organizations. There was a strong desire for political and ethical consistency between their work and personal values. Participants spoke of how their involvement brought significant meaning to their own lives, and of how, as a result, they strongly identified with an organization reflecting personal principles and ideals. This meant that they had poured themselves into what they saw as purposeful work. Foundational narratives allowed them to develop a philosophy, and they understood that it was then imperative to articulate that philosophy through action (Malcolm, 2001).

Consciousness of a goal or purpose and of being able to articulate these seemed to emerge from initial engagement in voluntary or civic action, but this was then constantly reshaped by subsequent involvement in socio-political activities. Integrity, making a difference, and creating change emerged as key themes in most responses, marking a sense of commitment that participants wanted to retain in the face of the tensions and compromises of a changed political reality. Immersed in day-to-day activities, the emotional impact of recalling these past histories of radical non-compliance led to a narrative arc emerging: one in which reflection on the past was interconnected with reflection on the present. Stories from the past solidified in reflections provoked by retelling these stories in the present. For most participants, these accounts were inextricably associated with struggle and alternative models, but also sometimes successes. Success was about recognizing that transformation occurred not only in the lives and experiences of the people they were working with but also in themselves. These stories described progressive actions, which were both psychologically rewarding and also served to strengthen the collective will to make change. Narrative had helped to shape organizational identities and contributed to justifying practitioners' distinctive ways of working within community-based services.

When first taking up their roles, the interviewees were not concerned with personal careers, but primarily with transforming conditions for people in difficult or unjust situations and, within that context, making discoveries and being transformed themselves. These were the foundational organizational stories (Schwabenland, 2006), including victories, struggles, and failures, that inspired and sustained the organizations and their workers. This ongoing desire to make a difference was now perceived as having been compromised through current organizational, economic, and political realities. However, the material problems within voluntary organizations were not seen as the root cause of the malaise, alienation, and low morale; instead, this lay in a fundamental commodification of virtue.

A significant thread to emerge from these narratives echoes Judt's (2010) conclusion that there is something profoundly wrong with current arrangements. Participants described how their core transformative and creative work was increasingly absent, as their focus was diverted towards initially monitoring and evaluating services and, subsequently, towards targets, output measurements, and competitive bidding. Organizational processes and systems had become privileged, displacing other meaningful service activities. Drawing on Winnicott (1965), the examples illustrate how some practitioners now work by stealth, producing a need to project a 'false self' to organizational leaders, funders, and the public, effectively constructing a defensive façade to protect the integrity of the work that they valued and their relationships with service recipients. Lisa expressed the fear that ultimately they would 'believe their false self is their true self'.

It meant that practitioners' roles were undertaken by stealth and deception, and the meanings that they constructed around their work were concealed. Consequently, their work was poorly understood and unsupported, making them subject to overload, depression, and burnout. There was an acute sense of loss, alienation, and, for some, a sense of shame arising from perceived feelings of failure. This compounded the shaming projected onto frontline services working with the worst off in society (Jo, 2013). Some interviewees were acutely conscious that activities which prioritized caring, support, and expressions of their 'true self' were now given little value and had effectively become hidden practices within organizational protocols. Increasingly systematized, technicist, and competitive processes and language had displaced person-centred practice and human relatedness.

Why eudaimonic well-being matters

Managerialist thinking has apparently invaded the heart of these organizations leading to acceptance of the dominant 'ways of doing things' (Hoggett, 2004: 119) and an associated loss of a relational language. Language and transactions have become symbolic. As more practitioners hide behind this symbolic use, real needs, meaningful approaches, and poor service practice are concealed, cementing managerial language and behaviours as norms. There is a loss of emancipatory vocabulary and associated aspirations and thinking. Thus, the requirement to be professional now encompasses a focus on winning funding, on meeting numerical targets, delivering generic services, reporting successes, and hiding failures. These have displaced local experience, specialist expertise, and more creative and caring approaches. These professionalized activities sanitize and displace earlier aspirational goals, values, and developed expertise, which were intrinsically linked to generating change and well-being for both workers and service recipients.

Has the present operational environment of voluntary services become detrimental to the well-being not only of practitioners, but also of members or service users? This chapter confirms that this is clearly the case in relational services such as those in this study, emphasizing the importance of eudaimonic well-being as a way to think about the state of welfare services more generally. Well-being cannot be equated with happiness or Well-being Plans, but needs to emphasize a return to meaning-making and a collective and conflictual understanding of what this process means. A positive relational environment among practitioners, members, and sometimes also grant-making bodies can, at times, involve intransigent, adversarial debate and that is the very stuff from which shared meanings arise and genuine bonds of shared purpose have been forged. This is a context where the othering of service users (and other potential allies) is avoided.

The sense of alienation and loss of well-being illustrated here is also confirmed in more recent research that reveals declining service provision in mental health and the increased use of para-professionals and volunteer or unpaid retired workers in staffing therapeutic services (Cotton, forthcoming). Further evidence demonstrates that this culture of alienation is present in voluntary services more widely (Unite, 2015). Preventative, effective early-intervention models and a collegiate approach (associated with well-being) are not compatible with a competitive, commodified environment grounded in a political economy of austerity, which instead generates a product within an industrialized response to social suffering.

Reframing language, practice, and strategic thinking in ways consistent with eudaimonic well-being would encourage a clearer focus on purposes associated with emancipatory or transformative service roles, genuinely centred on improving welfare experiences. It would also enable dissenting voices of individuals, groups, and organizations to reject the dominant discourse and reconstruct alternatives.

References

Aked, J., Mchaelson, J., and Steuer, N. (2010) *The Role of Local Government in Promoting Wellbeing*. London: Local Government Improvement and Development. Online. www.local.gov.uk/c/document_library/get_file?uuid=bcd27d1b-8feb-41e5-a1ce-48f9e70ccc3b&groupId=10180 (accessed 29 March 2014).

Armatrading, J. (2003) 'Less Happy More Often'. MetroLyrics. Online. www.metrolyrics.com/less-happy-more-often-lyrics-joan-armatrading.html.

Balbus, I.D. (2005) *Mourning and Modernity: Essays in the psychoanalysis of contemporary society*. New York: Other Press.

Baring Foundation (2012) *Protecting Independence: The voluntary sector in 2012*. Online. http://baringfoundation.org.uk/wp-content/uploads/2014/09/ProtectingIVS2012.pdf (accessed December 2016).

Barnes, M. (2007) 'Participation, citizenship and a feminist ethic of care'. In S. Balloch, and H. Hill, *Care, Community and Citizenship: Research and practice in a changing policy context*. Bristol: Policy Press.

Bond, E.J. (1996) *Ethics and Human Well-Being*. Oxford: Blackwell.

Cabinet Office (2010) *Building the Big Society*, 18 May. Online. www.gov.uk/government/publications/building-the-big-society (accessed December 2016).

Cahalane (2015) 'Charities risk losing staff if they fail to promote wellbeing'. *The Guardian,* 11 May. Online. www.theguardian.com/voluntary-sector-network/2015/may/11/charities-employee-mental-health-wellbeing (accessed 23 July 2016).

Challis, L., Fuller, S., Henwood, M., Klein, R., Plowden, W., Webb, A., Whittingham, P., and Wistow, G. (1988) *Joint Approaches to Social Policy: Rationality and practice*. Cambridge: Cambridge University Press.

Chamberlayne, P., Bornat, J., and Wengraf, T. (2000) *The Turn to Biographical Methods in Social Science: Comparative issues and examples*. London: Routledge.

Clarke, J., Gewirtz, S., and McLaughlin, E. (2000) *New Managerialism New Welfare?* London: Sage.

Cotton, L. (forthcoming) *Surviving Work: How to manage working in health and social care*. Gower Books.

Crystal, D. (2000) *Language Death*. Cambridge: Cambridge University Press.

Darcy, M. (2002) 'Community management: How management discourse killed participation'. *Critical Quarterly,* 44, 32–9.

Davies, W. (2015) *The Happiness Industry: How government and big business sold us well-being*. London: Verso.

Eagleton, T. (2003) *After Theory*. London: Allen Lane.

Ellison, N. (2011) 'The Conservative Party and the "Big Society"'. In C. Holden, M. Kilkey, and G. Ramia (eds), *Social Policy Review 23: Analysis and debate in socil policy, 2011*. Bristol: Policy Press, 45–62.

Harris, M. and Rochester, C. (2001) *Voluntary Organisations and Social Policy in Britain: Perspectives on change and choice*. Basingstoke: Palgrave.

HM Treasury (2002) *The Role of the Voluntary and Community Sector in Service Delivery: A cross-cutting review*. London: Treasury Office.

Hochschild, A.R. (1983) *The Managed Heart: Commercialization of human feeling*. Berkley: UCH Press.

Hoggett, P. (2004) 'Overcoming the desire for misunderstanding through dialogue'. In S. Snape and P. Taylor (eds), *Partnerships between Health and Local Government*. London: Frank Cass, 118–26.

— Wilkinson, H., and Beedell, P. (2013) 'Fairness and the politics of resentment'. *Journal of Social Policy*, 42 (3), 567–86.

Hood, C. (1991) 'A public management for all seasons?'. *Public Administration*, 69 (1), 3–19.

Ickle, F. (2010) 'Semantic infiltration'. *The American Spectator*, 10 July. Online http://spectator.org/39311_semantic-infiltration/ (accessed 10 July 2013).

Jo, Y.N. (2013) 'Psycho-social dimensions of poverty: When poverty becomes shameful'. *Critical Social Policy*, 33 (3), 215–33.

Judt, T. (2010) *Ill Fares the Land: A treatise on our present discontents*. London: Allen Lane.

Lister, R. (2013) 'Benefit cuts: How the language of welfare poisoned our social security'. *The Guardian*, 1 April. Online www.theguardian.com/commentisfree/2013/apr/01/language-welfare-social-security (accessed 1 June 2014).

Malcolm, N. (2001) *Ludwig Wittgenstein: A memoir*. Oxford: Oxford University Press.

McLaughlin, H. (2009) 'What's in a name: "Client", "Patient", "Customer", "Consumer", "Expert by Experience", "Service User" – what's next?'. *British Journal of Social Work*, 39 (6), 1101–17.

Milbourne, L. (2013) *Voluntary Sector in Transition: Hard times or new opportunities?* Bristol: Policy Press.

— and Murray, U. (2014) *The State of the Voluntary Sector: Does size matter? Paper 2* (NCIA Inquiry into the Future of Voluntary Services Working Paper 10). Online. www.independentaction.net/wp-content/uploads/2014/07/Does-size-matter-paper-2-final.pdf (accessed December 2016).

Miller, C., Hoggett, P., and Mayo, M. (2006) 'The obsession with outputs: Over regulation and the impact on the emotional identities of public service professionals'. *International Journal of Work Organisation and Emotion*, 1 (4), 366–78.

O'Hara, M. (2014) *Austerity Bites: A journey to the sharp end of cuts in the UK*. Bristol: Policy Press.

Pence, E. and McMahon, M. (1997) *Coordinated Community Response to Domestic Violence*. Duluth, MN: National Training Programme.

Power, M. (1997) *The Audit Society: Rituals of verification.* Oxford: Clarendon Press.

Ryff, C. and Singer, B. (2006) 'Know thyself and become who you are: An approach to psychological well-being'. *Journal of Happiness Studies,* 9, 13–39.

Schwabenland, C. (2006) *Stories, Visions and Values in Voluntary Organisations.* Farnham: Ashgate.

Sennett, R. (1998) *The Corrosion of Character: The personal consequences of work in the New Capitalism.* New York: Norton.

Stiles, W.B. (1995) 'Stories, tacit knowledge, and psychotherapy research'. *Psychotherapy Research, 5* (2), 125–7.

Thin, N. (2012) 'Counting and recounting happiness and culture: On happiness surveys and prudential ethnobiography'. *International Journal of Wellbeing, 2* (4), 313–32.

Tirado, L. (2015) 'America's "welfare state" is shameful: The UK shouldn't follow our lead'. *The Guardian,* 18 November. Online. www.theguardian.com/politics/2015/nov/18/us-welfare-shameful-uk-public-services-private-profit (accessed 23 May 2016).

Unite (2015) *A Strong Voluntary and Community Sector. The foundation for a thriving society.* London: Unite. Online. www.unitetheunion.org/uploaded/documents/0000042-Unite%20Manifesto_Our%20Society_A4_Finalv411-22933.pdf (accessed December 2016).

Weick, K.E. (1995) *Sensemaking in Organizations.* Thousand Oaks: Sage.

Winnicott, D. (1965) 'Ego distortion in terms of true self and false self'. In D. Winnicott, *The Maturational Process and the Facilitating Environment: Studies in the theories of emotional development.* London: Hogarth Press and the Institute of Psychoanalysis.

Worth, S. (2004) 'Narrative understanding and understanding narrative'. *Contemporary Aesthetics, 2.* Online. http://hdl.handle.net/2027/spo.7523862.0002.009 (accessed December 2016).

Chapter 12

Dangerous liaisons and spaces for resistance

Linda Milbourne and Ursula Murray

More than two decades of political realignment, growth, and widespread involvement in outsourced public services raise questions about the roles, values, and approaches that voluntary organizations are carrying into the future. There is also the bigger question of what an increasingly constrained civil society, illustrated both in service models and restrictions on speaking and acting freely, augurs for wider public services and the health of democracy. However, divisions and differences among civil society organizations are also increasing: between large national and international charities and small community-based organizations and between entrepreneurial service providers and those retaining advocacy roles; these are visible in contrasting examples in the book.

The success of neo-liberalism in embedding free markets and competitive, individualistic cultures, and in ushering corporations into domains previously occupied by public and voluntary services is therefore only a part of the story drawn from earlier chapters. The changes described are more pervasive than simply being about which sectors and agencies deliver services and extend beyond policy-driven, practical arrangements, although many of these are sufficiently damaging, as the rapid transformations in housing, probation, social care, and mental health services show.

Neo-liberal ideology has also had far-reaching and insidious consequences that are morally damaging to ideas of public welfare and an ethically rooted society. As a result, many actors in both public and voluntary services have refocused their priorities and the language of their daily transactions, losing sight of the importance of relationships and socially oriented goals. In pursuing aggressive competition for resources, they have lost their moral direction, alienating those that were previously allies. However, there are also voluntary organizations opting out and others mourning the current state of things, but feeling trapped in this destructive web.

The book began by mapping the reframing of welfare and the remodelling of the roles of many voluntary organizations, highlighting the extent to which many have departed from their philanthropic and campaigning roots. In chapter 2, we explored opposing concepts of civil society, emphasizing the extent to which compliance has become normative behaviour, in turn pervading ideas of volunteerism and non-adversarial, co-opted civil society activities. Thus, many voluntary organizations have adopted a stance that both compromises their own approaches but also contributes to the wider acceptance of lost freedoms and unchallenged assumptions about an increasingly privatized, market-driven environment. Pragmatism and survival have dominated many organizations' motivations, but, paradoxically, the consequence has been progressively relinquishing any political aspirations to criticize the way things are.

These brief reflections draw on core narratives emerging from earlier chapters, and provoke a series of insights discussed in this chapter, including questions about the future roles of voluntary organizations. The entrapment of many voluntary organizations in complicit relationships with the neo-liberal state and corporations also prompts the question of whether some will respond to the malaise that staff are clearly now experiencing and withdraw from the shackles of contract culture. Examining why so many have been drawn into these dangerous liaisons with neo-liberalism (Fraser, 2013), the chapter also considers other options for formal voluntary service organizations.

These questions outline the discussions that follow on voluntary organizations' complicity in damaging welfare and their potential loss of integrity. In seeking explanations, the chapter also examines the power of policy ideology in suppressing more emancipatory discourse around civil society's role, while reinforcing concepts of co-operative and associational organizations. The latter part of the chapter explores how things could be different, how organizations could escape the gilded web and create spaces for resistance, leading to a wider resurgence of more ethical alternatives and a more democratic future.

Dangerous liaisons and damage to welfare

Nothing changes overnight, and chapters 1 and 2 mapped transitions over several decades. However, the speed with which recent changes have been legislated and implemented has been remarkable even while writing this book. Chapter 3 provides a compelling illustration of the rapid transformations eroding social housing, with the Housing and Planning Act (UK Parliament, 2016) ensuring that short-term tenancies are now a reality for most new tenants. Large housing associations are relinquishing their primarily social aims and becoming quasi-private companies, heavily dependent on private investment. Together with the generous terms of right-to-buy accelerating the attrition of high-value social housing stock, these changes are turning social housing and affordable rents into rapidly vanishing possibilities. Insecurity is now facing tenants in both private and social housing and commentators are predicting not only a housing crisis, but also the demise of social housing with severe social fallout to follow (Beecham, 2016).

Loss of social housing is only one disturbing example of service providers shedding their previous philanthropic aims and aggravating unmet welfare needs. Food and affordable shelter are fundamental human rights, yet recent UK austerity policies have visibly worsened access to these basic commodities (Hills *et al.,* 2015), leaving few safety nets except through volunteer-led grassroots groups. Chapters 7 and 8 provide examples of faith-based groups and micro-organizations seeking to tackle growing welfare gaps, largely with inadequate resources. Together with chapter 6, they illustrate the struggle to maintain autonomous goals in the face of powerful mainstream arrangements. Reliance on ad hoc and emergency voluntary arrangements, such as homeless shelters, soup kitchens, and food banks seems shocking in a country previously reputed for its public welfare. It has also, however, focused the efforts of grassroots and specialist organizations on filling emergency welfare gaps, leaving little room for advocacy and dissent. Additionally, it has reinforced a broader ideology around the virtues and inevitability of voluntarism, absolving politicians, public agencies, and large service contractors from responsibility for their failures to adequately address needs.

Concepts of social protection, social insurance, and social security, which previously underpinned social policies, have apparently been displaced by a more restricted focus on welfare and benefits (largely for strivers). As chapter 11 indicates, this narrowed focus casts shame on service recipients for dependency, whereas the interdependence of welfare workers and service recipients, highlighted in chapters 10 and 11, is crucial but largely ignored in the current framing of welfare work. Some of the problems stem from the effectiveness of political ideology, which, with media help, has embedded a negative language of welfare dependency, alongside distinctions between strivers and scroungers, reminiscent of the nineteenth-century deserving and undeserving poor. This language has encouraged justification for rationing services and blames individuals for being in need, despite clear structural causes for their situations. These negative connotations affect the health of organizations and workers and also undermine services, leaving minimally resourced grassroots organizations carrying the burden for welfare gaps, as several chapters illustrate.

The new service industry

A massive scaling-up of public service contracts, largely awarded on the basis of financial criteria rather than proven records or experience, has ushered in corporations and large entrepreneurial charities, at the expense of small, local providers. Gagging clauses and threats to future funding widely silence criticism of provision, while tightly controlled specifications and restricted resources reshape the delivery approaches allowable and feasible. These damaging changes have been described in earlier chapters, illustrating the rapid transformation in service cultures and providers, often generating inadequate and fragmented provision. Disregard for specialist needs and the expertise of local providers pervade much commissioning, with mainstreamed models increasingly based on huge, standardized contracts. As chapters 5 and 6 illustrate, these strip out specialist expertise and ignore the diverse needs of different groups of people, also increasing subsequent costs for acute care.

The resulting landscape is one of corporations, gigantic housing associations, and major charities gaining contracts, while locally responsive providers struggle to survive or close, with bleak consequences for provision. Chapter 5 illustrates the loss of innovative projects supporting prisoners, their families, and vulnerable women following radical changes in the rehabilitation supply chain. Changes intended to personalize adult social care, as chapter 10 shows, have instead produced unsupported, time-poor workers, with prescribed tasks, often unable to respond to vulnerable older adults' needs and wishes. Equally, the failures in black and minority ethnic mental health support depicted in chapter 6 reveal vulnerable black people avoiding unwelcoming mainstream services and becoming seriously ill before reaching help. While not dismissing the enormous efforts of many frontline service workers to provide services to people in need, these are often against the odds, and as the chapters demonstrate, at considerable emotional cost. In each part of the book, the chapters provide a compelling case for reversing the direction of travel in these new service industries.

The damaging power of predatory charities

Pursuing growth and diversification of income sources has generated predatory behaviours among many large charities. These strategies are rationalized as protecting organizational resilience but they divert charities from their core purposes, while threatening existing local provision. Examples in chapter 5 show how some large charities have competed aggressively to partner with corporations in criminal justice programmes, effectively becoming 'corporate voluntary agencies' (Rochester, 2013: 236). Representatives of major charities have also been seconded into government as advisers, enabling access to valuable insider information that offers advantages in tendering for contracts. Additionally, the workers cited in chapter 9 report that contracts are frequently awarded unfairly to providers without experience of a service.

There are also examples of large charities using dedicated procurement teams to gain contracts in new service fields where they have no specialist knowledge, such as in the increasing takeover of local infrastructure services (CVS) (Milbourne and Murray, 2014a). This contrasts with the areas described in chapter 8, where CVS remain and still gain some local government funds for supporting micro-organizations. Collaboration can be another example of exploitative behaviour, however, and chapters 5 and 6 highlight incidents of large charities co-ordinating with small specialist providers but using them as 'bid candy' and then buying in other staff for delivery or heavily top-slicing income, reducing resources for frontline delivery.

The ways in which changes are being played out can depend on the political complexion and local relationships around commissioning in different areas and whether they are determined by national programmes and policies or by local budgets. As different chapters illustrate, allowing unbridled competition and cost-cutting to determine the winners and losers in welfare outsourcing raises questions about the overall quality and fragility of the resulting services. It is not hard to predict that further cost reductions will exclude more small organizations and exacerbate the inadequate provision for those with specialist and complex needs illustrated in chapters 6 and 10. As large contractors increasingly displace knowledgeable providers, service recipients are left confused and deterred as familiar centres close. If future services are underfunded or failing, corporations will withdraw, while voluntary organizations carrying too many risks will fold. In either case, provision changing hands rapidly can only aggravate existing failures. In the words of a participant from an infrastructure organization (Milbourne and Murray, 2014b: 6): 'It's building services on rocky ground, and sooner or later they'll collapse. … It's happening already.'

All this speaks of the dangerous liaisons that have entrapped many voluntary organizations. As chapter 11 shows, diverted from their core purposes, this entrapment is slowly destroying well-being in organizations and among workers, and undermining responsive service activities. However, the dangers extend beyond these concerns. If the greater part of public provision is outsourced to non-state providers, little democratic accountability remains, since neither charities nor businesses are publicly accountable. Chapter 4 illustrates ways in which accountability in an already multifaceted and fraught child protection system is becoming more fragmented, as more services are outsourced, suggesting the potential for further high-profile social work failures. The shortcomings of corporate contractors in welfare-to-work, adult social care, and prison management programmes (Long, 2012; Wright, 2013), including fraudulent reporting and the parking of costly cases, also offer salutary reminders of the potential for damage while companies profit from the public purse. Yet despite widely publicized investigations, governments have accelerated the outsourcing and privatization of services. The argument is often made that things would be much worse if left to the private sector alone, a view that we discuss below.

Charities: Fit for purpose?

How do the changes described above equate with the philanthropic and altruistic aims widely ascribed to charities? Delivering welfare services is readily associated with these aims but does little to address the underlying causes of growing welfare needs or the significant worsening of provision resulting from recent changes. Adopting the normative arrangements of the new service industry therefore fails to tackle the social changes that are needed to make a difference more widely. Arguably, such compliance offers little more than first aid, which, while hard to dismiss, also exposes the extent to which charities' founding social missions and broader aspirations have become tangential.

Voluntary organizations claim to be distinct as service providers, since they are neither motivated by profit nor governed by state hierarchies. Theoretically, this frees them to pursue more flexible, locally responsive, and socially purposeful aims. Yet this distinction is hardly visible in the behaviours and arrangements of charities heavily engaged in the new service industry. Trading on a trustworthy brand to gain new contracts and subsequently imposing poorer working conditions, or using community-based collaborators to win contracts and then discarding them are not compatible with altruistic purposes.

Despite these behaviours, it is still argued that charities' involvement will provide better services than if these are left to profit-seeking corporations. Charities are non-profits with governance structures that should ensure adherence to their missions. However, the extent to which charities are doing things better is questionable, as they become more immersed in business models, prioritizing service acquisition and financial investment, which displaces other concerns and deters active membership.

Major charities have successfully attracted corporate sponsorship to supplement their incomes, but dependency on corporate funds is becoming an indispensable way of life that may rebound, just as dependency on public funding has rebounded for smaller and medium-sized charities. Partnering with big business does not simply limit activities and openly expressed opinions through accepting money and goods in kind, it also empowers the neo-liberal drive of government, aggressive competition, and corporate models, weakening critical and alternative approaches. Public trust in charities has recently been shaken and their reputations risk further corrosion through association with unethical corporate practices. Barnardos, a well-known children's charity, has received a damning press for failing to challenge the harsh environment in detention centres where they provided services. The charity has since announced withdrawal from these G4S contracts, but its involvement in children's detention underlines the damage of such linkages.

For charities, therefore, corporate partnering raises crucial issues about charitable identity, roles, and purposes as their activities morph towards reinforcing the social, economic, and political systems that they originally aspired to reform. Chasing money and growth, with the associated behaviours described earlier, have transformed major social welfare charities into big business; and corporatization, as LeBaron and Dauvergne (2014) argue, narrows the limits of what else is possible.

What happened to integrity?

The refocusing and narrowing of activities described above shows charities entering willingly into restraints on their independent activities and voice, complicit in facilitating a changed ethos and generating a dominantly non-critical discourse. As chapter 9 illustrates, this pervasive apolitical organizational culture has negative impacts on workers' morale and what can be openly discussed. This is echoed in examples of legitimate and shadow conversations in chapter 10 and the longer-term transitions in language and culture mapped in chapter 11, revealing how, overtly, many organizations have moved from dominantly caring to transactional models as service providers.

This depoliticized positioning evolved as many voluntary organizations were drawn into public service provision and regeneration projects, with the increased income available from the late 1990s until 2010. The closer links with central and local government agencies served to subdue more strident voices and encouraged a seemingly neutral political stance, which increasingly became normative. Any privileges gained quickly dissolved with successive governments, but this positioning has been maintained, especially among national sector leaders hopeful of brokering, albeit fast-declining, funds and influence. However, this positioning has had little bearing on how effectively recent politicians have been able to marginalize voluntary organizations and dictate their own terms. Choosing whether to remain within the new service industry, silenced by recent legislative curbs on lobbying and gagging clauses in contracts, or whether to construct alternatives now seems unavoidable. Where previously it was feasible to operate within and against the state (Holloway, 2005), this position is increasingly problematic.

This depoliticized stance lacks integrity and self-reflection. Voluntary organizations involved in recent contractual settings can hardly be viewed as neutral but are actively colluding in changes, including reducing the quality of services, increasing their frailty and the likely demise of public welfare. By remaining silent in critical discussions about damaging changes and focusing instead on securing their own futures, many are complicit in the very agendas that undermine charitable aims. They are empowering business encroachment into public and charitable terrain, normalizing corporate behaviours and enabling a reshaping of much voluntary sector activity. There are examples of ethical and positive practices among both larger and smaller voluntary organizations and examples of dilemmas and questioning emerging, but these are outweighed by many major charities that have a significant public voice failing to confront negative trends.

Delivering frontline service activities by stealth, workers pressured to placate funders and managers, concealing service failures, gaming in performance reporting, and grossly unfair working conditions illustrate these trends in different chapters. Additionally, supressing critical reports that expose significant social injustices and concerns about poor services to avoid jeopardizing funding offer further examples from earlier chapters of unethical organizational practices. Even larger charities that retain campaigning roles may make choices to pull their punches.

Rather than focusing on wider welfare aims, these examples show organizations deeply embedded in a competitive ethos, constrained by audit requirements and often internally conflicted. Chapters 9, 10, and 11 all illustrate workers' disquiet and stress in seeking to manage these tensions, with organizational priorities to maximize funding and placate funders conflicting with the frontline service activities that they believe are vital. Chapters 6, 7, and 8 also highlight the acute dilemmas for ethnic minority, faith-based, and grassroots organizations in extending services to tackle social needs, while experiencing threats to their independent goals from mainstream arrangements.

Integrity is not altogether lost, and the suppressed disquiet and intense dilemmas that organizations and workers experience suggest potential for change. Organizations engaged in advocacy and campaigning alongside services, such as the grassroots organizations illustrated in chapters 6 and 8, depend heavily on activists and volunteers, who are questioning how they can retain values and purposes linked to social change and close neighbourhood ties amid the multiple pressures to remodel and professionalize. Community-based organizations such as these, and workers reflecting on their anxieties, find themselves in a dilemmatic space (Honig, 1996), facing a divided pathway, uncertain which direction to take. Should they strive to maintain services at any cost, because they aspire to be better than either large corporate or small entrepreneurial entrants to service markets? Or should they, like the two case examples in chapter 5, seek other ways to sustain some services and their campaigning roles, free from constraints on speaking out?

Recognizing the existence of this dilemmatic space and the existence of dissent among micro-level examples reopens the question of whether voluntary organizations can remain service providers while also challenging dominant cultures and arrangements. The discussion above concerning shifts in purposes away from fundamental charitable and welfare aims is central to this question. There is potential for the formal parts of the voluntary sector to realign their goals and act otherwise, to challenge dominant arrangements and make different alliances. However, many organizations seem to have recognized far too late the web of constraints that now entraps them and the distance that they have travelled from their ethical roots. Examples of large charities openly challenging involvement in compromising contracts are limited but there are a few, large and small: among others, the Refugee Council, Church Action on Poverty, and the smaller Southall Black Sisters, cited in chapter 6. Some have faced legal challenges for speaking out, but these positive examples indicate that there are alternatives to compliance.

The power of ideology

There is a difference between retreating from zealous neo-liberal behaviours to refocus on social and philanthropic aims and adopting a more adversarial stance to dominant ideology and arrangements. As Glasius and Ishkanian (2015) highlight, for some years the formal voluntary sector, together with its leadership bodies and research base, has separated itself from wider civil society and activist movements. Thus, the dominant discourse surrounding voluntary services has largely been detached from debates around civil society, social movements, and democracy. However, this apparently expedient positioning has also contributed to a failure to interrogate involvement in neo-liberal and often unethical arrangements, or to draw on historical or political analysis that might illuminate the dangerous web in which many voluntary organizations have become trapped.

In chapter 2, we discussed conventional theoretical explanations for voluntary services, many of which – including distinctiveness, added value, and the ability to provide creative alternatives in the face of state and market failures – offer poor justifications for current practices. How can we account for widespread submission to neo-liberal values and lack of dissent among many large charities in particular? The ways in which these cultures have become so normalized calls for further theoretical reflection if we are to learn and construct alternatives.

Leaving aside major charities and giant housing associations, the fact that so many other service-providing organizations have adopted these cultures unchallenged suggests that they have somehow been convinced of the strategic value of setting themselves apart from other parts of civil society, based on a continuing assertion of distinctiveness. However, this separation also signals a withdrawal from other important civil society roles, namely maintaining an independent locus and voice in pursuing a healthy democracy. Change is unavoidable, and adaptability is a particular strength attributed to voluntary organizations (Billis, 2010). However, if adapting to current dominant cultures and arrangements reduces them to unremarkable service providers, voluntary organizations have little distinctive purpose remaining. Nor is this the organizational identity that many workers signed up to, especially those committed to making a difference at grassroots levels.

Changing political ideology and socio-economic policies have been instrumental in shaping the roles and expectations of voluntary organizations and wider civil society. However, they offer insufficient explanation for the ways in which recent governments have been able to harness them so effectively into delivering government priorities and absorbing neo-liberal values. As discussed above, many arrangements through which change is implemented are promoted as consensual, discouraging spaces for dissent and stifling alternatives. Foucauldian governmentality provides a valuable analytical lens through which to understand how these supposedly consensual spaces and normative expectations operate, shaping communicative action and limiting individual agency and alternative approaches (Rose, 1999). Detailed technicist arrangements foster and reinforce the cultures of dominant discourse and arrangements, embedding a sense of inevitability around the way things are and suppressing alternatives. This analysis encompasses widespread acceptance of competitive practices, how services are commissioned and audited, their increasing privatization, and investment in financial markets, shedding light on how voluntary service cultures and activities have been harnessed and re-formed.

Conceptually, governmentality also accounts for the prevailing zeitgeist illustrated in the preceding chapters, with legitimacy proven through engagement in this ethos. Increasingly undemocratic management, extreme working hours, and discounting unionization as irrelevant are striking examples from chapter 9, which also depicts workers struggling to imagine alternatives, despite recognizing that their work overload swamps more creative thinking. Chapter 11 also describes the longer-term transformations in language and cultures now generating depression within organizations that have lost sight of the importance of relationships, which previously provided meaning to practitioners' work. However, growing malaise and more restrictive conditions can trigger resistance (Foucault, 1977), and challenges around future directions may spread. There is evidence of a growing critical perspective emerging (Body, 2016; King, 2016), together with new groups, and more explicit political alliances, and the question of whether voluntary service organizations can recapture alternative models is surfacing.

Reconstructing spaces for resistance

The power of ideology to reorient the values of so many voluntary organizations highlights the pressing need to construct new and alternative narratives. Competing for contracts has left organizations that previously promoted their complementary and particularistic service provision as essential qualities with an absence of rationale. In concert, a series of issues need to be analysed and confronted, not least the growing constraints on wider democracy and loss of creativity and dissent. Winnicott (1971: 65) observes that compliance always comes at a price and brings a 'sense of futility for the individual … associated with the idea that nothing matters and life is not worth living'. Part Three of the book reveals this malaise, with chapter 11 emphasizing how intolerable workers find it to contemplate the loss of meaning in activities that were once creative. Other chapters describe inertia and disempowerment, which at times are channelled into shadow conversations and covert activities. Alongside the dilemmas and tensions illustrated in Part Two, these chapters signal organizations and workers ill at ease with their current roles and potentially growing signs of disquiet and unrest, suggesting that some may start to redirect their efforts towards social change, whether within or beyond their workplaces.

Contemporary challenges and threats are numerous, and alongside constraints on lobbying, the current government has relegated the Office for Civil Society from the Cabinet Office to the Department of Culture, Media and Sports. This reinforces the associational view of civil society organizations as non-adversarial membership groups and clubs concerned with sports, arts, and cultural activities, while obscuring the wider role of civil society as an arena for critical discussion, opposition, and opinions outside formal political structures, which is a vital part of the public sphere (Edwards, 2009). The widespread absence of voluntary organizations (with key exceptions) from this critical public sphere is a major concern if we are to recreate an ethos among civil society organizations, no longer in thrall to the competitive individualism of current neo-liberalism.

Learning from history

The historical perspective included in earlier chapters contrasts the more progressive political environment and endeavours of voluntary organizations in the 1970s and 1980s with the present. It is important to interrogate how, from this wave of radical projects and alternatives, the social democratic agenda was so comprehensively eroded, enabling the focus on humane and socially inclusive values as underpinning society's rationale to cede to neo-liberal individualization and marketization. Drawing lessons from the 1980s, Fraser (2013; 2017) illustrates how the innovative veneer of neo-liberalism suggests openness to different approaches through criticism of traditional government and governance systems. This invites movements seeking change to participate, but they are subsequently domesticated and incorporated by powerful routines, avoiding fundamental challenges. The appearance of shared interests in making changes helps to explain the extent of entrapment among voluntary organizations and their absence in voicing opposition. Within this sphere, they can retain the illusion of distinctiveness from state and private sector activity.

The more radical and alternative approaches in both public and voluntary services, and the spaces previously enjoyed by civil society organizations from the 1970s into the late 1980s, were underpinned by supportive social democratic local governments. Thus, the challenges are greater and may demand different kinds of movements and alliances in the austere and punitive territory now faced. This prompts questions around whether emancipatory and social change movements need to work separately from organizations supporting social and welfare protection given the enduring tensions between social movements and the formal structures of trade unions and local authorities. Yet history illustrates times when the two allied in broad movements crossing political divides. More recent alliances, both locally and in wider movements, have also seen unions, social movements, and small civil society groups coming together, for example, in anti-racist, anti-austerity, and refugee defence campaigns.

Fraser (2013) emphasizes the need for new collaborations, for a 'triple movement' that recognizes the importance of alliances across different interests and across the political spectrum, if the current neo-liberal agenda is to change fundamentally. The harsher the conditions and the more that the traditional structures of social protection and civil society roles become weakened, the greater the logic for pursuing these broader alliances. Viewed from this perspective, there are spaces for service organizations to re-engage in social change activities and find a voice. The context is very different from past eras, but there are still lessons to learn, alliances and changes that can be made, alongside the growing examples of resistance rising.

Morality and ethics: Restoring relational spaces

Much of what has been discussed is intensely political, and the ethical and moral costs of neither questioning nor challenging involvement in the new service industry have unforeseen consequences, including operating in different moral territory. The private sector operates with different moral codes, driven by different purposes (Hoggett, 2006), and issues of integrity in welfare, also closely connected to public accountability, are of minimal concern for profit-driven businesses. Criteria for contracts and earlier concepts underpinning welfare are diverging, and contracts are not awarded on the basis of caring. Thus, many recent outsourced programmes offer little assurance of the safeguards needed to protect the most vulnerable in society.

Reawakening care and kindness in the social imagination, with commitment to the collective well-being of wider society, is therefore crucial if we are to move away from the individualized focus of current neo-liberalism. Historical experiences, such as those described in earlier chapters, suggest that things can be otherwise; and cases of legal challenge and refusals to compromise indicate that fighting back within the system, combined with campaigning, can be successful.

Yet unethical behaviours and reduced freedoms are everywhere, seemingly authorized by power and money. Workers talk about upping their game and aping corporate behaviours to compete better, and success is overtly judged in terms of market wins, despite organizations continuing to assert altruistic aims. In analysing how voluntary organizations became trapped within this uncharitable web, it seems as if the earlier seductions of sitting alongside power gave rise to hubris, with envy effectively driving the aspirations of charity executives competing for growth and status. Survival at any price has now trumped concern over damage to welfare services, with voluntary organizations seeking benefits from, rather than challenging, privatization. As Sennett (2003) argues, such cultural shifts are corrosive of character among welfare workers and undermine moral and ethical aspirations for services, and, consequently, for wider society.

Refocusing questions around whose reality counts and challenging limitations on diversity in ideas have become urgent tasks if we are to build changes based on critical reflection and shared human experiences. If workers can no longer make sense of their activities, they cease to feel significant and lose motivation. Different chapters highlight emotional worth as a feature that practitioners associate with working in voluntary organizations, but which they now regard as eroded. Reasserting the importance of relationships, human interdependence, and trust in welfare work have now become critical, together with confronting the cultures of individualization and blame that demean welfare recipients. Restoring relational priorities has the potential to rebuild the strengths of a currently troubled charity sector and to generate more creative developments in welfare work.

Change and diversity

Change is inevitable, but how it is managed, how people are treated, and how diverse groups of people are included are crucial but often complex issues. The Big Society and, more recently, devolution have caught the public imagination and promised much, including spaces for local voices and action; but the former was rapidly demonstrated as hollow, while the second has yet to demonstrate improved spaces for democratic participation. There is a tendency to celebrate the virtues of grassroots organizing and informal membership groups in achieving change, and several chapters illustrate the value of specialist local services and the gaps left behind when they fold. Yet grassroots groups can hardly offset the widespread failures of mainstream mental health services to provide care for black and minority ethnic patients. Furthermore, the abysmal failures in wider mental health and child protection services in large metropolitan cities with the workforce drawn from diverse populations suggest that overall service arrangements are at the heart of the problem. However, underlying these failures is a society with a crisis in care (Fraser, 2016).

Faith-based organizations are increasingly tackling pressing social needs, whether in food banks, housing shelters, or other needs, such as in projects run by the Black Majority Churches in chapter 7. Yet there are contradictions inherent in faith-led groups running services for wider communities in a predominantly secular society, in this case dependent on volunteers without geographic links to the area. However, their congregations and resources are flourishing while other grassroots groups are struggling to meet growing needs, posing political dilemmas for local governments with inadequate funding for services. Faith-based groups may hold values that conflict with those of the secular society they serve, including on sexual identities and abortion, offering advice at odds with that of other health or youth centres. Thus, the intersection of religion with civic life provokes wider, potentially fraught, questions around the cultures underpinning normative consciousness and solidarity among citizens, which we cannot disregard (Habermas, 2006) and needs fuller debate.

Further examples highlight different complexities involved in promoting change through grassroots activities, including new civil society groups that have evolved around action to defend existing neighbourhood identities against regeneration plans (Douglas and Parkes, 2016). The intolerance that emerged around arguments for Brexit also illustrates how campaigns born of dissent or a desire for change can exclude some groups in society at the expense of others, damaging wider democracy.

We do not propose to comment in detail on the fallout from the Brexit vote nor the arguments surrounding it. Our interest is in the contradictory paths in civil society, illustrated in how individuals and organizations demonstrate opposition to the established order. While many grassroots organizations have challenged growing inequalities and unmet needs in society through broad campaigns, there has also been a worrying growth of recent populist and racist movements, with groups of people seeking to exclude others who are culturally different, not only from association membership, but also from local areas, facilities, and even countries. This is often justified by a culture that locates blame for negative socio-economic experiences with others rather than with structural or institutional causes. A recent report (JRF, 2016) documents how the experiences of growing poverty and material inequalities, together with a seemingly uncaring government, have generated the increase in anti-establishment, insular, and prejudiced feelings underlying a part of the Brexit vote, while also apparently licensing racially motivated insults and violence.

These examples highlight the dangers of new spaces for resistance being suborned to negative or oppressive movements, whether led by populist sentiment or political elites, including growing racist movements and those based on cultural or religious intolerance. The relational spaces in which people come together to realize change are often uneasy alliances, full of contradictory voices and contain different visions and agendas that have to be addressed, if individualized interests and group cultures of othering are not to dominate but movements concerned with justice are to prevail.

Resistance rising?

It is clear that recreating spaces for alternative models is not straightforward. Turbulent times and governments constantly moving the goalposts around public welfare provision present significant barriers, alongside the visible mismatch between the stated purposes of many voluntary organizations and their actual practices. Yet, resistance is rising: dissenting voices are challenging the way things are (NCIA, 2015; Scott, 2016) and creative civil society activities and movements are evolving (Aiken, 2016). Alliances among those seeking changes are being forged in local campaigns, wider coalitions, and social media-inspired movements and are crossing generational, geographical, and traditional political boundaries. This demonstrates that despite the increasingly undemocratic landscape, alternatives to the limited consensual, civilizing view of civil society's role are both possible and growing.

Currently, examples of civil society groups challenging negative conditions, reclaiming spaces for dissent and reasserting an ethical vision of society and welfare are multiplying (Milbourne and Murray, 2015; King, 2016). Among examples are local movements, such as the PEER project – focused on space and land use and ownership - and Save Brixton Arches – resisting privatized redevelopment and gentrification at the expense of long-standing traders and residents. There are many wider campaigns, such as War on Want's international campaigns on trade partnerships, and a broad coalition of UK-based organizations (including Stand Up to Racism, People's Assembly Against Austerity, Unite the Union, Communications Workers Union, TSSA (Transport Salaried Staffs' Association), Stop the War Coalition, and the Muslim Association of Britain) and French NGOs working with activists and volunteers to support refugees. Environmental and climate change campaigns offer further recent examples of broad movements whose members span professionals, activists, practitioners, and academics, focusing on psychological barriers to change, international connections, and sometimes direct action. Examples of specific protests, such as Black Lives Matter's recent action closing the road to Heathrow airport, highlight the detrimental effects of polluted environments for UK and international populations.

Large charities and voluntary service organizations have been slow to challenge and seek alternatives to a now visibly tarnished web of arrangements. Except for the limited examples discussed earlier, they have largely disregarded the wider consequences. However, as some speak out or refuse untenable compromises in contracts, others sharing similar disquiet will find it easier to reconsider their options. Major charities and representative infrastructure bodies have the power and presence to voice concerns. Relinquishing self-interest and adopting a role and public voice more aligned with their supposed social and philanthropic purposes is badly needed and could foster a wider ethos of challenging current welfare and civil society arrangements, with broader benefits for democracy.

A strong civil society has often evolved in tandem with an effective local state, resourcing otherwise neglected services. The current dismantling of local government powers coupled with growing local competition for funding has wider ramifications for how power is played out locally in the absence of local government arbiters. The re-emphasis on the local economy and devolution without clear equitable resourcing strategies suggests a future landscape that may depend even more on competitive enterprise, entrepreneurial organizations, social investment, and private finance. Involvement in service delivery, co-produced services, and challenging injustice, wealth, and power are not mutually exclusive, but require a shared, mature local politics and intelligent, ethical approaches to commissioning. Some local authorities have engaged the expertise of small local groups in negotiating service criteria, aiming to improve commissioning, but such developments demand trust and mutual respect for different roles and are hard in a dominantly competitive and poorly resourced environment. However, if the continued commodification of needs and social life is to be challenged and a less hostile environment generated, stronger alliances need to be rebuilt with local authorities predisposed to seek alternatives. This demands better-developed relational skills to navigate the multiple layers of mistrust and conflict.

Many voluntary service organizations still appear trapped in the view that current arrangements are inevitable. A consideration must therefore be that organizations committed to change should abandon this formalized service industry and place hopes of more democratic models in alternatives. This may mean constructing provision with fragile funding and building new political alliances, as the cases in chapter 5 illustrate. It certainly means more acute reflection on recent discourse and actions that have contributed to damaging local services and suppressing diversity and dissent. Confronting power and the dominant consensus and the renewal of a democratic movement are uphill struggles. However, failing to seek different models to the current orthodoxy denies the roots of many voluntary organizations in politically engaged community action, in an era when many formed specifically to create critical alternatives to inadequate or discriminatory state services. Decoupling from a rapidly privatizing service industry appears a rational alternative, unless or until the political wind changes. However, dispensing with the state is a short-term solution, and ultimately the actions of civil society organizations are interwoven with the political complexion of the state and vital to the public sphere.

Locating sites and models for change

The discussion above considers whether changes can arise from resistance within existing settings, whether they demand separate (non-service-oriented) organizations or need to evolve from new movements. Should the focus for organizing be localized, specialist issues, confronting wider prejudice and discrimination, or the most pressing human needs? Rather than insisting on any one path, we would argue that all these are relevant but if organizing is local, fostering wider connections is important since many issues have regional, national, and international echoes. Considerable fragmentation is taking place among civil society organizations with the goals, behaviours, and arrangements of major charities and housing associations now markedly different from those of local micro-organizations and grassroots groups. However, examples also illustrate wider alliances being created to challenge injustices and, despite diverse approaches, movements are coalescing around different campaigns, including human rights, austerity, and environmental issues, building strength and spawning new groups. Alternative models constructed will inevitably encompass contradictions and struggles, and we also have to guard against exclusivity and intolerance.

Constraints on civil society organizations are equally challenges to democracy. This book argues a pressing need to counter the dominant discourse around the purposes of civil society and voluntary organizations with a new narrative, which will challenge the reduction of their diverse roles to consenting accomplices of state and market agencies or genial associations and clubs. Any new narrative has to abandon the focus on distinctiveness that has allowed so many voluntary organizations to hide behind the self-serving myth that they are somehow better than other sectors. It needs to be formed around a vision that draws compassion and politics together and recognizes the vital role of civil society in providing spaces for criticism and opposition.

There are three significant ways in which this can be addressed. First, organizations need to refocus their commitment on social values and independent purposes, aligning activities to these, rather than to external prescriptions or financial goals. Second, organizations and scholars need to prioritize rather than marginalize their critical roles, recognizing these as crucial to civil society's purposes in maintaining a healthy democracy. Third, for all those committed to an alternative vision, it means continuing to better understand the conditions in which civil society alternatives are already evolving as challenges to the dominant neo-liberal landscape, translating lessons from the past into the present and deploying organizational powers and voices towards strengthening growing movements. By exposing the narrow perspectives of many contemporary voluntary organizations and offering ways to understand their entrapment, we hope that this book has contributed to advancing alternatives.

Recreating an ethical society

Confronting the impoverished nature of welfare services and the loss of so many dissenting spaces is crucial to recreating locally responsive welfare provision that is not destined to fail, and to resurrecting commitment to alternatives. Challenge is also vital to restoring the well-being of organizations and workers. The diverse perspectives illustrated in the preceding chapters underline the widespread problems of this new service industry and the levels of dependency on localized voluntary efforts. As turbulent times and rapidly changing policies transform expectations among both providers and service recipients, the need for voluntary organizations to confront their entrapment is integral to the health of society.

This book has highlighted times when solidarity and community were more prevalent conceptually and in practice, and more recent settings where aspirations for a more ethical society are visibly reawakening in grassroots activities and social movements. Organizations are questioning their futures and the policy promises broken, but, while valuable, these reflections are not enough to check the continuing damage of contemporary neo-liberalism, which is currently reaping the whirlwind it has sown. Endemic self-interest and individualism are giving rein to rejection of authority, and emotional responses to dissatisfaction with current society are being played out in damaging ways, with unplanned consequences.

Participation and inclusion at the table have often been promoted as progressive, but have also resulted in incorporating and suppressing critical voices. Neither participation nor 'tinkering with policy' is enough to achieve fundamental social change (Fraser, 2016: 117). As competition for resources intensifies, the pressures to withhold criticism and to campaign with gloves on are ever greater, adding to complicity in an immoral society. Local strategies have to ensure responsive spaces for conflictual voices and self-organizing energy within civil society. Only then will they achieve practical changes that genuinely respond to popular narratives, while also helping to contain social anxiety and fear of difference, avoiding the damaging fallout of recent simplistic, anti-establishment feelings. In a fractured post-Brexit society, we are experiencing acute challenges related to ageing, the rapidly changing nature of work, and environmental degradation. The need for civil society to engage in the public sphere and contribute to new ideas about how society can collectively advance radical changes is vital. These are all spheres in which voluntary organizations could harness energy and voice imaginative ways forward.

This final chapter has argued that it is mistaken and short-sighted to assume that there are few alternatives to the way things are, which has persisted as a dominant narrative among voluntary service organizations and restricted their imagination and actions. The counter-agency of individuals and organizations to resist, subvert, and deflect the trajectories depicted as mainstream trends exists in the questioning and covert discussions and actions described in several chapters. Reawakening resistance revives dormant emotional energy, motivation, and meanings, and starting to redirect changes can create a powerful momentum. While many organizations and individuals have conformed, some are resisting, and the diverse strategies emerging highlight the dilemmas that organizations and individuals now face. The challenge faced by current democracy is such that if civil society organizations are to contest the entrenched forces of conservatism in society, they have to reinvent themselves 'from the bottom up' and reassert more ethical and transformational purposes as part of 'a counter-hegemonic force' for change (Powell, 2009: 52). These choices are now critical for the health and sustenance of an autonomous civil society ready to stand against the destruction, not only of public welfare, but also of the freedom to dissent.

References

Aiken, M. (2016) 'Tales we tell: Speaking out loud, story in the lives of activists'. Paper presented at the Voluntary Sector and Volunteering Research Conference, Nottingham, September.

Beecham, J. (2016) 'The stigma of renting and the legacy of new towns'. *The Guardian* Letters, 9 August. Online. www.theguardian.com/society/2016/aug/09/the-stigma-of-renting-and-the-legacy-of-new-towns (accessed December 2016).

Billis, D. (2010) *Hybrid Organizations and the Third Sector: Challenges for practice, theory and policy*. London: Palgrave Macmillan.

Body, A. (2016) '"A new and challenging landscape": Social skill and the mobilisation of ideological bias'. Paper presented at the Voluntary Sector and Volunteering Research Conference, Nottingham, September.

Douglas, P. and Parkes, J. (2016) '"Regeneration" and "consultation" at a Lambeth council estate: The case of Cressingham Gardens'. *City*, 20 (2), 287–91.

Edwards, M. (2009) *Civil Society*. Cambridge: Polity Press.

Foucault, M. (1977) 'Truth and Power'. In C. Gordon (ed.), *Power/Knowledge: Selected interviews and other writings 1972–1977*. New York: Pantheon.

Fraser, N. (2013) 'A triple movement'. *New Left Review*, 81 (May–June), 119–32.

— (2016) 'Contradictions of capital and care'. *New Left Review*, 100 (July–August), 99–117.

— (2017) 'The end of progressive neoliberalism'. *Dissent Magazine*. Online. www.dissentmagazine.org/online_articles/progressive-neoliberalism-reactionary-populism-nancy-fraser (accessed January 2017).

Glasius, M. and Ishkanian, A. (2015) 'Surreptitious symbiosis: The relationship between NGOs and movement activists'. *LSE Research Online*. Online. http://eprints.lse.ac.uk/63086/1/Ishakanian_Surreptitious%20symbiosis.pdf (accessed December 2015).

Habermas, J. (2006) 'Religion in the public sphere'. *European Journal of Philosophy*, 14 (1), 1–25.

Hills, J., Obolenskaya, C.J.P., and Karagiannaki, E. (2015) *Falling Behind, Getting Ahead: The changing structure of inequality in the UK 2007–2013* (Social Policy in a Cold Climate Research Report 5). London: CASE & London School of Economics.

Hoggett, P. (2006) 'Conflict, ambivalence and the contested purpose of public organizations'. *Human Relations*, 59 (2), London: Sage, 175–94.

Holloway, J. (2005) '*Change the World without Taking Power. The meaning of revolution today. 2nd ed*. London: Pluto Press.

Honig, B. (1996) 'Differences, dilemmas, and the politics of home'. In S. Benhabib (ed.), *Democracy and Difference: Contesting the boundaries of the political*. Princeton: Princeton University Press, 257.

JRF (2016) *Leave Voters Felt Ignored and Left Behind as Post-Brexit Poll Reveals Extent of Economic Division Across UK*. Joseph Rowntree Foundation. Online. www.jrf.org.uk/press/leave-voters-felt-ignored-and-left-behind-brexit-poll (accessed July 2016).

King, D. (2016) *Democratic Renewal in Civil Society Seminar Series*. Online. http://democraticrenewal.co.uk/about/ (accessed August 2016).

LeBaron, G. and Dauvergne, P. (2014) 'Not just about the money: Corporatization is weakening activism and empowering big business'. *Open Democracy*, 14 March. Online. www.opendemocracy.net/author/peter-dauvergne (accessed May 2014).

Long, J. (2012) '£46m payout for A4e – despite missing Work Programme targets'. *Channel 4 news*, 24 October. Online. www.channel4.com/news/46m-payout-for-a4e-despite-missing-work-programme-targets (accessed January 2013).

Milbourne, L. and Murray, U. (2014a) *The State of the Voluntary Sector: Does size matter? Paper 2* (NCIA Inquiry into the Future of Voluntary Services Working Paper 10). Online. www.independentaction.net/wp-content/uploads/2014/07/Does-size-matter-paper-2-final.pdf (accessed December 2016).

— (2014b) '*The State of the Voluntary Sector: Does size matter? Paper 1* (NCIA Inquiry into the Future of Voluntary Services Working Paper 9). Online. www.independentaction.net/wp-content/uploads/sites/8/2014/07/Does-Size-Matter-paper-1-final.pdf (accessed December 2016).

— (2015) 'Civil society organisations in a rapidly changing landscape: Space for alternatives or "another brick in the wall"?'. Paper presented at the Critical Management Studies Conference, Leicester, July.

NCIA (2015) *Fight or Fright: Voluntary services in 2015* (NCIA Inquiry into the Future of Voluntary Services Summary and Discussion of the Inquiry Findings). London: National Coalition for Independent Action. Online. www.independentaction.net/wp-content/uploads/2015/02/NCIA-Inquiry-summary-report-final.pdf (accessed December 2016).

Powell, F.W. (2009) 'Civil society, social policy and participatory democracy: Past, present and future'. *Social Policy and Society,* 8 (1), 49–58.

Rochester, C. (2013) *Rediscovering Voluntary Action: The beat of a different drum.* Basingstoke: Palgrave Macmillan.

Rose, N. (1999) *Powers of Freedom: Reframing political thought.* Cambridge: Cambridge University Press.

Scott, M. (2016) 'The voluntary sector as moribund and misleading terminology'. Paper presented at the Voluntary Sector and Volunteering Research Conference, Nottingham, September.

Sennett, R. (2003) *Respect: The formation of character in an age of inequality.* London: Penguin.

UK Parliament (2016) *Housing and Planning Act 2016.* The Stationery Office. Online. www.legislation.gov.uk/ukpga/2016/22/pdfs/ukpga_20160022_en.pdf (accessed December 2016).

Winnicott, D. (1971) *Playing and Reality.* London: Tavistock Publications Ltd.

Wright, O. (2013) 'Revealed: The great outsourcing scandal as firms "cut corners" to cream profits off public'. *Independent,* 18 July. Online. www.independent.co.uk/news/uk/politics/revealed-the-great-outsourcing-scandal-as-firms-cut-corners-to-cream-profits-off-public-8715119.html (accessed December 2016).

Appendix

Table 1: Type of housing association

Response	Number of participants	Percentage of participants (%)
LSVT[1]	16	34
Group Structure[2]	12	26
Large housing association (more than 5,000 units)	11	23
Medium housing association (1,000–5,000 units)	5	11
Other	2	4
Small housing association (fewer than 1,000 units)	1	2

Notes
[1] Large Scale Voluntary Transfer – these are independent housing associations created by local authorities in order to transfer their housing stock into the third sector.
[2] A form of housing association comprising several distinct associations grouped under a central banner, usually sharing central services such as IT and finance but with some degree of autonomous decision making.

Table 2: Results of sector positioning

	Number of responses in range on founding	Number of responses in range at present	Number of responses in range in 3 years
Public sector	20	9	1
Between public and third sector	8	14	11
Third sector	17	14	16
Between third and private sector	1	10	10
Private sector	0	0	9

Table 3: Position within sector by organization type

	Average position (LSVT)	Average score (Large HA and groups)
Position at founding	Public sector	Between public and third sector
Position at present	Between public and third sector	Third sector
Position in 3 years	Third sector	Between third and private sector

Table 4: Involvement in 'new opportunities' over next 3 years

New opportunity	Number of respondents	Percentage of respondents (%)
Affordable rents	38	90
Involving residents in governance structures	35	83
Supporting community organizations who provide services to organizations' residents	31	74
Big Society projects	30	71
Flexible tenancies	29	69
Running social/welfare contracts on behalf of government	18	43
Issuing a bond to raise money	17	40
Changing organization's legal status	8	19
Floating organization on the stock exchange	1	2

Table 5: In what way will the resident profile change?

Change to profile expected	Number of respondents	Percentage of respondents (%*)
More vulnerable residents	18	51
More full-time employed residents	7	20
More of both vulnerable and full-time employed residents	5	14
Other	5	14

*NB due to rounding, percentages do not total 100.

Index

Index

Index

violent crime 73
voluntarism 28; hiding failures 185
voluntary organizations: alternative approaches 130; bullying 140; business model 22, 118, 136; compliance 21; contracts 5, 10, 136, 138; criminal justice 73–80; critical voices 142–3, 162–3, 173–4, 193–5; depoliticization 189–90, 194; desire for growth 26–7; entitlement 78; ethical failure 78; the future 183–4; income 137–8; private and voluntary sector 20; survivalism 21; trade unions 142; workers and working conditions 135–48; workforce 138; *see also* advocacy; charities

War on Want 71, 198
Ware, P. 86, 90, 95, 97, 98
Welfare Reform Act (2012) 38

Welfare Reform Bill (2010–11): and voluntary organizations 22
welfare state 4
welfare to work 6
well-being 167–80; changing language 169; depression 167; eudaimonic well-being 168–9, 171–80; shame 178
Whitfield, D. 19, 25, 88, 136, 164
women's refuges 75
Work Programme 20
workers and working conditions 135–48; *see also* charities; well-being
workforce 138

xenophobia 28

Youth Justice Custody Pathfinders 73

zero-hours contracts 138